Practical Data Analysis and Reporting with BIRT

Use the open-source Eclipse-based Business Intelligence and Reporting Tools system to design and create reports as quickly as possible

John Ward

PUBLISHING

BIRMINGHAM - MUMBAI

Practical Data Analysis and Reporting with BIRT

First published: February 2008

Production Reference: 1140208

Published by Packt Publishing Ltd.
32 Lincoln Road
Olton
Birmingham, B27 6PA, UK.

ISBN 978-1-847191-09-0

www.packtpub.com

Cover Image by Wim Boucquaert (wim.boucquaert@gmail.com)

Credits

Author

John Ward

Reviewer

Meenakshi Verma

Senior Acquisition Editor

Douglas Paterson

Development Editor

Nikhil Bangera

Technical Editor

Mithun Sehgal

Editorial Team Leader

Mithil Kulkarni

Project Manager

Abhijeet Deobhakta

Project Coordinator

Patricia Weir

Indexer

Monica Ajmera

Proofreader

Chris Smith

Production Coordinator

Shantanu Zagade

Design Work

Shantanu Zagade

About the Author

John Ward is a consultant for Innovent Solutions, specializing in BIRT and e-commerce search and navigation solutions. Prior to that, John was an Assistant Vice President for Citibank, North America, managing the training MIS group and overseeing development of new technology-based training initiatives. John actively works with and tests BIRT — an open-source reporting platform built on Eclipse — including development work based on BIRT reports and the BIRT APIs. John also maintains The Digital Voice blog at `http://digiassn.blogspot.com`.

I'd like to thank my wife Claudia for her love, support, and patience throughout the writing of this book, my Grandfather and Father for their wisdom and advice, and my Mother for her encouragement and support.

Rich and Bamm, thanks for giving me the most tedious task in the department. Without it, this book wouldn't have been possible.

And Scott, thanks for talks about BIRT and help with presentations, which provided a good foundation to start with.

About the Reviewer

Meenakshi Verma has been part of the IT industry since 1998. She is experienced in putting up solutions across multiple industry segments using Java/J2EE technologies. Meenakshi has been helping with technical reviews for books published by Packt publishing across varied enterprise solutions. She is currently based in Toronto, Canada and is working with a leading North American Consultancy organization.

Table of Contents

Preface

BIRT, which stands for Business Intelligence and Reporting Tools, is an Eclipse-based open-source reporting system for Java and J2EE-based web applications. Including the word "Tools" in the acronym is appropriate, since BIRT is in fact a collection of development tools and technologies used for developing reports utilizing the BIRT runtime framework component on your application server. BIRT isn't essentially a product, but a series of core technologies on top of which products and solutions are built, similar in fashion to the Eclipse framework.

This book has a fast-paced, task-driven, tutorial style, which provides understanding and structure, not just lists of steps to follow. The focus is on the most visible and familiar product built with the BIRT framework, which is the BIRT Report Designer. The BIRT Report Designer is an Eclipse plug-in that utilizes BIRT technologies to allow users to design reports in the BIRT document format. Also covered is the BIRT Charting engine, which lets you add Charts to your application.

What This Book Covers

Chapter 1 introduces readers to the concepts of business intelligence and open-source software.

Chapter 2 discusses the different installation methods for BIRT, and the list of requirements needed to work with BIRT.

Chapter 3 provides an example of the creation of a simple report using the components of BIRT, such as the Navigator, the Outline, and the Property Editor.

Chapter 4 describes the various visual report elements that can be used to design BIRT reports, such as the Palette and Grid components.

Chapter 5 details the data components of BIRT (the Data Source and the Data Set), different types of data that BIRT supports such as XML files, flat text files, and databases, and the creation of all of the elements while connecting to Data Sources in reports and Report Projects.

Chapter 6 describes the Report Parameters and Data Set Parameters with their use in designing BIRT reports.

In *Chapter 7* readers are provided with the information related to Report projects, and made familiar with creating a shared development environment using Libraries.

Chapter 8 covers the creation of Styles and Themes to give a consistent appearance to a Reporting Project. It also describes the use of Templates in Report Designs.

Chapter 9 describes the role of Charts, Hyperlinks, and Drill-Downs to enhance the presentation of a report.

Chapter 10 covers some of the Scripting capabilities that BIRT has to offer with Expressions and Event Handlers.

Chapter 11 describes the process of deploying BIRT reports.

Chapter 12 shows a practical example of building reports for Bugzilla.

What You Need for This Book

- A basic understanding of the SQL language
- BIRT (version 2.2 is used in this book)
- For BIRT versions prior to 2.2, Java 1.4 is required; for 2.2 and later, Java 1.5 is required.
- iText is an optional requirement. For versions of BIRT prior to 2.2, iText version 1.3.2.2 is needed; for later versions, iText 1.46 is required.

Conventions

In this book, you will find a number of styles of text that distinguish between different kinds of information. Here are some examples of these styles, and an explanation of their meaning.

There are three styles for code. Code words in text are shown as follows: "Extract the `BirtSample.jar` file to a known location, such as in your workspace or a temporary folder."

A block of code will be set as follows:

```
var nameLengthCount = 0;
if (row["firstName"])
nameLengthCount = row["firstName"].length;
if (row["lastName"])
nameLengthCount += row["lastName"].length;
nameLengthCount;
```

Any command-line input and output is written as follows:

```
Set BIRT_HOME=C:\birt_runtime\birt-runtime-2_1_0\
```

New terms and **important words** are introduced in a bold-type font. Words that you see on the screen, in menus or dialog boxes for example, appear in our text like this: "Under the **Data Explorer** tab, right-click on **Data Sets** and select **New Data Set**."

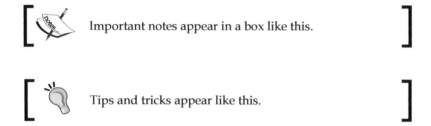

Important notes appear in a box like this.

Tips and tricks appear like this.

Reader Feedback

Feedback from our readers is always welcome. Let us know what you think about this book, what you liked or may have disliked. Reader feedback is important for us to develop titles that you really get the most out of.

To send us general feedback, simply drop an email to feedback@packtpub.com, making sure to mention the book title in the subject of your message.

If there is a book that you need and would like to see us publish, please send us a note in the SUGGEST A TITLE form on www.packtpub.com or email suggest@packtpub.com.

If there is a topic that you have expertise in and you are interested in either writing or contributing to a book, see our author guide on www.packtpub.com/authors.

Customer Support

Now that you are the proud owner of a Packt book, we have a number of things to help you to get the most from your purchase.

Downloading the Example Code for the Book

Visit http://www.packtpub.com/files/code/1090_Code.zip, and select this book from the list of titles to download any example code or extra resources for this book. The files available for download will then be displayed.

The downloadable files contain instructions on how to use them.

Errata

Although we have taken every care to ensure the accuracy of our contents, mistakes do happen. If you find a mistake in one of our books—maybe a mistake in text or code—we would be grateful if you would report this to us. By doing this you can save other readers from frustration, and help to improve subsequent versions of this book. If you find any errata, report them by visiting http://www.packtpub.com/support, selecting your book, clicking on the **Submit Errata** link, and entering the details of your errata. Once your errata are verified, your submission will be accepted and the errata added to the list of existing errata. The existing errata can be viewed by selecting your title from http://www.packtpub.com/support.

Questions

You can contact us at questions@packtpub.com if you are having a problem with some aspect of the book, and we will do our best to address it.

1
Introduction

At present, it's a very interesting time for open-source software. No longer is it a novel concept put forth by enthusiasts; new functionality is included into software that is changing our lives, and a lot of it is built on open-source technology. Having been an open-source advocate for some time now, I have seen a phenomenal amount of change and progress in the quality and quantity of **Open-Source Software (OSS)** projects. From the thoughtful minds of professional software developers, engineers, and hobbyists, tools have sprung up to support any discipline, from programmers to authors, office staff, teachers, students, media, and graphic designers. Where once there was only expensive proprietary commercial software to do particular tasks, now there are a whole handful of new and free alternatives based on OSS.

Open-source projects start—and also die—all the time. Each project starts to address what a user, or group of users, perceives as a relative shortcoming in the current computing landscape. OpenOffice.org was derived from StarOffice to address the lack of an open-source Office suite. Mozilla has grown from the ashes of Netscape to compete with IE (Internet Explorer), which led to the creation of Firefox—it has not only provided an alternative to IE but has also revitalized the browser wars, even garnering attention to its commercial competitor, Opera. Also, there is no end to the innovations that Perl and PHP have brought about.

Even non-free software benefits from OSS. Iterations of Microsoft Windows have utilized versions of FreeBSD-based implementations of the TCP-IP stack, for their network implementations. Commercial routers from companies like Linksys have embedded Linux in them; even gamers are affected, for example the Sony PlayStation 3 and Nintendo Wii are both designed to run Linux.

However, there has always been an area that is severely lacking, and that is the area of **business intelligence**. While there are solutions such as writing Perl or PHP scripts, these really don't leverage full-fledged business intelligence (the idea that reports and tools can be used by businesses to make strategic decisions, based on short-term and long-term data and trend analysis). There has not been an open-source tool that really addresses this shortcoming. Crafty developers can take the long approach and write out scripts and programs that automate data reporting tasks, but this is a long and complicated process. Proprietary software for doing reporting tasks has been around, such as the report developer inside Microsoft Access for reporting of Access databases or Crystal Reports. These are tools that have been built to automate reporting tasks—such as data retrieval, sorting, aggregation, and presentation—into a format that is meaningful to the user. These kinds of tools have been lacking in the open-source community, and have only begun to gain speed in the last few years.

Introduction to Business Intelligence

There are two major questions if you are reading this book that need to be answered at this point. What is business intelligence, and why do we need it? Business intelligence is a lot like many other technology buzzwords that get thrown around; many people say it, and many people will give you a complicated definition of it. However, the answer is really quite simple.

If I had to give it a formal definition I would say that business intelligence, as it relates to information technology, is any tool or method that allows developers to take data or information, process it, manipulate it, and associate it with related information and present it to decision makers. As for a simplified definition, it's presenting information to decision makers in a way that helps them make informed decisions.

Consider this scenario: You are a manager for a chain of retail stores. You need to figure out what products you should push to the forefront for the upcoming holiday season. You have a two-method approach: First you get the latest buzz from your marketers, who tell you what the new and upcoming products are; your second approach is to look at products that have traditionally sold very well.

In order to project how the current year may go, you need to look at the data you have available. What product categories have traditionally sold well over a 5-year period, or even a 10-year period? Has there been any sort of patterns to these sales figures? What individual items have sold well in that period? Are there any trends? When you look at these figures, can you give a projection on how well these products will do? What items should be put on sale in order to push for higher sales? These are the kinds of questions that a decision maker may need answered.

So the first step in the process is getting to this data, usually located in some place like a data warehouse. If you are looking at a regional level you may have this information stored separately in a localized data mart, with specific data. If you are looking at up-to-the-minute information: you may need access to transactional data. Either way, the first hurdle is getting access to the data.

What do you do once you have access to the data? How do you best format and present the data in some meaningful fashion that can be used to assist in the BI (Business Intelligence) process? This is where BI tools come into play. Using BI tools you have the ability to write reports that can present this oftentimes sporadic and confusing data, in some sort of format that is useful to decision makers. Once this data is presented, trends can be identified, total figures can be aggregated, and decisions can be made.

The Current State of the BI Market

The current state of the BI market is similar to the state of any technology field. It can change at the drop of a hat! At the time of this writing, you can divide the major players in this field into two categories: commercial offerings and open-source offerings. Each category has its own benefits and drawbacks. With the commercial offerings, typically you have familiar names such as Actuate and Business Objects, offering various tools aimed at different levels of business. Some of these tools are large and enterprise reporting platforms that have the ability to process, analyze, and reformat large quantities of data. With commercial offerings, you get product support and years of experience. Oftentimes with the big guys who offer consultation in developing your reports for a fee, you also get the professional services. One of the drawbacks of commercial offerings is the large price associated with them, both in terms of purchasing and in terms of running them. In some companies, in addition to the initial cost (which can at times be in the thousands of dollars) there is also a cost of yearly maintenance fees, upgrade fees, cost of licensing, and cost of ownership that may be typically overlooked. If you are building a large-scale custom application, are you allowed to integrate these products into your application? If so, with what restrictions? Finally, the years of engineering behind a product may leverage an obsolete methodology. Perhaps the technology behind these products is no longer viable or powerful enough to handle the demands of a growing enterprise.

Then, you have your open-source offerings. Currently there are three big names in the open-source reporting realm: JasperReport, Pentaho, and BIRT. Two of these projects, JasperReports and BIRT, are run by commercial companies who make their money by doing professional services for these offerings to small scale and private projects. Again, there are a number of pros and cons associated with open-source solutions. With open-source, you have full access to the source code of the platform you choose. This allows you to add in functionality, embed it with your existing applications, and actively participate in a development community that is oftentimes very large and around the world. There is little initial cost to open-source software in terms of purchasing, as open-source is free. The cons are that there is typically a cost associated with finding individuals who are knowledgeable in open-source.

Sometimes open-source software is not very user friendly. Finally, often there is little to no support for open-source products. This is not the case with large open-source projects, however. With large active development communities, and usually with open-source projects such as Linux, Eclipse, and Mozilla/Firefox, available answers are only an internet search away.

The Need for Open-Source Reporting

Some things are better illustrated with a story. So let me begin this with what brought me to the world of open-source business intelligence. My story starts on a late Sunday evening in 2001. At that time, I was a student intern for a midsized network security monitoring operation BATC (Ball Aerospace and Technologies Managed Network Security). Here I am, landing a dream job for a college student, a paid internship at a high-technology company, working in one of the most exciting fields in the tech industry, network security. From this single department came some interesting projects and concepts such as Sguil (the open-source network security analysis front end for Snort) and SanCP (a network session profiler). Concepts such as Network Security Monitoring (NSM) were being tested and proven over security appliances.

In this particular scenario: we are a department dedicated to providing customers with network security monitoring solutions, using open-source software. This entire NSM philosophy would later be expanded upon and described in "The Tao of Network Security" (Bejtlich 2004) yet, here I am, sitting in my cubicle with a broken keyboard, resting in an office where the A/C shuts off on a timer. So it's boiling hot! All this great technology and cool blinking lights, flashing screens, and on-the-cutting-edge monitoring of Internet traffic catching bad guys doing bad things. The whole setup is something right out of a spy movie, with exciting things happening; such a great opportunity for me, a young college student. Yet, on this particular evening, I am not enjoying my job.

My job here, this evening, is not to monitor the thousands of alerts; nor is it to inspect the exponentially higher amount of network packets, in an effort to protect networks from the insidious under doings of the digital underground. Instead, my job this evening is to do the most dreaded task in the entire operation: the weekly incident report.

Being a company dedicated to open-source, we had tons of open-source software proving that the open-source paradigm was a workable one. Our workstations were all Red Hat Linux systems, which were configured and customized to help us achieve our mission statement. Our back-end servers were all running FreeBSD. Our security console was a custom, in-house developed front-end built on open-source scripting tools (which was the base for what would later become the Sguil Project).

Our network sensors were all built on Snort, and dumped all transactional data into a PostgreSQL data warehouse. Our office productivity suite was an early release of OpenOffice.org. Yet we lacked one important piece of a customer-focused service group: a reporting system.

So, what tools did we use to address the area of reporting? We had scripts. Lots of tedious, boring, and manual scripts that generated lines and lines of ugly text. The scripts took hours to run, mostly due to lack of proper indexing on the reporting tables, because the DBAs refused to listen to us and focused on the transactional databases that housed all our live data. So the scripts were slow, and their output was ugly. The scripts may have outputted RTF documents, but no formatting tags were actually used. Part of our job was to go through each of these reports, cut out duplicate lines, change fonts and font weighting, and manually go through and confirm the accuracy of each of the counts in the summary. This was a time-consuming, tedious, and boring task that was highly error prone: as a result, it required longer validation time. Of course, due to the setup, the scripts were considered part of the Database Administrators' and the system developers' tasks; so we didn't have access to change anything in the event of an issue. If a query was returning funny results in the reports, too bad, because all we saw was an output page with no access to the code that generated it.

Now it's the middle of the night, we're tired, the other guy is griping about having to pick up the slack while I am doing the most tedious task of running the report. It's hot! I'm going through hundreds of pages of numbers, cutting out duplicates, changing summary numbers to reflect correct counts, and changing the formatting. I am sitting here asking myself the same question I ask myself each week when we run these reports: "Isn't there a better way?" This will become a question that always nags at the back of my mind, and it is one that I will always come back to as an unresolved question.

Fast-forward a few years. I have since moved on from BATC into a new role as senior software developer, for Citibank North America's National Training Department. It's the 2004 Actuate Users Conference in Los Angeles, California. Always on the prowl for innovative reporting technologies because of my encounters at BATC, I came to the conference to learn about the different products that Actuate had to offer. But the one thing that always stayed at the back of my mind was that nagging desire, to find an open-source reporting solution. So as a few days rolled on during the conference, I was getting a little annoyed at one of the product pitches. So on this particular day's keynote speech, the vice-president of some such department was talking on and on about all the products that Actuate had to offer. Of course, as I was already starting to zone out, I started doodling in my notebook with little caricatures of him doing sales pitches. But suddenly, as if I had a moment of clarity from a drunken stupor, this VP said the most remarkable thing. He said "Actuate realizes the importance for an open-source reporting product, which is why we have started on an open-source initiative with the Eclipse Foundation, to make an open-source report platform called BIRT."

It was as if he read my mind, and suddenly I couldn't help but listen to my new messiah. Apparently someone out there was listening, and someone had clued in to an untapped market. And thus was my introduction to BIRT.

However, this is actually a two-part question: While my story demonstrates the need for report developers, what about application developers? Well, let me give you a scenario. You work for the MIS/BI group in your company. For years you have leveraged hand-coded and database-driven web pages for your reporting. You have come to the conclusion that development time takes too long, and decide to leverage your existing J2EE platform; you decide it is time to change your report development habits.

After extensive research, you have come up with a list of requirements: Reports must have the ability to be accessible online, with the ability to export to common desktop formats, such as Microsoft Office formats and Adobe PDF. You need pagination and navigation of your reports. You would also like to take the hand-coding of reports out of the loop, to make them quicker to develop and deploy. As you work in a development group, you need the ability to share common reporting elements among your group. You would also like the platform to be flexible and dynamic, and need charting capabilities. However, you have no budget at this time for an enterprise reporting platform; so you decide on an open-source platform. After some research, you come across BIRT, and decide it is the way to go.

What is BIRT

If you are new to BIRT, or unfamiliar with Eclipse, you may be asking, "What exactly is BIRT?" The first thing that comes to mind is a fuzzy puppet with a unibrow. Well, this BIRT isn't related, although some may consider it fuzzy and cute. Others may think of a mustached rogue on a race to win money, running from the law. Well, this tough guy also isn't what we are talking about.

So what exactly is BIRT? This is a complex question to answer. Some people would tell you that BIRT is a Report Designer, built on top of Eclipse that provide users with a visual WYSIWYG design interface, for rapid report development. Others may tell you it is a plug-in for Apache Tomcat that allows you to view reports from J2EE web portals. And others still may tell you that it is a Report Engine that can be imported into Java applications. There is also a chart engine that may come up in some peoples answers.

Truth be told, all of these are correct. BIRT (which stands for Business Intelligence and Reporting Tools) is actually a development framework. Adding the word "Tools" to the title acronym is appropriate; BIRT is in fact a collection of development tools and technologies, used for report development, utilizing the BIRT framework. BIRT isn't necessarily a product, but a series of core technologies that products and solutions are built on top of, similar in fashion to the Eclipse framework.

The focus of this book will be on the most visible and familiar product built with the BIRT framework, which is the BIRT Report Designer. The BIRT Report Designer is an Eclipse plug-in that utilizes BIRT technologies, which allow users to design reports in the BIRT document format. Inside this application the Design Engine API, the Report Object Model, the BIRT Report Engine, the BIRT Chart Engine, and a number of other BIRT technologies are utilized to deliver a robust and capable report design environment.

Another product built with BIRT is the Web Viewer that comes with the Report Engine runtime. This is a product that is plugged into a J2EE application container, such as Apache Tomcat or BEA Weblogic, which utilizes the BIRT Report Engine to run reports and output to HTML and PDF. Several other applications are built with BIRT as well. Actuate BIRT Report Designer and Actuate 9 platforms are centered on BIRT technology.

By looking at the above examples, we can see that the core BIRT technologies can be leveraged to build a number of business intelligence products. Hopefully, this gives you an idea of what exactly BIRT is. For shorthand, we will refer to the BIRT Report Designer as BIRT throughout this book.

The Origins of BIRT

While the story I gave earlier in this chapter is great for telling my introduction to BIRT, and demonstrates the need for open-source reporting platforms, it is not the official origin of BIRT. For that, we need to turn to Actuate, and give a story that eventually intersects with my story.

Actuate has been a big player in the reporting arena for many years. Previously, it specialized in the realm of enterprise reporting applications. However, seeing a ripe opportunity to address a growing market, the idea of an open-source reporting platform was proposed.

Most applications have some sort of reporting requirement. Typically, the success or failure of a product is hinged on how well that reporting works. The problem with this is that oftentimes, reporting in the real world is a challenging issue. Data is typically spread out and not formatted for reporting purposes. There are several different sources, such as data warehouses, transactional systems providing website analysis, point of sale, data marts, and all sorts of different collections of data. To top it off, reporting requirements often change based on user requirements and market influences. So, creating flexible reports becomes a challenge.

Actuate decided to address these kinds of concerns, leveraging its years of experience, to create a more modern framework for report development. Keeping in mind the issues that came across, the Actuate developers focused on addressing these issues in a manner that can assist report developers, and reach a level of adoption of reports close to total. The Actuate philosophy has been stated on a number of occasions as that it seeks to create products that allow its customers to get to "100% adoption" of reports. Success of reports can be measured by how well these reports are consumed; oftentimes, if a report is successful, users will ask for more.

So the decision was made to create an open-source reporting platform; however, the open-source market is a funny industry. So Actuate joined forces with an already existing open-source development community—the Eclipse Foundation—to leverage their existing framework as a base line for its application.

BIRT has grown due to support and feedback from the community. The developers pay close attention to the groups out there, and listen for strengths and shortcomings of BIRT in order to improve upon it. Unlike a lot of open-source projects that have only part-time developers, BIRT has a team of full time developers, dedicated to improving the BIRT platform as a whole. BIRT even has a few "evangelists," dedicated to promoting understanding and use of BIRT in the developer community.

Features of BIRT

What does BIRT stand for? Certainly it's not everyone's favorite fuzzy unibrowed Muppet in the title slide. BIRT actually stands for Business Intelligence and Reporting Tools. Although not as cute, doesn't the definition just fill you with the same warm fuzzy feelings as a Muppet? It is an open-source report development environment built on top of the Eclipse framework. Now, I emphasize the term "environment" because, as some of us already know, Actuate doesn't just build "products," it builds full-fledged platforms for report delivery, and BIRT is no exception to this.

BIRT is what the Actuate Corporation sees as the future of its product line. While some may consider it in its "infancy," BIRT is actually a fairly mature product built on top of, and in conjunction with, the Eclipse Foundation and the Eclipse Platform. In the two years since BIRT's introduction at the 2004 Actuate Users Conference, BIRT has grown and matured to a full-fledged reporting platform, which is something that the open-source community has been severely lacking. Its announcement in 2004 really peaked my interest, as I was looking for a reporting platform to integrate into Sguil. Ever since my early introduction into the world of MIS and BI, I had to struggle with the lack of a decent open-source reporting product, and BIRT delivered on that and more.

At a high level, BIRT can be broken up into two main categories: The one most often considered "BIRT," is the report development environment that is used to design and develop reports. The graphical designer runs inside of Eclipse and leverages a highly customized workspace. It uses a familiar graphical development paradigm, similar to what Macromedia Dreamweaver or Nvu would use for designing web pages. It contains a number of "drag and drop" visual and data components. Visualize Actuates Enterprise Report Designer Pro, but with a managed layout instead of the free-form layout designer.

The second component of BIRT is the Java APIs. This is where BIRT gets so much flexibility from. This allows BIRT to be embedded into any number of Java or J2EE applications. For instance, these APIs provide the Java Servlet Report Viewer that allows for integrating a BIRT Report Engine into Apache Tomcat. I provide examples of this, and how to use these APIs on my website (`http://digiassn.blogspot.com/`).

Some of the features that the BIRT Designer provides out of the box, as of the 2.2 release, are as listed:

- JDBC Database reporting
- Extensible data capabilities through the Eclipse ODA data connection, and the ability to instantiate Java objects within reports
- Joined Data Sets to allow for multiple Data Sources in a single report
- Web-deployable
- Templates for rapid development of similar formatted documents
- Libraries for sharing common report elements among reports
- Scripting for adding in business logic and manipulating report elements
- Instantiation of Java objects in reports via Mozilla Rhino
- Full blown Chart Engine with Line charts, Bar charts, Pie charts, and a number of other chart types
- Cross-tab reports using the new BIRT cube designer

BIRT provides connections to existing database platforms via JDBC. So database back ends such as Oracle, MySQL, and Postgres are all environments that you can connect to and start reporting of. Even some of the lesser-known platforms that provide JDBC drivers, such as HyperSQL, which is the engine that Sun's Open Office uses, can be used.

For environments that don't provide JDBC, BIRT can leverage the Eclipse Foundation's ODA for building custom data connections. For example, Hibernate objects can be reported on via ODA, which is an example that Jason Weathersby from the BIRT Project Management team has demonstrated. If necessary, Plain Old Java Objects (POJOs) can be used as Data Sources via ODA and through BIRT's scripted Data Source.

BIRT also allows for joined Data Sets. This feature allows a user to join two separate Data Sources, regardless of physical data location, into one logical Data Set. So, say for instance, you have an HR database with employee information, and a training database with corporate training data; these two can be combined into a single logical dataset for use in BIRT reports.

BIRT reports can be distributed via the Web through Apache Tomcat, or any J2EE platform such as IBM WebSphere, using the BIRT Report View applet. While the BIRT Web Viewer is an example application, it already provides a full set of report viewing features, such as page navigation, exporting to CSV, and PDF format exporting. Plus, because it is open-source, its features can be extended to include authorization. It offers users a set of URL parameters for customizing report calls; or you can simply include the Report Viewer classes in your existing J2EE applications. This is great for integrating reporting into your own custom portal, using technologies such as Ajax and Reportlets, or to extend existing applications.

For the interface designers, things that we have come to expect from large projects, such as libraries and templates, are also features that BIRT has to offer. And of course, for the fan boys out there, including myself, it's open-source.

Eclipse Framework

If you've never been exposed to Eclipse before, it can seem somewhat overwhelming. In fact, I'm sure some seasoned Eclipse users would agree. The Eclipse Framework is a very interesting one to work with. What started as an Integrated Development Environment (IDE) for Java programming has grown into a full-fledge framework for application development. With Eclipse, it is possible to develop applications utilizing the already pioneered area of graphic development, using Eclipse SWT—the extended Eclipse functionality utilizing Eclipse's Plug-in architecture. Applications developed on top of Eclipse can then be deployed as extensions to an already existing Eclipse installation, or distributed as Rich Client Platform (RCP) standalone applications.

The way Eclipse works is: there is a series of core classes that are included with each Eclipse or RCP application. These classes contain all the necessary classes for building and managing the application and building the application interface. The core application is then extended using plug-ins. Things such as the Content Versioning System browser (CVS), Java IDE, C++ IDE, and various tools in the Web Tools Projects are all plug-ins to Eclipse. This is how the BIRT Report Designer works. The Designer API extends the core Eclipse functionality by providing the BIRT perspective with the report palette, the Report Designer, and ways to execute the BIRT Viewer for report previewing.

From the BIRT perspective, this provides some really interesting deployment strategies. For shops that are purely focused on report development, a BIRT RCP application can be deployed to the desktops for developers to work with, without being burdened down with any of the other Eclipse features. This is beneficial where simplicity is the key and developers might be confused with Eclipse concepts, such as having to change perspectives to have availability of the full features of an Eclipse plug-in.

For the more robust development house, the plug-in approach would be more ideal. This is beneficial for—let's say—building a larger enterprise web application utilizing the EclipseWeb Tools Project (WTP) for J2EE, and being able to switch over to and utilize BIRT to handle data reporting tasks for this application. This way you can get the best of both worlds. You would have the impressive set of features that WTP offers, such as web service creation wizards, server deployments, and the ability to debug applications in Eclipse. You would also be able to have the WYSIWYG report editor of BIRT, for rapid development of data-driven user-facing interactivity.

This also allows users to develop Java applications that leverage the BIRT Report Engine and quickly switch over to the Report Designer; so you can have you entire development process under one roof. Plus, you can get the added bonus of utilizing Eclipse's internal tools for team project management, such as the CVS tool, or using the free Sub-eclipse third-party plug-in for Subversion repositories.

Currently, BIRT already leverages ODA for data extensibility; so this is one example of how building on top of the Eclipse framework has benefited the BIRT project. By utilizing the Eclipse Data Tools Project, BIRT can leverage the already existing driver framework and not have to repeat the development cycle. Future plans include integrating with WTP and other Eclipse projects as well.

BIRT Distributions

As it stands right now, the BIRT Report Designer comes in two flavors: The distribution I will be discussing in this book is the Eclipse BIRT, available at `http://www.eclipse.org/birt`. The Eclipse version of BIRT (which is an open-source release under the Eclipse Public License) is the fly-by-the-seat-of-your-pants version of BIRT, with all the latest bells and whistles, actively supported by the BIRT community. This is where all the action is if you are into the development of an application and if you are a computer tweaker, or you like the latest and greatest features—a stable distribution is always available. This is the most popular version of BIRT.

The second version of BIRT is Actuate BIRT. Actuate BIRT is a corporate branded version of BIRT, put out by the parent company behind the BIRT project, Actuate. This version contains all the same features as the Eclipse BIRT, plus some features that are specific to the Actuate platform, such as integration into Actuate Iserver. Actuate's next generation of business intelligence solutions (Actuate 9) is built on top of BIRT technology, with Actuate's BIRT Report Designer, Business Reports Tools, and Iportal products all being heavily coupled with BIRT.

For the shirts out there who won't consider a product unless there is a professional support unit to call in the middle of the night, and scream bloody murder when things don't work, this is the option that you are looking for, as Actuate BIRT is fully supported by Actuate. Actuate BIRT is always based on the latest stable version of BIRT, with additional service fixes. It is also a standalone RCP product. While the Eclipse version is integrated into Eclipse and you can actively use other Eclipse products, the Actuate version is BIRT only.

Why BIRT?

As I mentioned before, there are other open-source reporting platforms out there. So what makes BIRT stand out over JasperReports or Pentaho? With JasperReports, in reality, it comes down to tastes. I prefer the "What You See Is What You Get" (WYSIWYG) designer of BIRT over JasperReports. I also like the fact that it does not require compiling of reports to run, and that it is an official Eclipse project. However, that is not to say Jasper is not without strengths of its own. Jasper does do pixel-perfect rendering of reports, which is something that BIRT does not do. Later versions of Jasper also support the Hibernate HQL language.

When compared to Pentaho, it's an even harder comparison to make. Part of Pentaho's business intelligence Platform makes use of the BIRT engine, demonstrating some of the flexibility of the open-source model. Pentaho also includes a wide range of tools for business intelligence operations as a whole, such as Pentaho Data Integration Project, formerly known as Kettle—a tool used for Extraction, Transformation, and Loading (ETL) of data from one source to another. BIRT's primary focus is on reporting and does not include other tools as such.

Conventions Used in This Book

The purpose of this book is to familiarize users with the BIRT Report Designer. In order to do so, I have decided to alternate between two different scenarios in order to demonstrate the capabilities of BIRT, to familiarize you—the reader—with BIRT features, and to allow you an opportunity to follow along.

One set of reports will be built using the **Classic Cars** example database that comes with every BIRT distribution. This gives us an opportunity to allow you to follow along with examples, and try them out on your own. The data schema used in Classic Cars is a very simple schema, and will require only a basic understanding of SQL to follow along. This will allow us to give you some basic reporting examples, such as listing reports, Drill-Down reports, some basic charts, and some of the other BIRT features; other features of BIRT include parameters, scripting, and the BIRT report emitters.

However, unlike most other books, I am also providing you an opportunity to follow along with a real-life reporting scenario as well. I am also including examples of reports for the BIRT Bugzilla database. I feel these are beneficial to readers not only as a source of learning, but as an example of how the BIRT platform can be used in a real-world scenario. This lets the user know that a whole lot of theory and sales pitches aren't the only thing BIRT is good for, but that there is also a real-world use of BIRT. Likewise, this also allows us a chance to demonstrate some of the more advanced capabilities of BIRT.

Summary

In this chapter, we took a look at the concepts of business intelligence and open-source software. You got a brief introduction to some of the other players in the open-source business intelligence community, such as JasperReports and Pentaho. Also, you got a little background of some real-world needs for open-source reporting projects.

2

Installing BIRT

I'm sure after discussing the features of BIRT that you're excited to jump right on in. Well you're in luck, because I am excited to show you. BIRT is a powerful application to meet your reporting needs, but the first step is to get BIRT and install it. This can be a bit daunting, as BIRT comes in so many different flavors.

In this chapter, we will discuss the various methods of downloading BIRT and installing it. Once completed you will know:

- Where to go for BIRT
- How to install the standalone **BIRT Report Designer**
- How to install the BIRT Eclipse Plug-in through the Eclipse update manager
- How to install the BIRT Eclipse Plug-in manually
- How to build BIRT from source.

Requirements

BIRT has a fairly small set of requirements to run, depending on your use. There are no Operating System requirements to run BIRT, as it is a Java application and should run on any platform that Java will run on. For the BIRT Report Designer, any platform that will run Eclipse will work. Personally I have successfully run and developed reports under Windows, Linux, and Mac OSX. A fair word of warning to the Mac folks: you are probably better off running under Parallels due to Eclipse's poor performance under native OSX.

As far as hardware requirements are concerned, I would recommend at least a Pentium 3 processor with at least 512 MB of RAM for the BIRT Report Designer. The standalone Report Engine has much less stringent requirements, as it does not run a full-blown instance of Eclipse. I would say 256 MB of RAM would be sufficient, depending on the requirements of the application it is being embedded into.

Where Do I Get BIRT?

First, you want to download BIRT. The typical location for everything that is related to BIRT is going to be the Eclipse website, at `http://www.eclipse.org/birt/phoenix`. This will bring you to the BIRT homepage. Here, you can get the latest news on BIRT, including status of upcoming releases, news on books, conferences, and access to the BIRT newsgroups where you can ask questions about BIRT. The newsgroups are an excellent resource for BIRT questions, as they are frequented by the BIRT developers and BIRT Project Management Committee members.

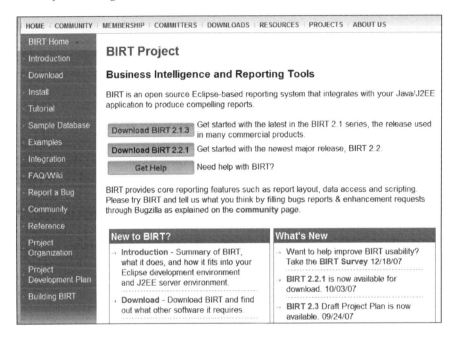

The homepage is also where you can get the various BIRT distributions, such as the All-In-One Eclipse package (which is Eclipse pre-packaged and configured with BIRT), the BIRT Standalone Report Designer, and information about retrieving and building BIRT from source.

For the following installations, we will use the **BIRT 2.2** release.
There are several installation paths to choose from. The one I highly recommend to people is the BIRT All-In-One package. You can also install BIRT as a plug-in to go into an already existing Eclipse installation, or you can retrieve the BIRT Standalone RCP package. I will go into depth about each one of these packages, and the benefits of and reasons to use each in the following sections.

Installing BIRT from the All-in-One Installation

The BIRT All-in-One package is the easiest one to install for BIRT, so it will be the first one I demonstrate. The BIRT All-in-One package is a BIRT distribution that contains a full Eclipse installation, pre-configured with BIRT. I usually use this as the base installation for Eclipse, and add plug-ins accordingly. BIRT can have some tricky issues with configuration that I have come across in the past, and since then, I avoid these by installing the All-In-One package.

As with most BIRT installations, the **All-in-One** package is available from the **Download BIRT** link, as shown previously. This will typically take you to the current and stable release of BIRT. The developers seem to agree that the All-in-One package is the typical way to go, as it is the first link on the page. Following is the screenshot of what the BIRT download page looks like:

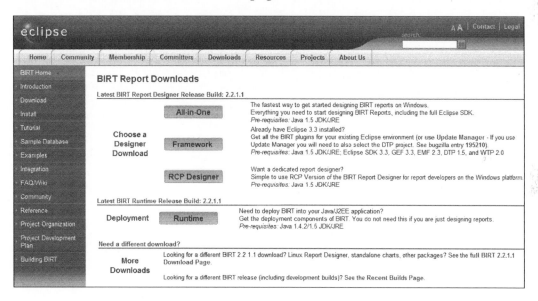

Additionally, older and pre-release versions of BIRT are available from the **More Downloads** section of the BIRT Download Page. From this link, you can retrieve older releases, current milestone builds, and the latest nightly release for those who want to stay on the cutting edge.

BIRT Downloads for build 2_2_1_1 created on 2007-11-01 16:10:01

Build Documentation

BIRT provides a single download that works on all supported platforms.

- ⊡ **License** – These downloads are provided under the Eclipse.org Software User Agreement.
- ⊡ **Install** – Complete download instructions for BIRT and the software it requires.
- ⊡ **Other Builds** – Check for the latest builds and find general information about BIRT builds.
- ⊡ **Language Packs** – Language Packs Available for BIRT.

Eclipse Project Dependencies

BIRT has dependencies on the following Eclipse projects. In certain downloads such as the Allinone these are already included, but in others such as the framework you will be required to download them.

- Eclipse Version 3.3.1.1 SDK
- DTP Version 1.5.1
- GEF Version 3.3.1
- EMF Version 2.3.1 EMF+SDO+XSD
- WTP Version 2.0.1

Report Designer Full Eclipse Install

This Download includes the BIRT Reporting Framework, Eclipse SDK, GEF and EMF and Axis downloads. It includes everything you need to get started.

Availability	Platform	Download
✓	Windows	birt-report-designer-all-in-one-2_2_1_1.zip (md5)

Report Designer Full Eclipse Install for Linux

This Download includes the BIRT Reporting Framework, Eclipse SDK, GEF and EMF and Axis downloads. It includes everything you need to get started.

Availability	Platform	Download
✓	Linux	birt-report-designer-all-in-one-linux-gtk-2_2_1_1.tar.gz (md5)

Report Designer

The BIRT designer is a set Eclipse plugins that lets you build reports as a perspective from within Eclipse.

Shown in the previous screenshot is the full download page for **BIRT 2.2.1.1**. From here, I can retrieve the various installation packages, such as the RCP Standalone Report Designer, the BIRT Source Code, and various other runtime libraries and demo databases. As I am installing the All-in-One package, I downloaded the release for Windows.

The BIRT All-in-One installation package is a large ZIP file (roughly 240 Mb); so for individuals who already have an Eclipse installation and are limited by a small amount of bandwidth, this may not be an attractive option. But for individuals with access to high-speed Internet or not having an existing Eclipse installation, this works out fine. This ZIP file contains a full Eclipse installation, with the BIRT plug-ins already installed and pre-configured for use.

Installation of the BIRT All-in-One package is as simple as opening the ZIP file in an archiving utility such as WinZip and extracting the contents to an installation directory of your choice. I typically use `C:\Eclipse` as my base installation directory.

Installing BIRT All-In-One under Linux

In Linux, installation is very similar. The archive file containing the All-in-One package is a standard Linux tarball file. One recommendation for the Linux installers: I recommend using Sun's Java instead of the GNU Java. The GNU Java is compliant to an older specification of Java than BIRT requires, and some features will not work correctly under Linux. Installing Sun Java under Linux can vary, based on the distribution of Linux you use and the distributor's views of the Sun license on Java. I have chronicled my experiences getting Sun Java to work under Ubuntu Linux, a free desktop-oriented distribution of Linux based on Debian, as well as CentOS, a free alternative to Red Hat's Enterprise Linux, on my blog (`http://digiassn.blogspot.com/`). For your distribution, see the appropriate documentation on getting Sun Java installed, and getting it to execute as the default Java Runtime.

Also, based on the version of BIRT you run, you will need one of the two different Java versions. For BIRT versions prior to 2.2, you will need **Java 1.4**; for 2.2 and later, you will need **Java 1.5**. This is the same for Windows or any UNIX-like Operating System.

Once installed, extract the BIRT All-in-One archive to your target location. This will vary based on the philosophy of file management and purpose of the system in question. For example, on a multi-user desktop system, you may choose to extract this archive to the `/home/yourUserName` folder to allow only yourself access to BIRT.

If you are setting this up on a single-user desktop, or for multiple users, you may set this up under /, /usr, /usr/local folder, or some other dedicated folder location.

```
Output - Notepad
File  Edit  Format  View  Help
Archive:  birt-report-designer-all-in-one-2_2_1_1.zip
   creating: eclipse/
   creating: eclipse/plugins/
   creating: eclipse/plugins/com.lowagie.itext_1.5.2.v20070710/
   creating: eclipse/plugins/com.lowagie.itext_1.5.2.v20070710/META-INF/
   creating: eclipse/plugins/com.lowagie.itext_1.5.2.v20070710/about_files/
   creating: eclipse/plugins/com.lowagie.itext_1.5.2.v20070710/lib/
   creating: eclipse/plugins/org.apache.derby.core_10.1.2.1/
   creating: eclipse/plugins/org.apache.derby.core_10.1.2.1/META-INF/
   creating: eclipse/plugins/org.apache.derby.core_10.1.2.1/about_files/
   creating: eclipse/plugins/org.eclipse.birt.chart.cshelp_2.2.0.v20070625/
   creating: eclipse/plugins/org.eclipse.birt.chart.cshelp_2.2.0.v20070625/META-INF/
   creating: eclipse/plugins/org.eclipse.birt.chart.doc.isv_2.2.0.v20070625/
   creating: eclipse/plugins/org.eclipse.birt.chart.doc.isv_2.2.0.v20070625/META-INF/
   creating: eclipse/plugins/org.eclipse.birt.chart.integration.wtp.ui_2.2.1.r221_v20070828/
   creating: eclipse/plugins/org.eclipse.birt.chart.integration.wtp.ui_2.2.1.r221_v20070828/META-INF/
   creating: eclipse/plugins/org.eclipse.birt.chart.integration.wtp.ui_2.2.1.r221_v20070828/icons/
   creating: eclipse/plugins/org.eclipse.birt.chart.integration.wtp.ui_2.2.1.r221_v20070828/runtime/
   creating: eclipse/plugins/org.eclipse.birt.chart.integration.wtp.ui_2.2.1.r221_v20070828/templates/
   creating: eclipse/plugins/org.eclipse.birt.cshelp_2.2.0.v20070622/
   creating: eclipse/plugins/org.eclipse.birt.cshelp_2.2.0.v20070622/META-INF/
   creating: eclipse/plugins/org.eclipse.birt.doc.isv_2.2.1.r221_v20070913/
   creating: eclipse/plugins/org.eclipse.birt.doc.isv_2.2.1.r221_v20070913/META-INF/
   creating: eclipse/plugins/org.eclipse.birt.doc_2.2.1.r221_v20070919/
   creating: eclipse/plugins/org.eclipse.birt.doc_2.2.1.r221_v20070919/META-INF/
   creating: eclipse/plugins/org.eclipse.birt.integration.wtp.ui_2.2.1.r22x_v20070830/
   creating: eclipse/plugins/org.eclipse.birt.integration.wtp.ui_2.2.1.r22x_v20070830/META-INF/
   creating: eclipse/plugins/org.eclipse.birt.integration.wtp.ui_2.2.1.r22x_v20070830/icons/
   creating: eclipse/plugins/org.eclipse.birt.integration.wtp.ui_2.2.1.r22x_v20070830/runtime/
   creating: eclipse/plugins/org.eclipse.birt.integration.wtp.ui_2.2.1.r22x_v20070830/schema/
   creating: eclipse/plugins/org.eclipse.birt.integration.wtp.ui_2.2.1.r22x_v20070830/templates/
   creating: eclipse/plugins/org.eclipse.birt.report.data.oda.jdbc_2.2.1.r22x_v20070919/
   creating: eclipse/plugins/org.eclipse.birt.report.data.oda.jdbc_2.2.1.r22x_v20070919/META-INF/
```

```
Output - Notepad
File  Edit  Format  View  Help
 inflating: eclipse/plugins/org.eclipse.wst.wsdl.ui_1.2.1.v200709112242.jar
 inflating: eclipse/plugins/org.eclipse.wst.wsdl.validation_1.1.201.v200706062140.jar
 inflating: eclipse/plugins/org.eclipse.wst.wsdl_1.1.100.v200707201214.jar
 inflating: eclipse/plugins/org.eclipse.wst.wsi.ui.doc.user_1.0.203.v200706120315.jar
 inflating: eclipse/plugins/org.eclipse.wst.wsi.ui_1.0.300.v200706062140.jar
 inflating: eclipse/plugins/org.eclipse.wst.wsi_1.0.105.v200706120315.jar
 inflating: eclipse/plugins/org.eclipse.wst.xml.core_1.1.201.v200709201331.jar
 inflating: eclipse/plugins/org.eclipse.wst.xml.ui.infopop_1.0.2.v200706110217.jar
 inflating: eclipse/plugins/org.eclipse.wst.xml.ui_1.0.301.v200709112242.jar
 inflating: eclipse/plugins/org.eclipse.wst.xmleditor.doc.user_1.0.300.v200705302225.jar
 inflating: eclipse/plugins/org.eclipse.wst.xsd.core_1.1.201.v200707172046.jar
 inflating: eclipse/plugins/org.eclipse.wst.xsd.ui_1.2.1.v200709112242.jar
 inflating: eclipse/plugins/org.eclipse.wst.xsdeditor.doc.user_1.0.300.v200705302225.jar
 inflating: eclipse/plugins/org.eclipse.wst_1.0.2.v200706120315.jar
 inflating: eclipse/plugins/org.uddi4j_2.0.5.v200706111329.jar
 inflating: eclipse/plugins/org.apache.batik.bridge_1.6.0.v200706111724.jar
 inflating: eclipse/plugins/org.apache.batik.css_1.6.0.v200706111724.jar
 inflating: eclipse/plugins/org.apache.batik.dom.svg_1.6.0.v200706111724.jar
 inflating: eclipse/plugins/org.apache.batik.dom_1.6.0.v200706111724.jar
 inflating: eclipse/plugins/org.apache.batik.ext.awt_1.6.0.v200706111724.jar
 inflating: eclipse/plugins/org.apache.batik.extension_1.6.0.v200706111724.jar
 inflating: eclipse/plugins/org.apache.batik.parser_1.6.0.v200706111724.jar
 inflating: eclipse/plugins/org.apache.batik.pdf_1.6.0.v200706111329.jar
 inflating: eclipse/plugins/org.apache.batik.svggen_1.6.0.v200706111724.jar
 inflating: eclipse/plugins/org.apache.batik.swing_1.6.0.v200706111724.jar
 inflating: eclipse/plugins/org.apache.batik.transcoder_1.6.0.v200706111724.jar
 inflating: eclipse/plugins/org.apache.batik.util.gui_1.6.0.v200706111724.jar
 inflating: eclipse/plugins/org.apache.batik.util_1.6.0.v200706111724.jar
 inflating: eclipse/plugins/org.apache.batik.xml_1.6.0.v200706111724.jar
 inflating: eclipse/plugins/org.w3c.css.sac_1.3.0.v200706111724.jar
 inflating: eclipse/plugins/org.w3c.dom.smil_1.0.0.v200706111724.jar
 inflating: eclipse/plugins/org.w3c.dom.svg_1.1.0.v200706111724.jar
```

Installing iText for PDF Support

One optional element that needs to be downloaded is iText. iText is a Java library written by Bruno Lowagie and Paulo Soares, which allows Java programs to output in the Adobe PDF format. Without iText, reports cannot be exported to PDF. iText is available from Bruno Lowagie's website at `http://www.lowagie.com/iText/`.

iText is the cause of one of the most commonly occurring issues with BIRT. As of the time of this writing, iText is not distributed with BIRT at the request of Eclipse itself, due to the fact that it has not completed its intellectual property verification. While using iText is perfectly legal, and the maintainer has given full permission for use of iText in BIRT, the legal folks at Eclipse are just being safe. As a result, installation of iText is a manual procedure. Fortunately, it is a very easy installation process.

For versions of BIRT prior to 2.2, use **iText version 1.3.2.2**; for later versions, use **iText 1.46**. Installation for all versions remains the same. Installation of iText under the BIRT Report designer is as simple as copying the `iText.jar` file to the appropriate location. This is located under the `eclipse\plugins\com.lowagie.itext_<version>` folder.

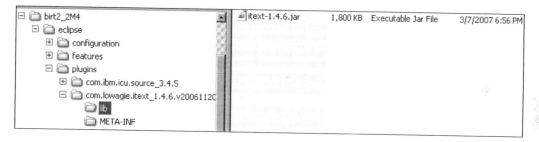

Once it is copied to this location, you will be able to export report designs as PDF documents. Instructions for installing iText to the J2EE web viewer are a little different, and will be covered in Chapter 11 under the section about the Web Viewer Installation.

Installation of BIRT through the Eclipse Plug-in Update Program

The next section covers how to install BIRT using the Eclipse plug-in manager. Let's say that you already have an Eclipse instance that you use regularly. As Eclipse can typically be a rather large package, installing a separate instance may not be feasible due to disk space constraints, policy, or some other limiting factor. In cases such as these, it is more appropriate to add on to your existing Eclipse installation.

Keep in mind that if you take it upon yourself to install BIRT as a plug-in, you must also install all the prerequisite plug-ins that the BIRT designer is built on top of. This part is what makes the All-in-One installation method preferable to the manual installation of plug-ins. Another reason is that this is the avenue in which I have traditionally encountered most installation problems, such as dependency problems.

In order to proceed, you must first make sure that the following dependency packages are installed with BIRT:

BIRT 2.2	BIRT 2.1
Eclipse 3.3	Eclipse 3.2
Graphical Editor Framework 3.3	Graphical Editor Framework 3.2
Eclipse Modeling Framework 2.3	Eclipse Modeling Framework 2.2
Java Runtime Environment 1.5	Java Runtime Environment 1.4.2
Data Tools Project 1.5	

These requirements can be installed separately alongside your BIRT plug-in installation, given that you include the appropriate repositories. Plug-in installation is done through the Eclipse Software Update menu, located under the **Help** toolbar menu, under **Software Updates**.

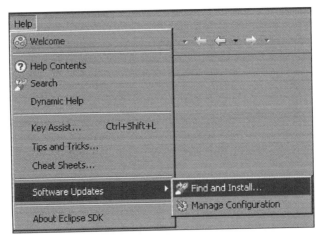

Once in the software update tool, there are two options you can select: You have the option of searching for updates, or to install new features. If you do not already have BIRT installed, you should choose Install New Features. Otherwise, you can get updates for your existing BIRT installation by choosing **Search for updates**.

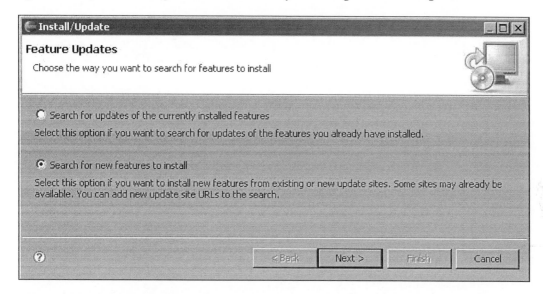

If you choose to update existing software, the software update tool will prompt you to verify your repositories or mirror sites to check for updates. If you chose to install new updates, you will have to complete an extra step in choosing the list of repositories to search for new software. Because BIRT has been a member of the Eclipse consortium since 2004, the BIRT project is listed under the sites to include in your search. You will not need to add BIRT as a new repository to search under. This makes things much easier.

However, as BIRT is collaborating with a number of other Eclipse projects in order to leverage their tools—such as the Web Tools Project for site deployment and the Data Tools Project for a future revision of the query editor inside of BIRT—you will need to include other repositories as well in your update search path.

I recommend at least all of the sites listed in the following screenshot:

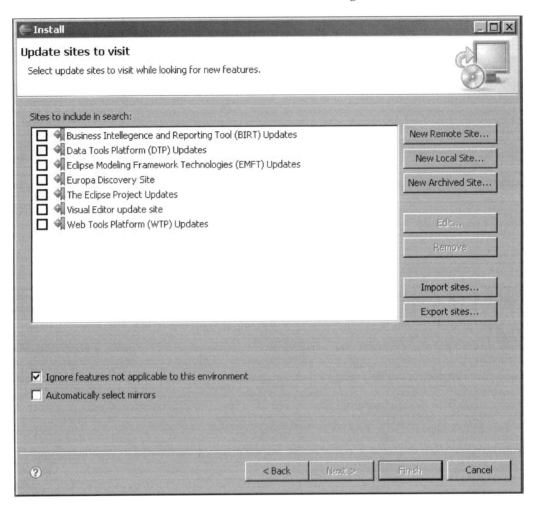

Now, with the correct repositories selected, you can click **Finish**. A list of mirrors will be shown for each repository given. I will typically use the default or first on the list, but this is up to the user. A rule of thumb is to choose a location close to you.

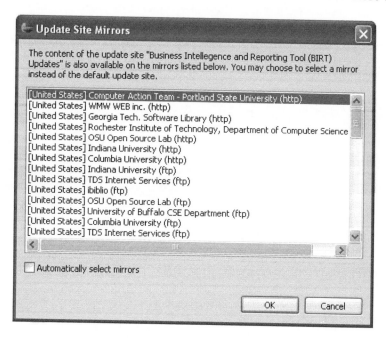

Once you have chosen all of your sites, you will be brought to the package selection screen. Here you can choose which packages to install. BIRT, of course, and all BIRT packages should be chosen.

Sometimes, you will get a notice that a required package has not been chosen. This can be due to various versions in the selected repositories, or because a particular package is not in the chosen repositories, in which case, you will need to add a new repository to your list. Sometimes you can just click on the **Select Required Packages** button, and the necessary packages will be selected from the chosen repositories. This delicate balance of choosing the correct packages, required dependency packages, and repositories is the reason I usually recommend that people use the All-in-One installation method.

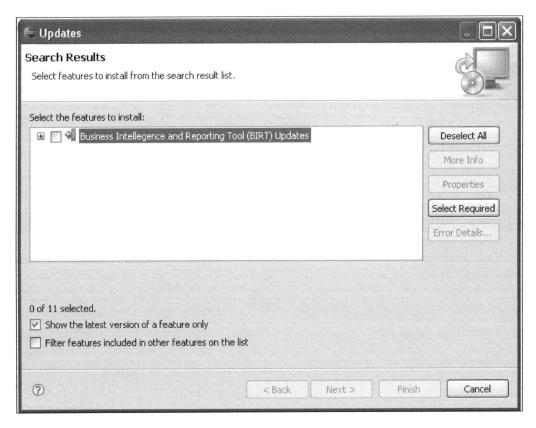

Now, with your packages selected, you can click on **Next**. The packages will then be downloaded from the selected repositories. Once finished downloading, a prompt will come up to install the packages you selected. You can either confirm each package individually, or just select **Install All**. Once completed, you will be asked to restart Eclipse. At this point, you can follow the steps to install iText given earlier, and your BIRT installation will be complete.

Summary

By now, you should have chosen your preferred method of installation and have a working copy of BIRT installed on your machine. We have looked at a number of different installation methods, including:

- The All-in-One Package
- Installing through the Eclipse Software Update Manager
- Installing the Plug-in Manually

We have seen where to get BIRT, how to install it, and a list of requirements needed to run BIRT. This is great because we can now get into the heart of BIRT (report design); but first, we will get acquainted with the BIRT development environment.

3

The BIRT Environment and Your First Report

OK, so now you have BIRT installed; what now? You have heard so many great things about the BIRT Report Designer, and are eager to jump into creating some reports. However, you haven't ever worked with Eclipse or BIRT for that matter. At first glance the BIRT Designer can look a little intimidating, and in some cases you may not even see the BIRT Designer on your first run. That's OK. In this chapter we will get acquainted with the BIRT working environment, also known as the BIRT Perspective in Eclipse lingo, and we will get started on creating a basic report.

A Basic Scenario

When I teach people about development topics of any sort, I like to use scenarios. This book will be no different. These scenarios provide a basic context for the learner to relate the topic information to, and hopefully facilitate absorbing the information.

In this chapter we will look at a very simple scenario, in order to get us started with our first report. You work for a toy company called **Classic Cars**. Classic Cars specializes in selling models of classic cars and motorcycles. Classic Cars uses a centralized database for all company operations, such as employee listing, offices, customers, products, and sales history. This information is in a relational database that is stored locally on your machine, as Classic Cars is a small company.

Through this chapter, I will walk you through creating your first report, which will be a list of all employees who work for the company. I choose this for a number of reasons. First, it is a fairly simple database query to build and understand. If you are not familiar with the SQL language—don't worry—I will provide the queries that you will use. However, I highly recommend getting some basic familiarity with database concepts, and SQL in particular.

In walking through this report, I will introduce you to the BIRT working environment, and show you where to get access to the various portions of the BIRT Designer. Finally, I will show you where you can go through another guided tutorial, accessible from right within the BIRT environment. You might as well have access to all available resources for further learning.

The BIRT Perspective

So we are ready to begin. We have defined a clear objective for our basic report, and now is the time to jump into the basic concepts of the BIRT Environment.

Once you start BIRT/Eclipse the first time, you will be asked to select a location for a **Workspace**.

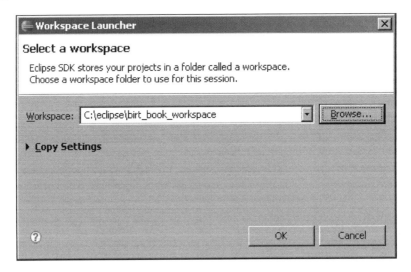

A Workspace is a location where projects get stored. This is very useful for Java developers, who may want to re-use projects; however for a report developer, a single Workspace should suffice. In our case, we will set our **Workspace** to **C:\eclipse\birt_book_workspace**.

If you're running the BIRT All-in-One package, you will start up in the default Eclipse screen and will need to change to the BIRT report perspective. Eclipse uses different **perspectives** as interfaces for different functionality and tools for particular tasks. For instance, if you are writing a Java program, you would use one of the several Java perspectives available, which would allow you access to outlines, class views, and other tabs. If you are debugging a program, you would use the debug perspective, it gives you access to a tab with variables, tools bars for controlling the flow of programs, breakpoints, and other debugging functions.

For our purposes, we will use the BIRT reporting perspective, which will give us access to the BIRT report-building elements that we need in report development. The BIRT report perspective can always be accessed from one of the several ways to open perspectives in Eclipse. One such way is from the menu bar, under **Window/Open Perspective**, **Report Design** (if available), or under **Other/Report Design**. Typically on the upper right-hand side is the **Open Perspective icon** for quicker access.

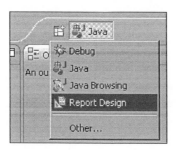

The BIRT Workbench

In Eclipse, the main work area is called the workbench. Once you open the BIRT perspective, you will be looking at the Eclipse workbench with the BIRT perspective.

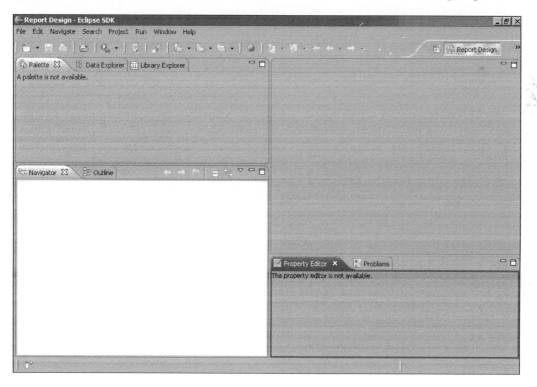

The BIRT perspective is broken up into several different sections by default, but is customizable by the user. For this book, we will keep this default. However, if you wanted to change the layout, you would only need to "drag and drop" any of the workbench tabs to another section.

The Navigator

The first section under the BIRT workspace that we will discuss is the Navigator. The Navigator is fairly universal among Eclipse perspectives, as it is what is used to browse the current workspace for contained projects. Under the navigator, you can create and manage projects, reports, libraries, templates, and various other files that would be contained in your projects. If you wanted to rename the folder or create folders to organize report elements—such as file locations—it can all be done under the Navigator. The Navigator can be used to do many of the same functions that you can perform under the menu bar, under the **File** section. If your workspace contains many different reporting projects, you can also use the Navigator to go into those projects, so that other projects are not visible during editing.

In the next screenshot, I have a single project called **StyleSheetExample** with a single report design file and a report library, which we will discuss in Chapter 9 From this menu, you can see that the right arrow is available to allow me to go into the **StyleSheetExample** project, which is like double-clicking on a folder in Windows Explorer. I also have the Sync with Editor double-arrows clicked, which allows me to automatically give focus to each of these items if they are open in Eclipse.

So when would you use multiple reports in a single project, or why would you want to break out projects instead of storing all your reports in a single project? This is really a matter of preference. I will typically store reports based on real-life projects. So if I were doing an earnings report for the 4th quarter, I would create a single project called 4th Quarter Earnings Report, with a summary report containing graphs, high-level areas such as regions of the country, and all my detailed reports—that would get linked in when a user clicks on a portion of the graph or region in a single project. This allows me to keep report and projects separated. If I were building an online reporting portal that uses many shared components, I would also put all reports in their own project, with a library housing the shared components. This is useful because online reports have the tendency to require multiple sub-reports, and very rarely can be captured in a single report. There is more on using libraries and on linking in reports in Chapter 7.

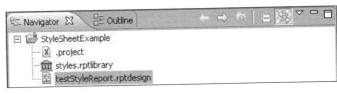

Another useful function of the Navigator is that it gives you quick access to actually run BIRT reports. This will actually run a report in a separate and interactive instance with full export capabilities, which differs from the **Preview** tab under the Designer pane. Things that you get with actually running a report instead of previewing are the navigation features, pagination, table of contents functionality, and the ability to see how reports would look in built-in BIRT Web Report Viewer. Running a report from the Navigator is available from the report submenu when you right-click on a **Report** design file under the **Navigator**, as illustrated in the following screenshot.

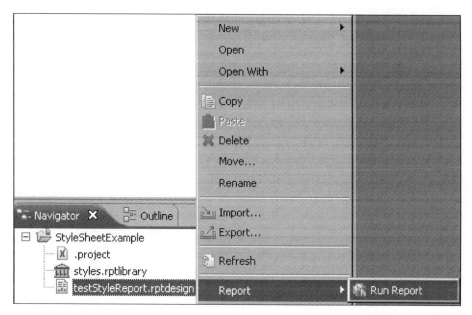

The Outline

Next on the agenda is the Outline. Now if there were one portion of the BIRT perspective that is often overlooked, yet provides good return value when used, it would be the Outline.

The Outline provides a hierarchical view of a reports structure that you can use to select, edit properties, view events, and edit scripts. Oftentimes, it is the best way to get access to particular elements of a report for editing with precision, without the hassle of attempting to select them in the graphical Editor. It is very easy to select and expand high-level elements to easily select contained report elements, such as rows, cells, and groups. Rather than having to muck around with the Report Designer to find the element you are changing, you have it right at your fingertips with the Outline. It also makes things easier when you begin scripting, to ensure that you are writing script for the correct components. I can tell you this from my experience; it is an incredibly useful view, and learning how to use it can save time and headaches in the long run.

In the following example image, I am showing an expanded view of a very simple report demonstrating the different elements of reports that are visible in a report **Outline**. Here I am showing my **Data Sources**, **Data Sets**, the fields in the **Data Sets**, the visual report elements, my **Libraries**, and library components.

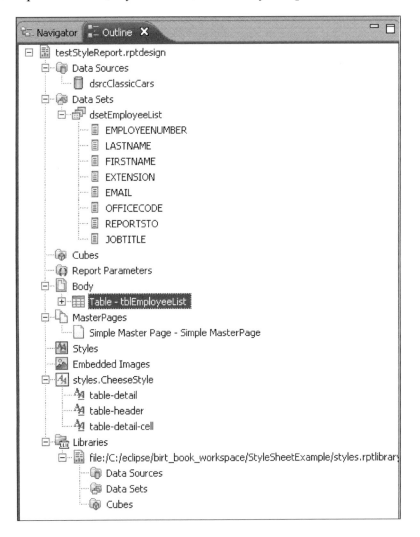

The Palette

Now, taking a page from many other visual IDE's, BIRT provides a component Palette that contains visual report design components. Just as in Visual Basic you can "drag and drop" components like buttons, text boxes, and labels into a form, BIRT allows you to "drag and drop" visual report components such as labels, data text items, HTML text items, graphics, and layout modifiers such as grids and tables. In the next chapter we will cover the various report components, their purpose, and how each one is used in a report.

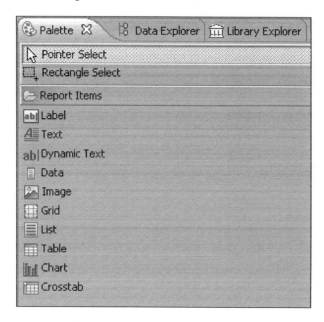

Now although we have not gotten into the topic of scripting in BIRT, it is worth mentioning that the Palette does change when you open up the Script Editor in BIRT, to give a simplified view of different low-level script objects that are available. If this is a topic that we have not gotten to, why do I mention it here? Because this is one of those things that I wish I had known early on in my BIRT development experiences, which I didn't find out until later and kicked myself for not knowing about it. As strange as that sounds, you will thank me when we get there.

The following figure shows the BIRT **Palette** when editing script, showing available functions and objects:

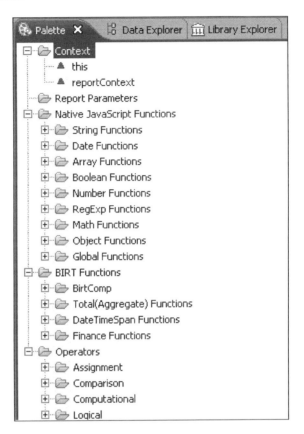

The Data Explorer

A report development environment would not be very useful if it didn't have a means or mechanism to manage data connections. The Data Explorer is such a place.

The **Data Explorer** provides several different data-related functions. From here you can manage data connections to your **Data Sources**. For example, this is one of the locations where you can manage your database connections and drivers and any sort of custom data adapters. You will also manage your data queries from this pane. Finally, this is the place where you will manage your **Report Parameters**, which the report consumer will use to interact and pass in data to your report for processing. New in **BIRT version 2.2** is the ability to manage **Cubes**, which we will cover later on in this book. This option did not exist in the previous versions of BIRT.

It is important to note that this is not the only place where you can manage your data-related objects. You can also manage these items from your report outline. This gives you a little bit of flexibility depending on which views you may have opened.

Property Editor

Now with any visual development IDE, you have the ability to change and manipulate various properties for visual components. BIRT provides this ability through the Property Editor. Things that you would expect such as font attributes—like size and weighting, alignment, and color—are available through the Property Editor. But there are other features of the Property Editor such as value formatting, hyperlinking, Table of Contents entries for online reports, element to data binding, the ability to set conditional visual properties known as highlights, and enumerated value replacements called Maps—all available from the Property Editor.

For example, let's say I was doing a financial report. Now with a column of financial data, I would want to right-justify it so that the decimal numbers line up. I would also want to bold my column headers, set the values to display as currency with a preceding dollar sign, and only display two decimal places. This is all set through the Property Editor.

In addition, if an account status is stored as a number, and I want the report to display an actual text representation—assuming that there is not a table in my database that contains this mapping—I would assign a map to my display element with the possible values and their display representation. I would also set a Highlight to bold the accounts that were in danger of defaulting.

The Property Editor is a particularly large beast that we will be revisiting many times throughout the course of this book. As I indicated in the Outline section, the Property Editor and the Outline make a very useful combination when setting report parameters, especially with visual elements in complex reports.

The properties pane allows users to set various properties for report elements. Things such as font size, boldness, and italics can be set here for text-based elements. Data bindings for list elements and table elements are set here, and really tricky things such as highlighting conditions for setting up alternating colors for rows are set here.

Report Designer

In any visual IDE on the market, there is a part of the user interface that allows a developer to manipulate the look and feel of what they are developing. In programming environments such as Visual Basic, this would be the **Form designer**. In web development environments such as Adobe Dreamweaver, this is the **Designer** tab. In BIRT, we use the **Report Designer**. The Report designer is the section of the BIRT workspace that takes up the most real estate, by default. It is denoted by the title of the report design that is currently open, and has multiple tabs on the bottom part.

Reports need to have an interface to the user, and this is where you design that. This is where you drag the visual components from the Palette in order to work with, and get that exact look and feel necessary to display your information. Working with the Report Designer can be a little tricky if you do not know what to expect; so let me set your expectations now. BIRT is not a pixel-perfect "What You See Is What You Get" (WYSIWYG) development environment. So if you are expecting things to design perfect visual layouts for reports for use in printing, or a pixel perfect design interface like Visual Basic, BIRT does not provide this out of the box. BIRT is designed as a primarily online report technology, and as such it is heavily HTML-driven. So it uses a design interface similar to Dreamweaver or NVU. BIRT, out of the box, does not provide layers. In the Report Designer, components will be resized, shaped, and adjusted to give an approximation on how an HTML engine will render them. For such design principles in their strictest sense, this is a much better method as it does most of the alignment and proximity rendering for you.

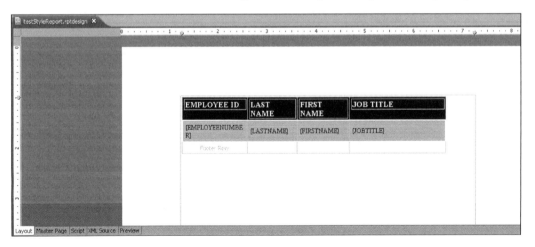

The designer also has several other tabs associated with it. The **Master Page** tab will open a designer that allows users to design a constant header and footer layout that will remain persistent on multi-page reports. These would be separate from the table headers and rows used in the Layout Editor.

The **Script** tab is for more advanced report developers, and allows for overloading report events associated with report elements. BIRT uses an event-based model for report rendering; so overloading particular events allows the user to control and manipulate at a much finer level the way a particular report will be displayed to the user. This also allows report developers to add in advanced business logic to report designs. BIRT utilizes the Mozilla Rhino JavaScript engine to accomplish this. In addition to internal report script, BIRT also allows developers to provide event handlers in external Java objects.

The next screenshot shows the BIRT Script Editor overriding an event for a **Table** object. You will notice the drop-down box displays the event method **onPrepare** that is being overridden. Next to it is a button labeled **Reset Method**, which will delete all code in the Editor and bring the event handler back to a default state. And next to it is a label **Table**, which indicates the name of the element that we are setting an event handler for.

It is important to note from experience that again, the Outline provides an invaluable tool for script editing in that it allows a developer to ensure that they are developing an event handler for the correct component. Too often with report development in BIRT, a developer will select the wrong component using the **Layout** Editor. Also, because the **Layout** Editor is not visible when the **Script** Editor is open, the Outline provides a convenient mechanism to switch between elements.

```
//We only want to add this into our code when the value is set to true to
//hide the report table
if ( params["rprmAddGroup"] == true )
{
    //Bring in the BIRT Report Model API scripting elements for using the StructureScriptAPIFactory
    importPackage( Packages.org.eclipse.birt.report.engine.api.script.element );

    //Create a dynamic sort condition
    var groupCondition = StructureScriptAPIFactory.createGroup();

    groupCondition.setKeyExpr("row[\"A\"]");

    //set condition to ascending order
    groupCondition.setSortDirection("asc");
    groupCondition.setSortType("asc");

    //Add to the table
    this.addGroup(sortCondition);
}
```

For those who are gluttons for punishment, you can view the actual **XML Source** for a report page. Personally I rarely ever use the **XML Source** viewer, except to copy report source code when helping individuals in the BIRT newsgroup.

Finally, there is the report **Preview** tab. This is a convenient way to preview how a report will look, without having to have the application launch a separate window with the report viewer. This is different than actually running the report using either the **Outline** or the **Run** options under the **File** menu. For one, it does not provide pagination, so report previews will come out as one giant HTML page. There are no navigation options under the report preview either.

Setting up a Simple Project

So now that we are familiar with the different aspects of the BIRT Workspace, what now? What does it all mean? How does it all work together? And how do we use it? Well, that is what we are going to explore next as we build a very simple report. We will describe components more in detail in the next chapter; so for now just follow along and see how to navigate in the BIRT environment.

The first thing we want to do when setting up our simple report project is to define what the project is going to be, and what our first simple report will be. Our first report will be a simple dump of the employees who work for **Classic Cars**.

So, the first thing we need to do is set up a project. To do this, we will use the Navigator. Make sure you have the BIRT report perspective open, as described earlier. Use the following steps to create our project:

1. Open up the **Navigator** by single-clicking on the **Navigator** tab.
2. Right-click anywhere in the white-space in the **Navigator**.
3. Select **New** from the menu, and under **New** select **project**.

4. From the Dialog screen, select **Business Intelligence and Reporting Tools** from the list of folders; expand that view, and select **Report Project**. Then click on the **Next** button.

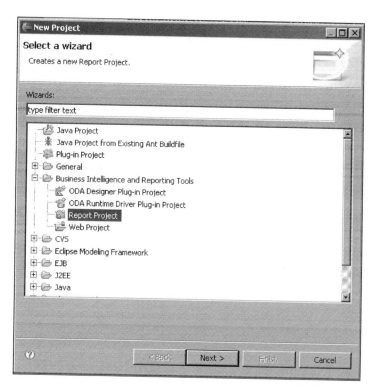

5. For the Project name, enter **Class_Cars_BIRT_Reports**. You can either leave the **Use Default Location** checkbox checked, or uncheck it and enter a location on your local drive to store this report project.

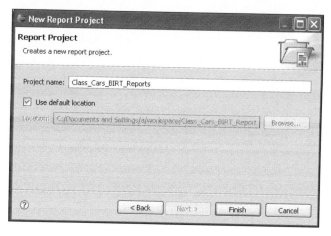

Now, we have a very simple report project in which to store our BIRT reports that we will build in the first few chapters of the book.

Creating a Simple Report

Now that we have our first project open, we will look at creating our first report. As mentioned earlier, we will create a basic listing report that will display all the information in the employees table. In order to do this, we will use the following steps:

1. Right-click on the **Class_Cars_BIRT_Reports** project under the **Navigator**, and choose **New** and **Report**.

2. Make sure the **Class_Cars_BIRT_Reports** project is highlighted in the new report Dialog, and enter in the name as **EmployeeList.rptdesign**. I chose this name as it is somewhat descriptive of the purpose of the report, which is to display a list of employees. As a rule of thumb, always try to name your reports after the expected output, such as **QuarterlyEarningReport.rptdesign**, **weeklyPayStub.rptdesign**, or **accountsPayable.rptdesign**.

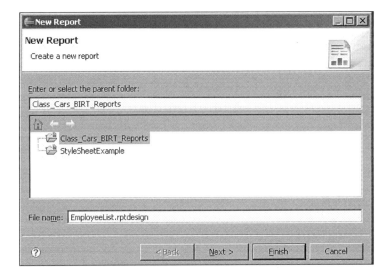

3. On the next screen is a list of different report templates that we can use. We will select **Simple Listing** and then click on the **Finish** button.

4. Go to the **Data Explorer**, right-click on **Data Sources**, and choose **New Data Source**.

5. From the New Data Source Dialog box, select **Classic Models Inc. Sample Database** and click on the **Next** button.

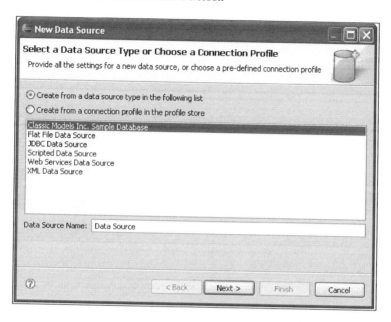

6. On the next screen, it will inform you of the driver information. You can ignore this for now and click **Finish**.

7. Under the **Data Explorer**, right-click on **Data Sets** and choose **New Data Set**.

8. On the next screen, enter the **Data Set Name** as **dsetEmployees**, and make sure that our created **Data Source** is selected in the list of Data sources. You can click **Next** when this is finished.

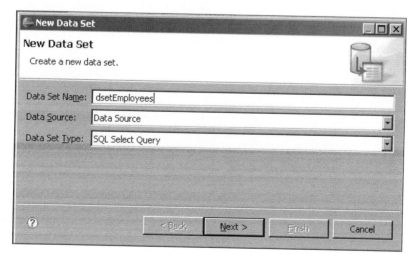

9. On the Query Dialog, enter the following query and click **Finish**:

```
select
*
from
CLASSICMODELS.EMPLOYEES
```

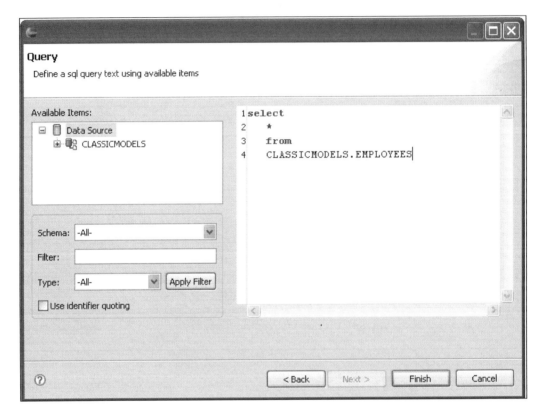

10. On the next screen, just click **OK**. This screen is used to edit information about Data Sets, and we will ignore it for now.

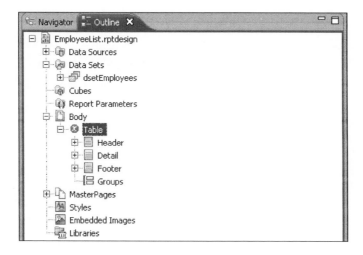

11. Now, from the **Outline** select **Data Sets** and expand it to show all of the fields. Drag the **EMPLOYEENUMBER** element over to the Report Designer, and drop it on the cell with the label of **Detail** Row. This will be the second row and the first column.

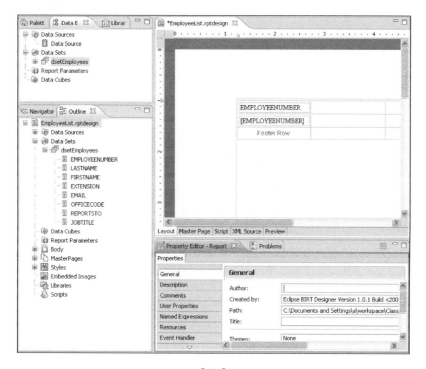

12. You will notice that when you do this, the header row also gets an element placed in it called **EMPLOYEENUMBER**. This is the Header label. Double-click on this cell and it will become highlighted. We can now edit it. Type in "**Employee ID**."

13. Drag and drop the **LASTNAME**, **FIRSTNAME**, and **JOBTITLE** to the detail cells to the right of the **EMPLOYEENUMBER** cell.

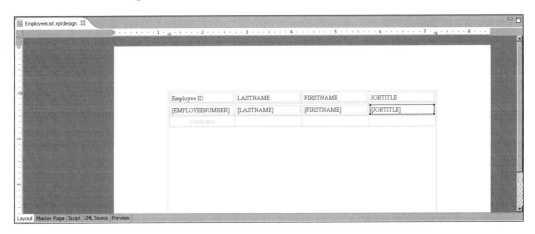

14. Now, we want to put the header row in bold. Under the **Outline**, select the **Row** element located under **Body/Table/Header**. This will change the Property Editor. Click on **Font**, and then click on the **Bold** button.

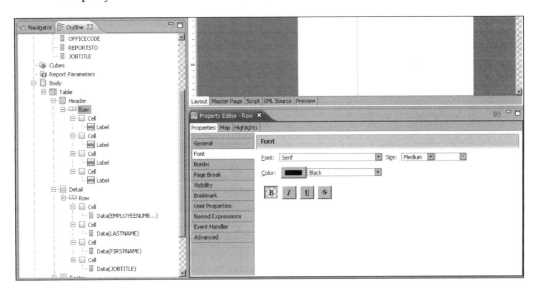

That's it! We have created our first basic report. To see what this report looks like, under the Report Designer pane, click on the **Preview** tab. This will allow you to get a good idea of what this report will look like. Alternatively you can actually Run the report and get an idea what this report will look like in the BIRT Report Viewer application, by going up to **File/View Report/View Report in Web Viewer**. This option is also available by right-click on the report design file under the **Navigator**, and choosing **Report** followed by **Run**.

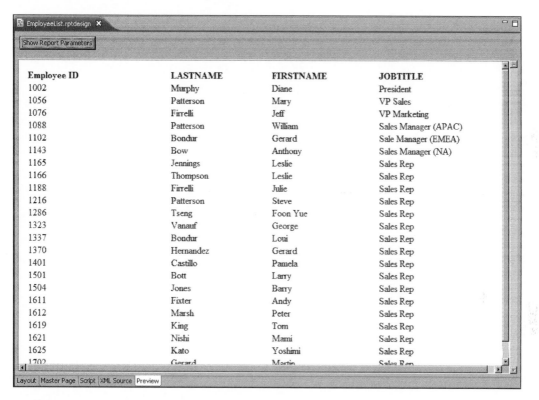

Although it may be a simple report, this exercise demonstrated how a report developer can get through the BIRT environment, and how the different elements of the BIRT perspective work together.

Summary

For a very simple report design, we utilized all of the major areas of the BIRT perspective. We used the Navigator to create a new report project and a new report design, the Data explorer to create out data connection and Data Set, dragged elements from the Outline to the Report Designer to get the data elements into the right place, and used the Property Editor and Outline cooperatively to bold the text in the table header.

In the coming chapters we will build more complex reports, and in the process, explain what the various BIRT report elements are and what they can do.

4

Visual Report Components

In the previous chapter, we looked at the BIRT workspace. You should be familiar with the environment you will use to build BIRT reports. Now we get to take a look at each of the individual BIRT report elements, some of their uses, and some of their common properties. By gaining some familiarity with these components, you can save yourself a good amount of headache in working with BIRT. A surprising number of questions come up on performing some of the more common functions with BIRT components, such as how to format numbers as currency or limit decimal places, how to format dates, and other questions about features that can be influenced by using simple BIRT properties.

BIRT report components aren't radically different from other visual components, used in other visual development environments and Report Designers. You have some of the more common visual components, such as text labels, data-bound text elements, and graphics. For those who are already familiar with Web development environments there are formatting components that you might already be familiar with, such as grids that are similar in function to HTML tables. Then, there are some more advanced components such as graphs, tables, and in later BIRT releases the cross-chart component.

In this chapter, we will take a look at a number of these components and some of their common uses. In the last chapter, we worked with a few of these components, such as the data element, text label, and table, and their properties. Report components are available from the Palette, and their properties are accessible from the Property Editor. So in this chapter, we will be working mainly with the Palette, the Property Editor, and the Report Designer panes in the workbench.

Adding Labels

In almost any development environment, you have static text elements. These are text elements that for one reason or another will not change. Common uses of static text elements are for field identifiers in online Web forms, identification of what some piece of data is, instructions for how to use an application, on-screen prompts, and titles. Reporting is no exception to this rule. In reporting, you see this type of static text content used as column headers for listings, report titles, and footer information, such as copyright lines. BIRT provides this in the form of Labels. Following is the icon used on the development Palette for the Label:

In the previous chapter, we saw Labels used as the column headers in our Employee Listing report, although we didn't have to explicitly create them. We got to see one of the properties of Labels when we changed it and made them bold. This illustrated one of the most common properties of the Label component: font information. This will be the most common property you work with when working with Labels; however, it is not the only one.

As this is the most common and least technical property to work with, we are going to create a simple report to demonstrate the properties used with this component. Go through the following sequence of steps:

1. Right-click on the **Class_Cars_BIRT_Reports** project under the **Navigator**, and choose **New | Report**.

2. Make sure the **Class_Cars_BIRT_Reports** project is highlighted in the **New Report** Dialog, and enter in the name as **HelloWorld.rptdesign**. You will notice that I don't use a space in the filename. The reason is that some operating systems have issues with spaces in names, and it is considered bad etiquette in others to use spaces even if it is allowed.

3. Select **Blank Report** from the list of **New Report** templates, and click **Finish**.

4. From the **Palette**, click on the **Label**, and "drag and drop" it over to the Report Designer pane. You will have a blinking cursor on the Label component you just dropped on to the Report Designer. If you do not have a cursor, double-click on the Label component, and type in **Hello World**.

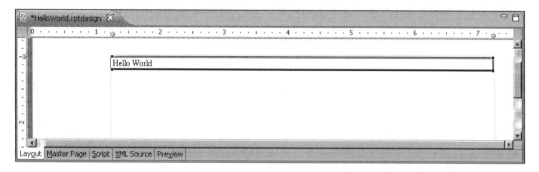

5. Under the **Property Editor**, the **General** tab should be be highlighted. If it is not, go ahead and click on it. The General tab is where elements such as the element name, font selection, font color, alignment, and style sheet selection are located. Under the **Name** option, type in **lblHello** to name the component.

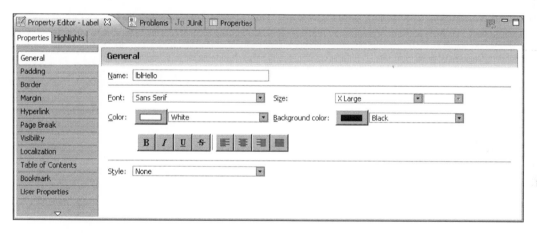

6. Under **Font**, choose **Sans Serif.** You can use any font here that you would like; I chose **Sans Serif** because it is a commonly used font for reading text on screen.

7. Under **Size,** choose **X-Large**. This will make it easier to read.

8. Click on the button next to the **Color** option, and select the color **White** from the available colors. We want a slightly different contrast than black on white to make it stand out a little.

9. Click on the button next to the **Background color** option, and select the **Black** color. Now, click on the ▣ button to make the text bold. Finally, click on the **Preview** tab in the Report Designer to see the finished report.

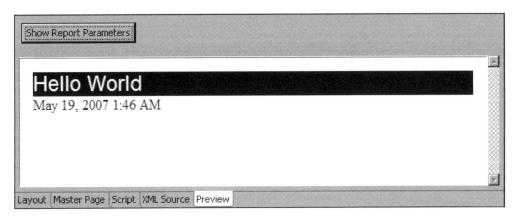

Just shown is the screenshot of the finished report. We were able to easily manipulate some basic visual elements of the Label Component, using the **Property Editor**. There are a number of other elements that we will cover more in depth later, such as conditional hiding and hyperlinks. The important thing to remember about the Label is that it is a text component that is not bound to data in any manner.

Adding Images

The next component we will talk about is the Image component. The Image component is a mechanism for putting in static graphics, such as company logos, into a report page. The BIRT Image component has lot of capabilities that allow for dynamic image usage based on data, including image data in Report Designs for easier distribution of single reports, and using image files from a resource location or Library to allow for single images to be used across multiple reports. A lot of these features we will discuss later in the book. Following is the icon used on the development Palette for the Image:

In the following exercise, we are going to insert a logo from the Eclipse home page at the top of the Hello World report.

1. Open the **HelloWorld.rptdesign** from the **Classic_Cars_BIRT_Reports** project. From the **Palette**, drag an **Image** object over to the Report Designer pane, just above the **Hello World** label.

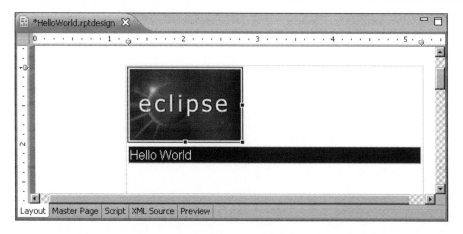

2. The **Edit Image** Dialog pops up. From the Edit Image Dialog there are several options for putting images in reports. You can put in a URL for a remote image hosted on a Web server. You can add an **Embedded image** from your local file system that will get stored in the report itself. If you have an image stored in your resources (more on that later), you can add it from there. You can also set a **Dynamic image**, which based on particular conditions can change the image file; this is useful if you want to pass in a value for different companies, and have different report headers be displayed. For this exercise, keep the **URI** option highlighted, and enter the following URL: `http://www.eclipse.org/artwork/images/eclipse_bckgr_logo_fc_sm.jpg`. Be sure to put double quotes around the URL, otherwise you will get an error.

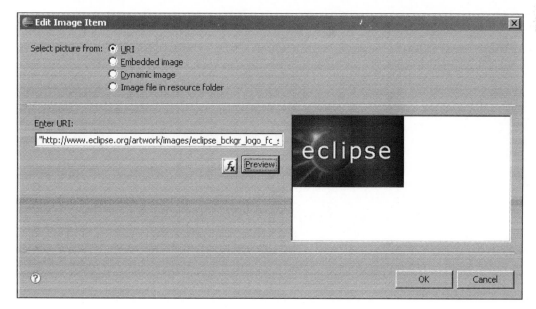

3.   Hit **OK**. The report preview is illustrated as follows:

Using Text and Dynamic Text

Text components are very similar to Label components. They provide much more flexibility than Labels in that they allow HTML formatting within the definition for the text. They also allow for some special tags that will display data from a JavaScript environment. It is even possible to put in images without using the BIRT Image component and anchor tags. Following are the icons used on the development Palette for the Text and Dynamic Text:

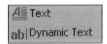

For the following example, we will build on to our Hello World report, by adding in a list that will be formatted with HTML. The items will be Item 1, Item 2, and Item 3 respectively. Item 1 will be set to bold using HTML; Item 2 and Item 3 will remain unchanged. For the purpose of this example you do not need to be familiar with HTML, as I will walk you through the steps. A detailed tutorial on HTML is outside of the scope of this book.

1.   Open the **HelloWorld.rptdesign** from the **Classic_Cars_BIRT_Reports** project. From the **Palette**, drag the **Text** object over to the Report Designer pane, just below the **Hello World** label. The Text element icon is illustrated at the beginning of this section.

2.   The **Edit Text Item** Dialog will pop up. Here, we can edit the type of text we want to be appeared, control the HTML formatting of the text, and get access to quick menus that will allow us to see a small sample of HTML code that we can embed in a text object. At the very top, change the type of text from **Auto** to **HTML**.

3. Go ahead and play around with the different types of formatting menus here. You can see the drop-down box that says **Formatting**. Change that from **Formatting** to **Lists**. Hit the **<DL>** button that appears to the right of the drop-down list. You can see that it will automatically create both the opening and closing tags for the list.

4. Now, click on the **<LI>** button. Do this three times. In between the **<LI>** and **</LI>** tags, put one of the following labels in order:

   Item 1

   Item 2

   Item 3

5. Now, using your mouse, highlight the Item 1 text between the first **<LI>** and **</LI>** tags. With **Item 1** highlighted, click on the **<B>** button at the top of the **Edit Text** Dialog. This will automatically surround the **Item 1** text with the tags **<B>** and **</B>**.

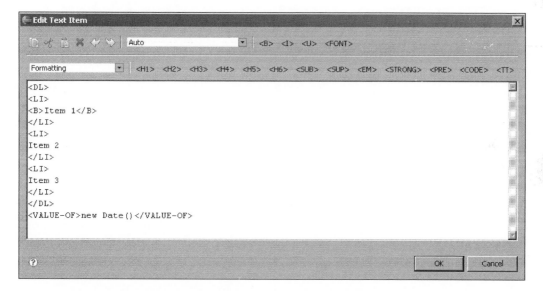

6. Move the cursor below the **</DL>** tag. Select the **Dynamic Text** tag from the drop-down list. Click on the **<Value-Of>** button, which will insert a **<Value-Of>** and **</Value-Of>** tags at the position of the cursor. The Value-Of tag is a special BIRT tag that will insert dynamic text based on any number of values — such as JavaScript results or data values — at the time of the report generation.

7. In between the **<Value-Of>** and **</Value-Of>** tags, put in **new Date()**. This is a small piece of JavaScript code that will retrieve the current date.

8. Hit **OK**. Now, click on **Preview**. You can see that the **Item 1** text is now in bold, and the place where the **<Value-Of>** tag was located now contains the current date and time. You will notice two different dates and times. One is from our Value-Of expression. The other is located in an area called the Master Page, which we will discuss later.

Of course, there is a lot more you can do with this by having some understanding of HTML. The <Value-Of> tag also gives you a lot of flexibility once data becomes part of the picture, which we will see later on. With a little understanding of JavaScript, you can make some really dynamic things happen. With the combination of HTML and JavaScript, you can add some report interactivity.

The Dynamic Text component is very similar to the Text component using the <Value-Of> tag, except that it uses JavaScript and the BIRT report objects to display its text. For the time being, we do not need to know much more about this because we will be covering this more in depth during Chapter 12. For now, we will go through a simple exercise to demonstrate how the Dynamic Text component can be used with JavaScript. In the following exercise, we will take a very simple phrase, and using the Javascript function to convert to upper case, we will display the text in all caps. A discussion on JavaScript and JavaScript programming is outside of the scope of this book. For this exercise you will not need to know JavaScript; just understand that we are taking a string and converting it to uppercase.

1. Open the **HelloWorld.rptdesign** from the **Classic_Cars_BIRT_Reports** project. From the Palette, drag the **Dynamic Text** object over to the Report Design pane, just below the Hello World label or the Text object from the previous exercise.

2. The **Expression Builder** will pop up. You will notice that this looks really different than the **Edit Text Item** Dialog from the previous exercise. The Expression Builder is a Dialog that will be used a lot in BIRT. It is used to edit small and short JavaScript expressions that will usually return single data items. When we cover scripting more in depth, we will discuss the differences between the Expression Editor and the Script Editor Pane used in the Report Designer. Type in the following text: **"Good-Bye World"**.

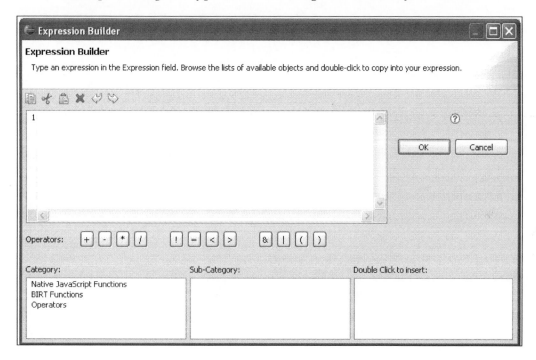

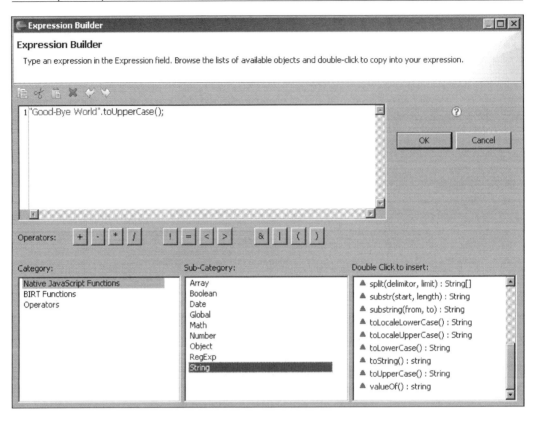

3. At the bottom of the **Expression Editor**, you will notice three different list boxes. These are used as a quick reference for JavaScript objects and methods that can be used in an expression. Put a period at the end of the **"Good-Bye World"** text. Then, under the **Category** list box at the bottom of the **Expression Editor**, choose **Native Javascript Functions**.

4. A whole list of items will appear under the **Sub-Category** list box. These are types of objects and methods we can work with. Because **"Good-Bye World"** is a text string, select the **String** item.

5. Now, we have a list of methods we can use with the string **"Good-Bye World"**. Make sure the cursor is after the period that was added after the **"Good-Bye World"** text. In the third list box, find and double-click on the **toUpperCase() : String** item. When you do that, you will notice that the method will get added to where the cursor is located.

6. Hit **OK**, and **Preview** the report.

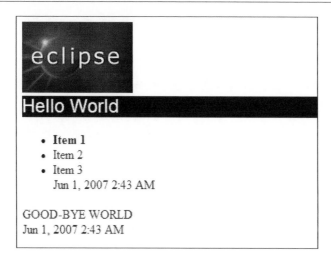

In the finished report, the string **"Good-Bye World"** now reads **"GOOD-BYE WORLD"**. This is a useful component when you need to perform operations on data values, perform calculations, and do a few other things that would require dynamic and calculation-driven text. There are properties of components that can do similar things, such as Maps and Highlights that can perform dynamic text substitutions, enumerate data values, and change formatting of text based on certain conditions. We will discuss these elements in depth later in the book.

Adding Grids

The Grid component is used to visually arrange components in a BIRT report, in a particular layout. BIRT is not a pixel-perfect Report Design environment. In terms of visual arrangement of elements on a page, BIRT is very similar to static HTML. As such, the way to arrange elements in BIRT reports is to use elements such as the Grid, the Table, and the List. The Table and List components are similar to Grids, except that they are bound to data. Following is the icon used on the development Palette for the Grid:

In Chapter 3, we already saw an example of a Table component. We will cover these two components more in depth in the next chapter, when we start to cover data interaction.

In the following exercise, we are going to take a Grid component and use it to change the arrangement of the elements we already have in our existing Hello World report. While this won't be the prettiest visual layout around, it will effectively demonstrate how to interact with the Grid while designing reports, and how it affects report layout.

1. Open the **HelloWorld.rptdesign** from the **Classic_Cars_BIRT_Reports** project. From the **Palette**, drag a Grid object over to the Report Designer pane, just below the **Hello World** label or the **Text** object from the previous exercise.

2. In the **Insert Grid** Dialog, choose **2** columns and **2** rows and hit **OK**.

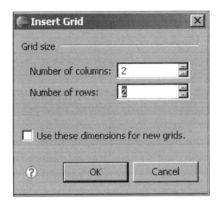

3. Now, in the Report Designer pane, click on the Eclipse Image component and drag it over to the cell in the first column and first row.

4. Now, to change things up a little, open up the **Outline**. We are going to look at manipulating elements using the Outline view instead of using the Report Designer. Under the **Body** item, expand. You can see the **Label**, the **Text** element, the **Dynamic Text** element, and the **Grid**.

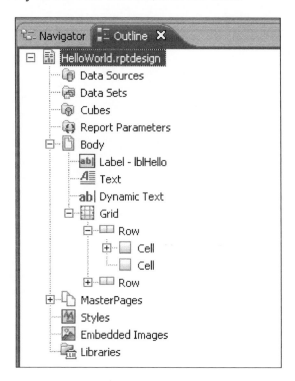

5. Expand the **Grid**. You should see two **Row** items. Expand the first **Row**, and you should see two **Cell** items. The first **Cell** will have the option to expand. This is because we have the Eclipse Image in that cell.

6. In the **Outline**, select the **Label**, and drag it onto the second **Cell** object under the first **Row**. You can see that the **Cell** gets the **Label** added under it, making the **Label** the lowest item in the hierarchy. It will also move the **Label** with the **Hello World** text in the Report Designer pane into the second column, first row cell.

7. **Collapse** the first row item. Right-click on the second row item. A Dialog with the option to insert a new row above or below the current row appears. In our case, it really doesn't matter which one you pick, as the current row is empty. Go ahead and select **Insert row below**. A new row gets added, and we can see visually a new row appears in the Report Designer.

8. In the Report Designer, move the mouse to the **Grid** until a little tab pops up that says **Grid**. When it does, click on that tab. In the Report Designer pane, this is usually the way you will need to get the option to select an entire container component, such as a Table, Grid, or List.

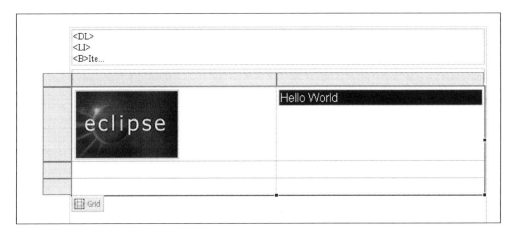

9. We want to combine the cells in the second row into a single cell. Move the mouse cursor into the cell in the first column, second row. Now click and hold the mouse button. Drag the mouse cursor over to the second column, second row, and release the mouse button. This will select both the first and second column cells in the second row. Right-click on the selected cells and choose **Merge Cell**.

10. In the Report Designer, select the **Text** component and drag it over to the newly merged cell.

11. Drag the **Dynamic Text** Component to the cell in the first column, third row. Be sure to observe how the different objects are now placed in the **Outline**. You can see that the hierarchy of components is now set.

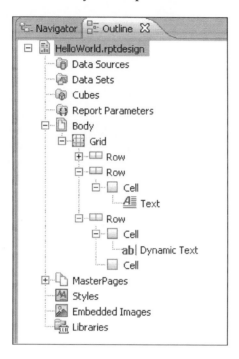

12. **Preview** the Report. With the finished report, you can see how the visual arrangement of the report elements has changed from the previous report previews.

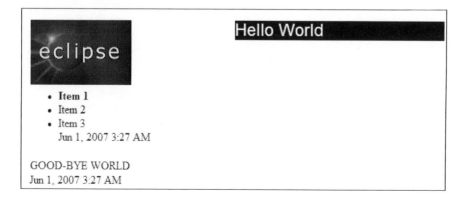

While the report just developed is not the prettiest report in the world, you get the idea of how to work with the visual elements in the BIRT Palette.

Summary

In this chapter, we discussed the various visual report elements that you can use to design BIRT reports. We had the opportunity to see how the various panes in the workspace cooperate together to create BIRT reports, such as using the component Palette to drag components over to the Report Designer pane, selecting elements in the Outline, moving objects in the Outline under other components, and changing their properties in the Property Editor. We caught a brief glimpse of some of the more advanced BIRT report development topics (like the Expression Editor) and got an idea of how BIRT stores reports internally (the hierarchy from the Grids exercise). By now, you should feel pretty comfortable with dragging elements around the BIRT workspace, how to get access to properties, and how to work with the Outline to select components and move their position in the BIRT report layout.

You may notice that I left a few components of the Palette out of our discussion, such as the Table, the List, the Chart (and the Crosstab if you are looking at BIRT 2.2). The reason is that these are data bound components, which require a Data Source. While we discussed this briefly in Chapter 3, I want to discuss this more in depth in the next chapter.

5
Working with Data

The previous chapters have focused on the BIRT working environment and the visual elements used to develop reports, *sans* the data element. In this chapter, we are going to focus on the data-specific elements of the BIRT environment, build some example reports using data from the example **Classic Cars** database, and work with a separate MySQL database.

BIRT Data Capabilities

As BIRT is a Java-centric reporting environment built on top of Eclipse, many different data tools provide BIRT with their data capabilities. JDBC can be used to provide connection to many of the popular Relational Database Management systems out on the market—such as Oracle, MySQL, Microsoft SQL Server, and PostgreSQL.

In addition to the classic client/server-based reporting capabilities afforded to BIRT through this mechanism, BIRT also offers some extensible data handling capabilities through a number of different mechanisms. The Eclipse Data Tools Project is being leveraged by BIRT for its XML Data Source handling. The Eclipse Open Data Access allows developers to build custom drivers for data connections that JDBC doesn't actually provide connectors for. The Classic Cars sample database was built using ODA. For the Java-centric developers who are looking for more flexibility, or with specific needs in mind: BIRT's extensible event handling model allows Java programmers to write scripted Data Sources, where the data is populated either through Java code or JavaScript code at run time.

Most of these are topics that are beyond the scope of this book. In this chapter, we are going to focus primarily on using the Classic Cars example database, and configuring BIRT to use a JDBC database connection to MySQL. This will give the reader some familiarity with the basics of how to establish a connection to a database, using JDBC drivers. Some familiarity with SQL is assumed; however, the queries used in the exercises and examples will be provided for those who are not familiar with SQL.

In Chapter 3, we looked at a very simple employee listing report, using the Classic Cars database. To avoid duplicating exercises, we will leverage that report in the following discussions, in order to demonstrate the remaining data-centric components of BIRT. It will also illustrate how to get data from data containers into reports.

Understanding the Data Components of BIRT

BIRT's data connection capabilities can be broken up into two main logical constructs. Well, actually there would be three; however, for the purposes of our discussion, we only need to think about two. The first is the **Data Source**. A Data Source is information about physical connections to Databases, text files, or some other data source. In the Classic Cars example, the Data Source is the ODA connection information. If we were connecting to a MySQL database, the Data Source would contain information such as the IP Address or DNS name of the database server, the database name, and the user name and password we are using to connect to the database. The Data Sources themselves do not usually contain any data that we will display in our report. There are exceptions, but they are few.

The second is the **Data Set**. For our purposes, the Data Set will contain a description of the data we want to retrieve, such as SQL queries or custom code that will populate the data in a scripted Data Source. At run time, the Data Set will actually contain the data that is described by the SQL query. This is where it gets confusing. In reality, The Data Set description and Data Set instance are two separate things; however, for the purpose of report development, we don't need to concern ourselves with that just yet.

The way this works is that Data Sets are dependent on Data Sources. Without a valid Data Source, the Data Set has no way to retrieve data. That Data Source can contain information on any number of different Data Sources, such as databases, flat text files, XML data files, a special kind of Data Source called a scripted Data Source (that lets BIRT know we will build our own Data Source by hand using Java or JavaScript), or a custom data driver built using the Eclipse ODA framework. The Data Source does the work because it knows how to communicate with the Data Source back end; the Data Set tells the Data Source what to retrieve and then stores the results.

There are a couple of other data components in BIRT. The Report Parameter is a way the report developer can interact with the report user. Report Parameter serves as both an input mechanism and a variable for BIRT reports. Let's say you have a report that returns the information about an Employee, such as their first name, last name, department, and a history of performance reviews used in an HR system.

The report would need some way to know about what Employee you wanted information. A Report Parameter would provide that mechanism. The report developer would create a Report Parameter to get the Employee ID from the user, and would pass that Employee ID to the Data Set to request the relevant information. Report Parameters can also be used as a means to allow the user to control the logic and layout of BIRT reports.

New to **BIRT 2.2** is Cubes. We will be discussing Cubes a little later in the book. To keep you heads up, a Cube is a way of grouping data in a way that allows report consumers to "cut" and "slice" data in a 3D sort of way.

The Data Source

As mentioned earlier, the Data Source is your conduit to your data. Data Sources are the developers' way to specify where data is located, how to get access to that data, and provide a mechanism to retrieve that data from a data location. Out of the box, BIRT provides six different Data Source types:

- The Classic Cars Sample Database
- DTP XML Data Source
- Flat File Data Source
- Scripted Data Source
- JDBC Driver
- Web Services Data Source

We have already seen the Classic Cars Sample Database with the Employee Example, in Chapter 3. This Data Source is not meant to be a production Data Source, and a report environment would not be used in a real-world development shop. It is provided as an example Data Source, which is used as a teaching aid, and demonstrates how an ODA Data Source would function in BIRT. When using this Data Source, you provide no information as it is all self-contained in the Classic Cars Data Source itself. We will use this Data Source in a number of examples throughout this book.

The second Data Source is the DTP (Data Tools Project) XML Data Source. The XML Data Source is a driver that allows developers to use XML files as a data source.

Let me give you an example of this. Let's say I have an XML file containing some entries with Employee information. I want to use this XML data file as a Data Source for a report. The XML file looks like the following:

```
<?xml version="1.0" encoding="UTF-8"?>
<Employees xmlns:xsi="http://www.w3.org/2001/XMLSchema-instance">
  <Employee>
    <firstName>John</firstName>
    <lastName>Ward</lastName>
    <jobTitle>Developer</jobTitle>
  </Employee>
  <Employee>
    <firstName>Bunson</firstName>
    <lastName>Honeydew</lastName>
    <jobTitle>Professor</jobTitle>
  </Employee>
  <Employee>
    <firstName>Bert</firstName>
    <lastName></lastName>
    <jobTitle>Fuzzy Muppet</jobTitle>
  </Employee>
  <Employee>
    <firstName>Ernie</firstName>
    <lastName></lastName>
    <jobTitle>Sidekick</jobTitle>
  </Employee>
</Employees>
```

Notice that I am not using any namespacing prefixes in the XML elements. This will simplify this example. The XML file is saved as EmployeeData.XML. In order to use this, I need to set up a Data Source. I will take the following steps to do so:

1. Create a new **Report Project** called **BIRT Book Chapter 5**.

2. Create a new report called **EmployeeReportCH5.rptDesign**. Use the **Blank Report** template.

3. Under the **Data Explorer** pane, right-click on **Data Sources** and select **New Data Source**. Under the Data Source Type, select **DTP XML Data Source**. As the **Data Source Name**, put in **dsXMLEmployee**.

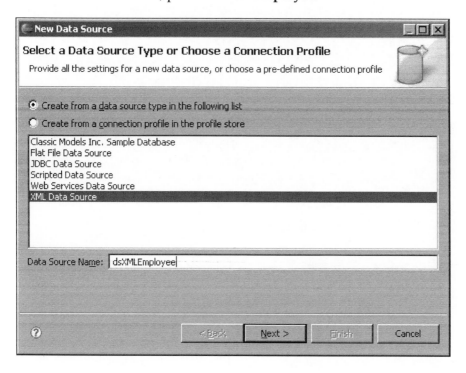

4. Under the location Dialog, select the location where the XML file resides. If available, select a DTD file to verify the schema of the XML file. In my case, my XML file resides under the same workspace location as the Classic Cars examples. Once selected, you can test the file by clicking on **Test Connection**, or just click on **Finish**.

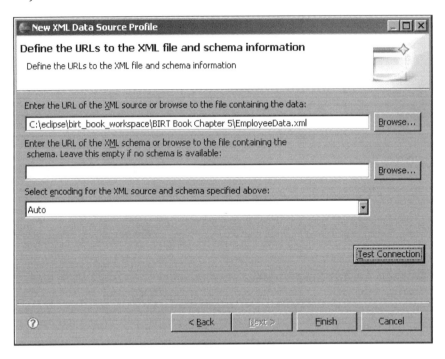

Now we have a Data Source containing Employee information. We will work with this a little more when we get to work with Data Sets. For now, we can hold on to this Data Source for use in a later example.

The next type of Data Source we will look at is the flat file data adapter. The flat file data adapter is pretty much exactly like you would expect. It is an adapter that provides connections to flat data files, such as Comma-Separated text files and other delimited text file types. The one limitation with this adapter is that there is no way to explicitly use a particular type of delimiter. You are stuck with commas, pipes, tabs, and spaces. This should cover most types of flat files you will come across.

In the following exercise, we will cover creating a connection to a flat text file that contains employee pay information. The format of the text file is fairly simple. The file will be a Comma-Separated text file, with the fields displayed in the following format:

First Name | Last Name | Payment Date | Payment Amount

An example of the file is as follows:

```
John,Ward,1/2/2007,500
John,Ward,1/3/2007,600
John,Ward,1/4/2007,900
John,Ward,1/5/2007,400
Bunson,Honeydew,1/1/2007,300
Bunson,Honeydew,1/2/2007,300
Bunson,Honeydew,1/3/2007,200
Bunson,Honeydew,1/4/2007,100
Bert,Unibrow,1/1/2007,230
Ernie,,1/1/2007,275
```

Here, we can see that there is no header row to tell us what the column names are; so it will be up to us to name those in our Data Set later on. Save the above information as `paymentInfo.csv`. Now, to create a Data Source based on this file, follow these steps:

1. Create or open the report **EmployeeReportCH5.rptDesign**. Select the **Flat File Data Source** and name the Data Source as **dsFlatFilePayments**.

2. Select the folder where the text files will reside. Each **CSV** text file under this folder will be seen as its own unique table in any Data Set that we use later on. Specify the character encoding used, and the type. In the case of my example, I am using a **CSV** set as a **UTF-8**-encoded file.

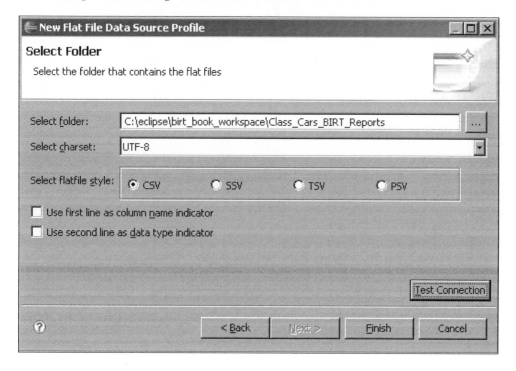

Much like the XML Data Source, we will use this a little later on too, when we build the Data Sets. For now, we have created the Data Source that will be used to retrieve our employees' payment information.

We are going to skip the scripted Data Source for the time being. This is a special Data Source that is meant to be a placeholder for data, which gets built manually using BIRT's scripting capabilities, either through Java Event Handlers or through JavaScript. We will discuss these more in depth in Chapter 10 on *Scripting*.

New in BIRT 2.2 is the Web Services Data Source. The Web Services Data Source functions in the same way as the other Data Source adaptors, except that it allows the developer to use a Web Service as a Data Source.

The JDBC Data Source

The Data Source we are going to look at in detail is the JDBC Data Source. This will, more than likely, be the Data Source you use most often. It has the largest set of options and facilities for the out-of-the-box Data Source types, which is why I have included it in a separate section. It is used to connect to a RDMS that has supplied a JDBC driver. Most widely used enterprise RDMS already provide these, such as Oracle, Microsoft SQL Server, MySQL, PostgreSQL as well as many others. Other embedded database platforms, such as HSQL and Apache Derby, also provide JDBC drivers for accessing data; in some cases, it may be the only way to access data stored on those platforms.

One thing to note about JDBC drivers is that the JDBC connecting URL is different for each platform. The JDBC URL for Oracle is not going to be the same as that for MySQL or Derby. Check your documentation for your platform. Once you have a basic template, you can set up a basic URL for future projects based on that platform, when you manage your drivers.

So let's go through an example to get acquainted with the JDBC Data Source. In the following example, we are going to work with the Classic Cars database that is provided with BIRT. In the previous example using it, we used a built-in ODA Data Source that was based on the JDBC driver. In this example, we will use the actual JDBC driver for Derby.

1. Create or open the report **EmployeeReportCH5.rptDesign**.

2. Under the **Data Explorer** tab, right-click on **Data Sources**, and select **New Data Source**. Under the list of available drivers, select **JDBC Data Source**, and use the name **dsSampleDataBase**.

3. The following screen is where all the JDBC connection information is put in. From the drop-down list for Driver Class, select the **org.eclipse.birt.report. data.oda.sampledb.Driver** class. It will automatically fill in your database URL with the appropriate JDBC URL for the sample database.

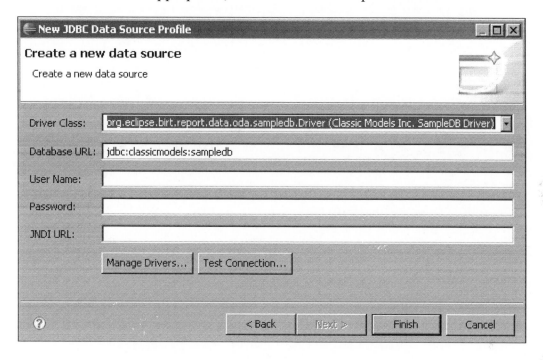

4. Click on **Test Connection** to make sure you can connect. Then, click **Finish**.

For the sample database this was very simple, because the JDBC URL template was already filled in for us. Let's say we didn't have the JDBC URL automatically filled in for us. Let's look at using the Derby JDBC driver that is set up, and explore the Manage Drivers Dialog a little:

1. You will need to extract the Sample Database from its archived format in the BIRT plug-ins folder. For this you will need to know where you have BIRT installed. In my case, I have the BIRT Report Designer installed under `C:\eclipse\birt_2_2\eclipse`. So I need to open the file `C:\eclipse\ Birt_2_2\eclipse\plugins\org.eclipse.birt.report.data.oda. sampledb_2.2.0.v20070531\db\BirtSample.jar` in an archive program, such as WinZip or WinRAR. Don't worry about the extension being .jar instead of .zip. The file is still a ZIP file.

2. Extract the `BirtSample.jar` file to a known location, such as in your workspace or a temporary folder. I chose a folder under my Workspace for this, so I extracted the file to `C:\eclipse\birt_book_workspace\BIRT Book Chapter 5\`. This will create a folder called BirtSample under that folder. (For more information on extracting an archive, consult the documentation for your archive program.)

3. Create or open the report **EmployeeReportCH5.rptDesign**. Under the **Data Explorer tab**, right-click on **Data Sources**, and select **New Data Source**. From the drop-down list, select **JDBC Data Source**, and enter the name **dsDerbySampleDatabase**.

4. Select **org.apache.derby.jdbc.EmbeddedDriver (Apache Derby Embedded Driver)** from the drop-down list for drivers.

5. Under **Database URL**, put in the following URL:
    jdbc:derby:<Location where .Jar file was extracted>
    In my case, I used the following URL:
    jdbc:derby:C:/eclipse/birt_book_workspace/BIRT Book Chapter 5/ BirtSample
    Be sure to use the forward-slashes in my example instead of back-slashes.

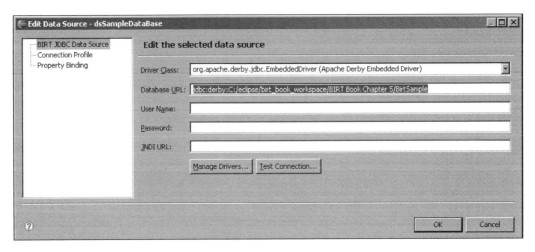

6. At this time, go ahead and click on the **Manage Drivers** button.

This brings up the Manage Drivers Dialog. This is where you would add new JDBC drivers that are not already in BIRT, such as if you have an external Oracle, MySQL, or MS SQL Server JDBC driver. You would do so by clicking on the **Add** button, and navigating to the location with the driver.

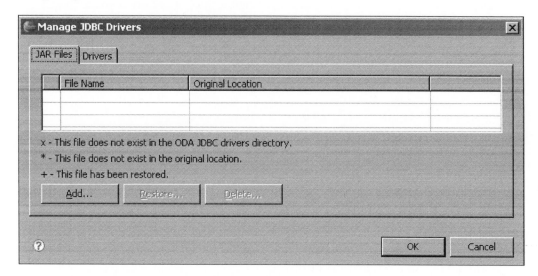

1. Click on the **Drivers** tab.

2. Here is where you can set the various properties for the JDBC drivers, such as the driver name and the default JDBC URL. Click on the Derby Embedded driver, and then click on the **Edit** button. You can see that the default JDBC URL is already filled in. Anytime after you have registered a new driver, you can always come here to change the default JDBC URL and driver name.

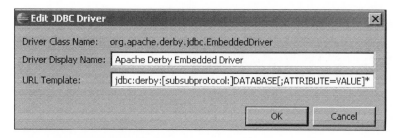

3. Click on **OK** to exit the Edit Dialog. Now, click on **OK** to exit the Manage JDBC Drivers Dialog. Finally, click on **Finish**.

Data Sets

With the preceding examples completed, you should have four Data Sources in your report. The reason we kept each of these Data Sources is to demonstrate the differences in each when setting up Data Sets. As mentioned before, Data Sets are basically descriptions of the data you want to retrieve. Each type of Data Source is going to contain different Data Set types. In the following examples, we are going to create five different Data Sets, of which four are going to be based on each of the different Data Sources we have created, and one will be a Joined Data Set or combination of two of the existing Data Sets.

First we are going to build a simple Data Set from the XML Data Source, dsXMLEmployee. Building the XML Data Set consists of defining columns to be built, and then resolving them to XML paths using XPath expressions. This can be a bit tricky if there are namespaces used in the XML file. For our example, namespaces are not used in the XML Data Source.

1. Open **EmployeeReportCH5.rptDesign**. Under the **Data Explorer** tab, right-click on **Data Sets**, and select **New Data Set**.

2. Enter the following information:
    Data Set Name: dsetXMLEmployee
    Data Source: dsXMLEmployee
    Data Set Type: XML Data Set

3. On the next screen, make sure the **Use the XML file defined in Data Source** is checked and click **Next**.

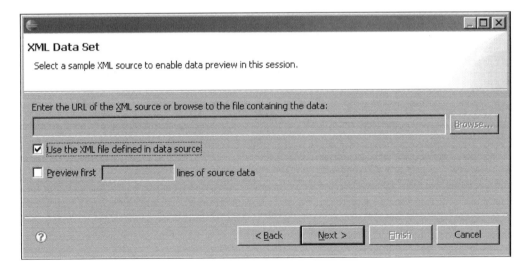

4. On the Table Mapping screen, use the following XPath Expression: **/Employees/Employee**.

5. On the next screen, click on each on the nodes, and then click on the 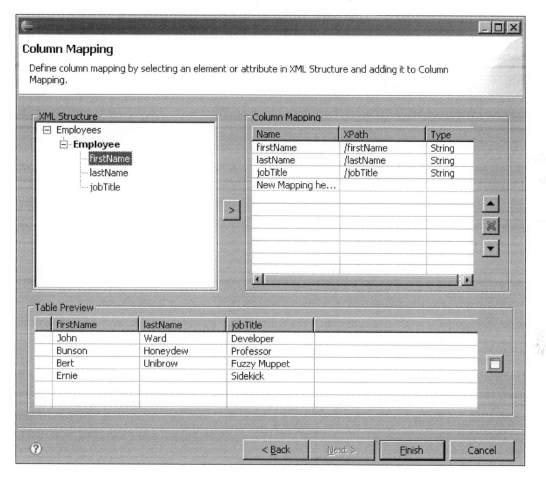 button to create a new field mapping. You can click on the preview button to make sure your field mapping works correctly.

Column Mapping

Define column mapping by selecting an element or attribute in XML Structure and adding it to Column Mapping.

XML Structure
- Employees
  - **Employee**
    - firstName
    - lastName
    - jobTitle

Column Mapping

Name	XPath	Type
firstName	/firstName	String
lastName	/lastName	String
jobTitle	/jobTitle	String
New Mapping he...		

Table Preview

firstName	lastName	jobTitle	
John	Ward	Developer	
Bunson	Honeydew	Professor	
Bert	Unibrow	Fuzzy Muppet	
Ernie		Sidekick	

< Back   Next >   Finish   Cancel

6. Click **Finish**.

The next screen allows us to edit the Data Set after we create it. This allows us to do things after the fact, like filter through the data and create additional columns based on computations. Let's take a look at doing that for this Data Set. Let's say we want to filter the data returned by this Data Set, to only return people with the jobTitle of Developer. If you are going into this example right from *Step 6* of the last example, you can skip the first few steps.

1. From the Data Explorer tab, double-click on **dsetXMLEmployee**.

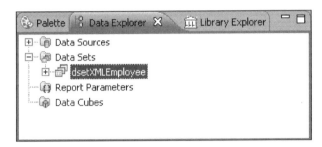

2. Go ahead and click on each of the categories on the left-hand side. The ones that are unique to the XML Data Sets are the ones we have already seen—the **XML Data Set**, **Table Mapping**, and **Column Mapping**.

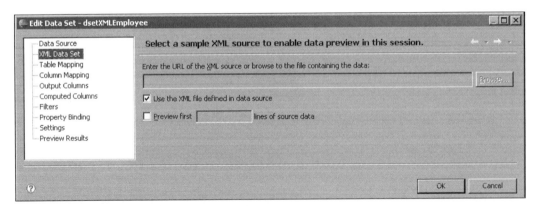

3. Go to the **Filters** category.

4. Click on the **New...** button, and enter the following information:
   Expression: row["jobTitle"].toUpperCase()
   Operator: Equal To
   Value 1: "DEVELOPER"

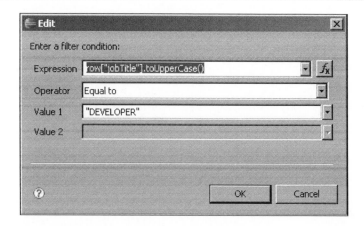

To make the Expression editing easier, you can use the function button f_x located next to the Expression text box, to build your expression using the expression editor. When you do so, you will see an extra category called **Available Data Sets** that was not visible before, when we saw the Expression Editor. This Category is only visible when working with Data Sets or components that are bound to data.

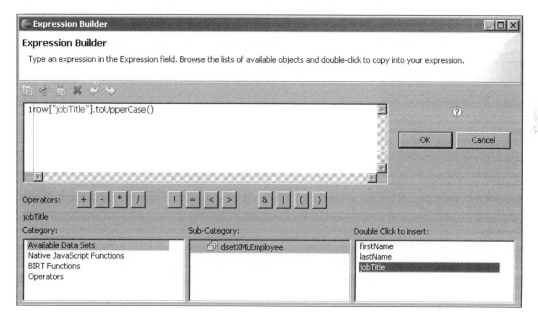

5. Hit **OK**. Now, we can see the filter expression in our list of filters.

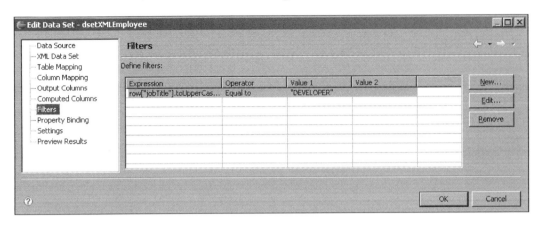

Filters are useful when you are dealing with non-database Data Sets, or any Data Set for which the back end does not have any sort of filtering capabilities. So now, let's say you wanted to add a computed column that will return the number of characters in the first name and the last name. We could do this from the **Computed Columns** category, under the Data Set Editor. Let's take a look at how to do this:

1. Under the **Data Explorer**, double-click on **dsetXMLEmployee**. Now, Click on the **Computed Columns** category.

2. Click on the **New...** button, and enter the following information:
   Column Name: **nameCount**
   Data Type: **Integer**

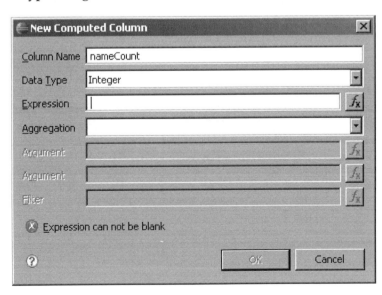

3. Click on the function button next to **Expression**, and enter the following expression:

```
var nameLengthCount = 0;
if (row["firstName"])
nameLengthCount = row["firstName"].length;
if (row["lastName"])
nameLengthCount += row["lastName"].length;
nameLengthCount;
```

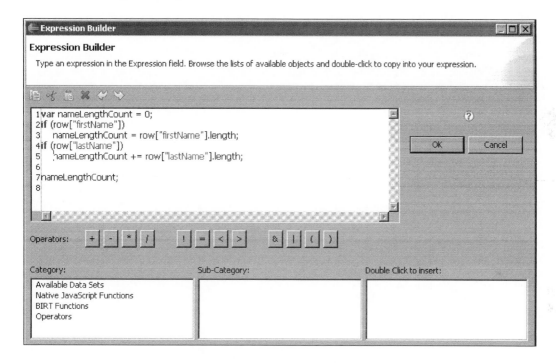

4. Hit **OK**. Now, go down to the **Preview Results** category. See how the Filter is only allowing employees with the job title of Developer to be displayed, and now there is an additional column called **nameCount** with the number of letters in each employee's name.

The example just shown is not very useful in most reports, but it does demonstrate the Filter and Computed Column functionality. Computed Columns become more useful when dealing with numerical data that you may need to perform aggregation on.

Data Set for Flat Files

Next, we are going to create a Data Set based on the **Flat File Data Source**. This interface will look a little different than the XML Data Source, but the basic idea is still the same. We will define each column's name and data type, and create any filters or computed columns that are necessary. In this example, we will just be defining the columns though.

1. Under the **Data Explorer** tab, right-click on **Data Sets** and select **New Data Set**.

2. Enter the following information:
    Data Set Name: dsetFlatFilePayments
    Data Source: dsFlatFilePayments
    Data Set Type: Flat File Data Set
    Click **Next**.

3. As the **Flat File Data Source** defined a directory where the data files are located, we need to select the appropriate text file from the **Select file** drop-down list. Choose the **paymentInfo.csv** file created during the Data Source exercise.

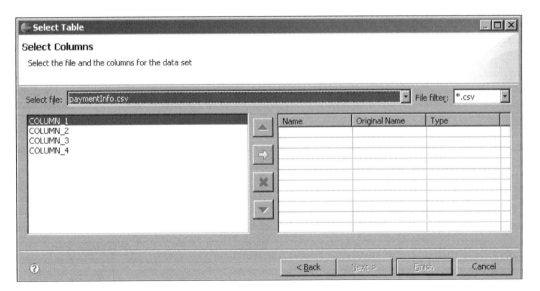

4. There should be four columns labeled **COLUMN_1, COLUMN_2, COLUMN_3**, and **COLUMN_4** respectively. If we had chosen the option to have a header row during the Data Source creation, these columns would be named whatever the values were in the first line of the text file. For each column, click on it, and then click on the right-pointing arrow button 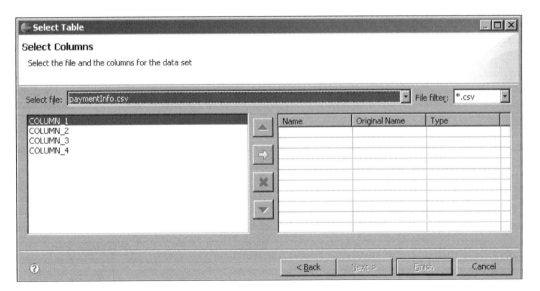.

5.   Each of the columns should be in the grid. You can change the values of each of the columns, such as original name, name to be used in the Data Set, and the data type. Enter the following information for each of the columns:

COLUMN_1: Name = firstName Type = String
COLUMN_2: Name = lastName Type = String
COLUMN_3: Name = paymentDate Type = Date
COLUMN_4: Name = paymentAmount Type = Double

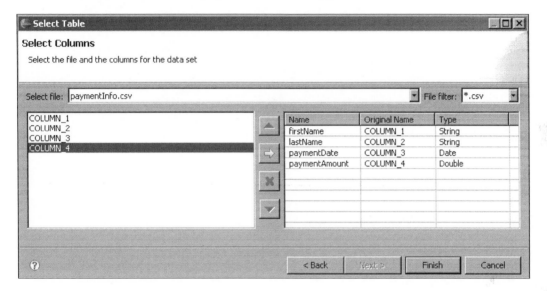

6.   Click **Finish**.

Just as with the XML Data Set, once you finish the initial setup, you enter the edit Data Set Dialog. From here, you can create filters and computed columns, in addition to the columns outputted by the data adapter itself. With the XML Data Set, flat file Data Set, and the scripted Data Set that we will look at later, the ability to create filters inside of BIRT is very useful when there is no back end filtering capability, as there would be with a database system using the WHERE clause in an SQL statement.

With the two non-JDBC Data Sets out of the way, we can now create the Data Set for our JDBC Data Sources. Typically, this is where you will spend most of your report development time. I know in my experience, I have used these types of Data Sets more than any of the others because so many applications use a RDBMS back end to store data. In the following example, we are going to create only one Data Set, as the two JDBC Data Sources we have point to the same set of data. In this Data Set, we want to retrieve a listing of Orders and Order Details, using an SQL statement to join the two tables. I will not assume any prior knowledge of SQL for this example; instead I will give you the SQL statement to use.

1. In the **Data Explorer** tab, right-click on the **Data Sets** folder, and choose **New Data Set**.

2. Enter the following information:
   Name: dsetOrders
   Data Source: dsDerbySampleDatabase
   Data Set Type: SQL Select Query

   Notice that under the **Data Set Type**, there is an additional option to use an SQL Stored Procedure. This was not an option with the other Data Set. This is only applicable to Data Sources that are DBMS-based. As our example—Derby Database—does not have any stored procedures, this doesn't do us any good. We can ignore this and click **Next**.

3. The next screen is the SQL Editor. Here, you can play around with the left-hand tree view, to see the available tables and columns in our database. You can either drag tables or columns over to the text editor on the right-hand side, or you can move the cursor someplace in the text editor and double-click on the table or column you want to add. In doing so, you automatically put in the fully-qualified path to that table or column. You can also filter down to see tables in particular schemas, in databases where you have access to more than one. Additionally, you can type in a filter to limit based on table name. A word of caution: In my experience this is case sensitive, or "order" is not the same as "ORDER." Put the following information in the Filter data and click on **Apply Filter**:
   Schema: CLASSICMODELS
   Filter: ORDER
   Type: Table

4. Use the following SQL query:

```
select
*
from
    CLASSICMODELS.ORDERDETAILS,
    CLASSICMODELS.ORDERS
where
    CLASSICMODELS.ORDERDETAILS.ORDERNUMBER =
    CLASSICMODELS.ORDERS.ORDERNUMBER
```

Feel free to experiment with "dragging and dropping" the columns and tables, to get a feel for how that mechanism works.

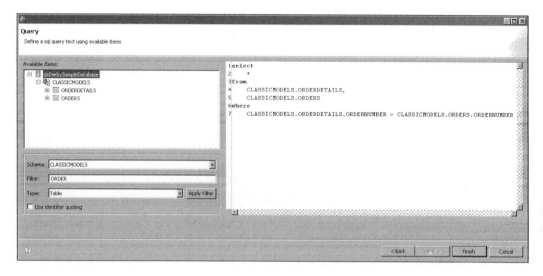

5. Click **Finish**.

The final type of Data Set we are going to create is called the **Joined Data Set**. This is a type of Data Set that will combine the results of two existing Data Sets into one logical Data Set. This is a very useful feature when you are joining data from two unrelated Data Sources, such as with a database and a text file, or from two separate databases. In the following example, we will join the **dsetFlatFilePayments** with the **dsetXMLEmployee**. To show that there are a few different ways to create Data Sets, we will also create this one using the Outline view instead of the Data Explorer.

1. From the **Outline** view, right-click on **Data Sets** and select **New Joined Data Set**.

2. Enter the information as illustrated in the following figure:

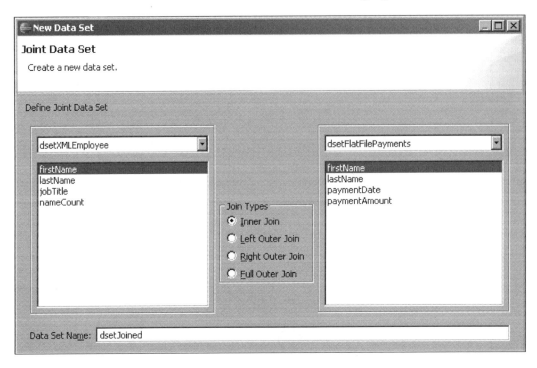

If you kept the filter in **dsetXMLEmployee**, you will see that information for only **John Ward** comes back with the payment information. This is because the filter on that Data Set, in combination with the Inner Join, is preventing any data from **dsetFlatFilePayments** from coming back, except the information related to John Ward. Feel free to remove this Filter to see the full join.

Tables

In the example *Employee Listing report* from Chapter 3, we used a visual report element called a Table, even if we didn't know it. The Table is similar to the *Grid* component we saw in Chapter 4, except that it is data bound. What this means is that the contents of this component are populated by data stored in a data container, such as a Data Set. In the Employee Listing report, we saw a shortcut method for creating a Table. This is very useful when you are building simple listing reports. However, when you need more precision over your Table, you can also do it manually using the component Palette.

The Table is divided into three logical groups: The header that will contain the name of each report column in the report; the Details section (which will actually contain the data returned from the bound Data Set), and the Footer (which will contain ending summary or aggregate information about a report). In the following example, we are going to demonstrate two different ways to create tables. First, we will use the shortcut "drag and drop" Data Set method. Second, we are going to manually build a Table, bind it to a Data Set, and populate the element of the table.

Creating Tables Using Drag and Drop

First, we want to get the data from dsetJoined and move it over to our Layout view. There are a couple of different ways in which this can be accomplished. We can drag it over from the Data Explorer just like we did in Chapter 3, or we can drag it over from the Outline view. If we right-click on the **dsetJoined**, we can also choose the Insert into Layout option. The caveat with this is that if there is already any element in the layout, you will need to click on an empty space in the Layout editor for this option to be available.

1. In the **Data Explorer**, under **Data Sets**, right-click on **dsetJoined** and choose **Insert in Layout**.

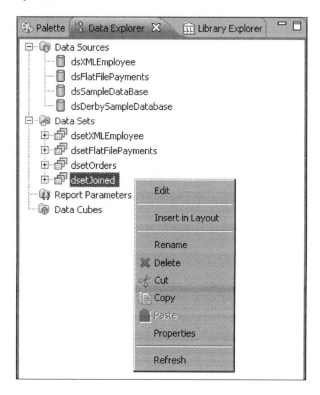

2. From the **Outline**, under the **Body** branch, select **Table**.

3. Under the **Property Editor**, change the **Name** to **tblEmployeePayments**.

4. In the **Layout** Editor, find the cells that say **dsetFlatFilePayments::firstName** and **dsetFlatFilePayments**. Click on the gray square above these labels to select that entire column. Then right-click, and choose **Delete**. Repeat for both columns.

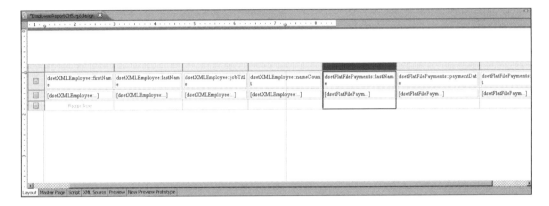

5. We need to change each of the column header's contents, so that they do not contain **dsetXMLEmployee::** or **dsetFlatFilePayments**. To do this, you can either double-click on each of them, or you can use the **Property Editor**. To use the **Property Editor**, select the **Label** element in the **Layout** Editor; or using the **Outline**, select the **Label** under each of the **Body**, **Table**, **Header**, **Row**, **Cell**, **Label** components. Then in the Property Editor, scroll down to **Advanced**, and select **Content**. Change each **Label** to an appropriate title.

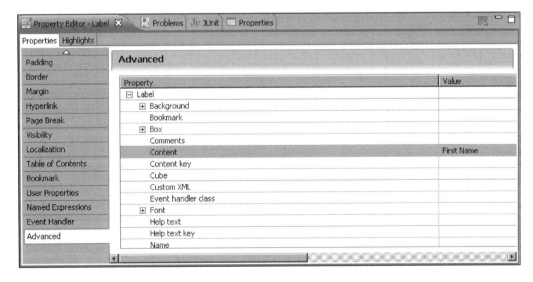

6. Select the **Row** from the **Outline** view, under **Body\Header\Row**. In the
    Property Editor, choose the **Font** category, and change it to Bold.

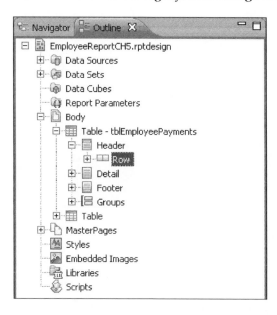

7. In the Layout Editor, click on the **Detail** cell under the **Payment Amount**
    column. Under the Property Editor, under the **Format Number** category set
    the **Format as** property to **Currency**. Click on the **Use 1000s separator** check
    box, and select $ for the **Symbol**.

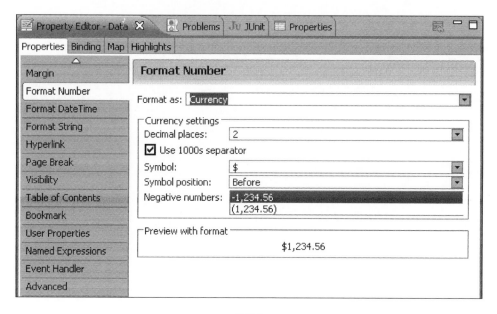

8. Now, we want to add an aggregation for the **Payment Amount** column. New in **BIRT 2.2** is a quick component that will do aggregates for you. You can drag the **Aggregation** component over from the Component **Palette**. Drag the component over to the **Footer Row**, in the **Payment Amount** column.

9. Enter the following information:
   Column Binding Name: agrPaymentTotal
   Display Name: Payment Total
   Data Type: **Any**
   Function: **SUM**
   Data Field: select **PaymentAmount** from the drop-down list.

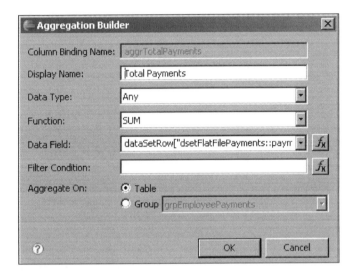

10. Click on the **agrPaymentTotal** component, and format it as **Currency**.

11. Click on **Preview** under the **Layout** Editor.

First Name	Last Name	Job Title	Name Count	Payment Date	Payment Amount
John	Ward	Developer	8	Jan 2, 2007	$500.00
John	Ward	Developer	8	Jan 3, 2007	$600.00
John	Ward	Developer	8	Jan 4, 2007	$900.00
John	Ward	Developer	8	Jan 5, 2007	$400.00
					$2,400.00
Jun 18, 2007 11:11 PM					

So, creating a simple report that way is easy enough; but how would we do so manually? Well, that's exactly what we are going to do next.

Creating Tables Manually

We want to create a table right below this one, with the information from the dsetOrders. We will create this one manually, as we do not want to display all the information in that Data Set, but only certain columns. As you should be fairly familiar with using the Component Palette at this point, we are going to create this table directly in the Layout Editor.

1. Right-click in the area below the tblEmployeePayments, and choose **Insert | Table**.

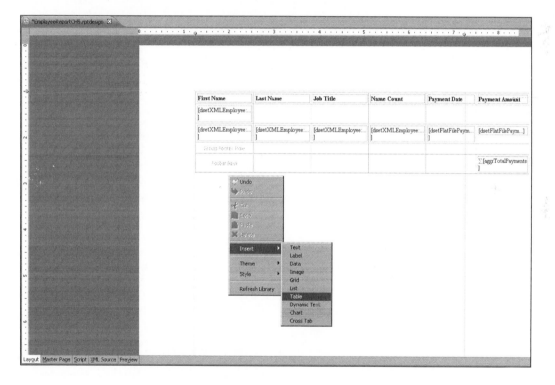

2. For dimensions, use **6** columns, **1** Detail Row, and use **dsOrders** as the **Data Set**. In the **Detail Row** (first column), right-click, and choose **Insert | Data**.

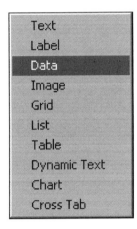

3. Enter the following information:
    Column Binding Name: **cbOrderNumber**
    Display Name: **Order Number**
    Data Type: **Any**
    Expression: **row["ORDERNUMBER"]**

    Here, we manually created a data element in the Detail Row. Note the **Expression**. This **Expression** is telling BIRT to use the value as **ORDERNUMBER** in the current row because the detail band in a table will cycle through every record returned in a Data Set. Hit **OK**.

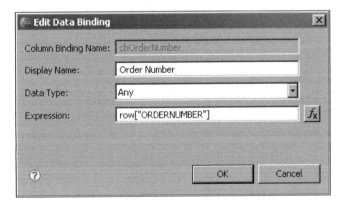

4. Right-click in the **Header Row**, first column; choose **Insert | Label**. For the value, type in **Order Number**.

5. Now that you have seen how to do that manually, here is an easier way. Open up the **Data Explorer**, and expand on the **dsetOrders** node. Drag over the **CUSTOMERNUMBER** field to the **Detail Row**, second column. You will notice that the header label was automatically created.

6. Repeat for the **PRODUCTCODE, PRICEEACH,** and **QUANTITYORDERED** fields.

7. Click on the gray square at the top of the last colum to select the entire last column. Once done, right-click and select **Insert | Column to the Right**.

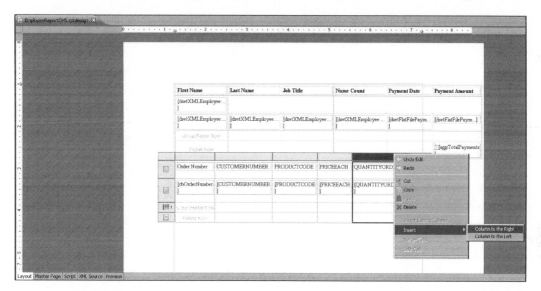

8. Right-click on the new Detail cell, and insert a new Data Element. Use the following information:
    Display Name: Product Total
    Data Type: Any
    Expression: row["PRICEEACH"] * row["QUANTITYORDERED"]

9. Create a Label for this column titled **Product Total**. Format both the **Product Total Detail** cell and the **PRICEEACH** cell as **Currency**.

10. Save and **Preview**.

First Name	Last Name	Job Title	Name Count	Payment Date	Payment Amount
John	Ward	Developer	8	Jan 2, 2007	$500.00
John	Ward	Developer	8	Jan 3, 2007	$600.00
John	Ward	Developer	8	Jan 4, 2007	$900.00
John	Ward	Developer	8	Jan 5, 2007	$400.00
					$2,400.00

Order Number	CUSTOMERNUMBER	PRODUCTCODE	PRICEEACH	QUANTITYORDERED	Product Total
10100	363	S18_1749	$136.00	30	$4,080.00
10100	363	S18_2248	$55.09	50	$2,754.50
10100	363	S18_4409	$75.46	22	$1,660.12
10100	363	S24_3969	$35.29	49	$1,729.21
10101	128	S18_2325	$108.06	25	$2,701.50
10101	128	S18_2795	$167.06	26	$4,343.56
10101	128	S24_1937	$32.53	45	$1,463.85
10101	128	S24_2022	$44.35	46	$2,040.10
10102	181	S18_1342	$95.55	39	$3,726.45
10102	181	S18_1367	$43.13	41	$1,768.33
10103	121	S10_1949	$214.30	26	$5,571.80
10103	121	S10_4962	$119.67	42	$5,026.14
10103	121	S12_1666	$121.64	27	$3,284.28
10103	121	S18_1097	$94.50	35	$3,307.50
10103	121	S18_2432	$58.34	22	$1,283.48
10103	121	S18_2949	$92.19	27	$2,489.13
10103	121	S18_2957	$61.84	35	$2,164.40

Groups

Grouping, much as in an RDBMS, is a mechanism used to group data that falls into a similar category. This can be done with an SQL `Select` statement using the GROUP BY clause; or in BIRT, it can be done by adding a grouping to a Table or List. We are going to add to the previous examples by adding groups.

1. In the **Outline** view, select **tblEmployeePayments**.

2. In the **Property Editor**, open the **Groups** tab and click on the **Add** button.

3. Use the following information:
   Name: grpEmployeePayments
   Group On: dsetXMLEmployee::lastName

4. Hit **OK**.

Now, when we preview the report, we can see that it adds an extra header with last names, and groups all the like payments together. Of course, this will be better illustrated with the next example, where we modify the Order table to display groupings by order number.

1. Add a new group to the table with the **Orders**.

2. Use the following information:
   Name: grpOrderInfo
   Group On: ORDERNUMBER

3. Under the **Outline** view, select **Body\Table** (the one with **Orders**, not the **tblEmployeePayments**)**\Groups\Table Groups\Header\Row**. Delete the **Row**.

4. In the **Layout** Editor, select the **Order Number** column. In the **General** Tab, click on the **Suppress Duplicates** checkbox.

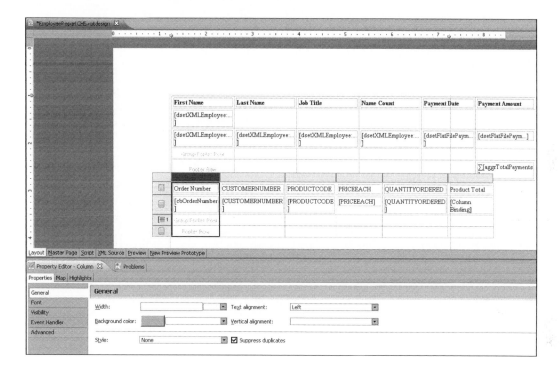

5. Do the same thing for the **Customer Number** column.

6. Click **Preview**.

Now, when we click on Preview, we can see that the orders are all grouped by the Order Number, and instead of repeatedly displaying the Order Number and Customer Number for each line as in the previous previews, it will now only display it once.

Lists

Lists work in a similar manner to tables, except that they do not have the ability to have multiple columns. This is useful for single column tables or when using one Data Set to drive the results of another during render time or to create lists of tables based on a single value. Lists are created the same way as Tables are created manually, and only support a single column.

Aggregation

Often, when working with groups of data, it is desirable to perform aggregations on one of the values. For example, if you have a report listing employees' sales for a year, you may want to create a sub-total for each month and a grand total for the year. In such cases, you are creating an aggregation.

In the following example, we are going to create a simple count of employees that work at a particular office, using the BIRT Aggregation component.

1. Create a new report called **employeeCount.rptDesign**.
2. Create a new Data Source based on the Classic Cars Data Source.
3. Create a new Data Set called **employeeList**.
4. Use the following query:

```
select
CLASSICMODELS.EMPLOYEES.EMPLOYEENUMBER,
CLASSICMODELS.EMPLOYEES.LASTNAME,
CLASSICMODELS.EMPLOYEES.FIRSTNAME,
CLASSICMODELS.EMPLOYEES.OFFICECODE
from
CLASSICMODELS.EMPLOYEES
```

5. Drag the **employeeList** Data Set over to the Report Designer.
6. Select the new **Table**, and under the **Property Editor**, select **Groups**.
7. Create a new **Group** called **groupByOffice**, and **Group on** the **OfficeCode**.

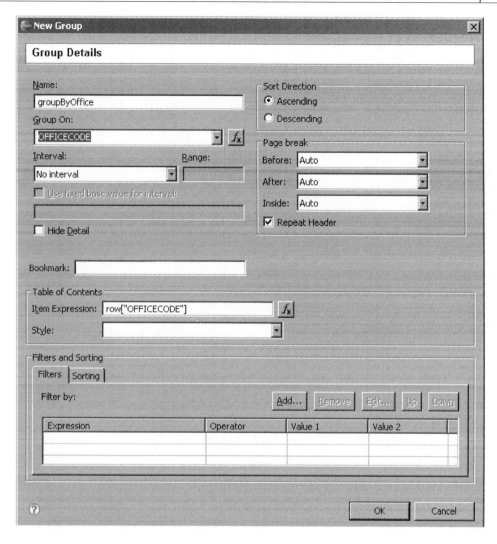

8. In the Report Designer, select the last column with **OFFICECODE** and **Delete** it.

9. Select the **Group Header Row** with **OfficeCode**, right-click, and select **Insert | Row | Below**.

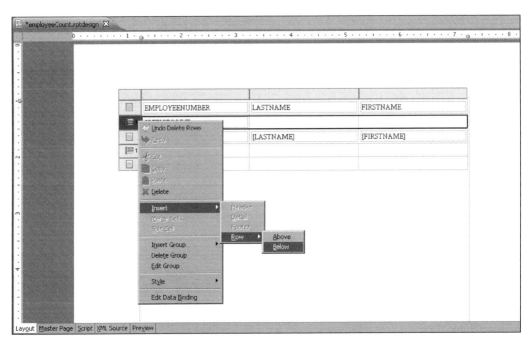

10. Move the three column Labels to the newly created row.

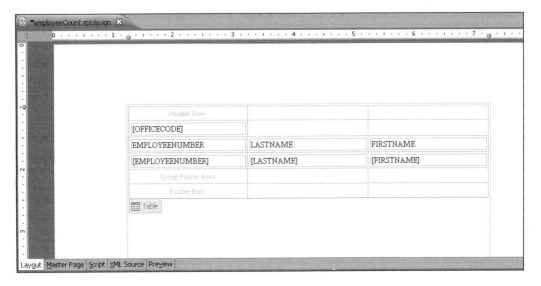

11. In the **Group Footer Row** (first column), insert a new Label, and for the text use **Number of Employees**.

12. Drag over an **Aggregation** component to the **Group Footer Row**, second column.

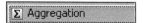

13. When you drop the component, a Dialog for the **Aggregation** will pop up. Name the component as **countEmployees**. Change the **Function** to **Count**, and set the **Aggregate On** to **Group | groupByOffice**.

14. This pretty much finishes up the functional part of the report. Now we need to format it just a little. Select the **Group Header Row**.

15. In the **Property Editor**, under the **General** tab, change the **Background color** to **Black**.

16. Click on the **Font** tab. Change the Font **Color** to **White**, and bold the text.

17. Select the **Group Footer Row**.

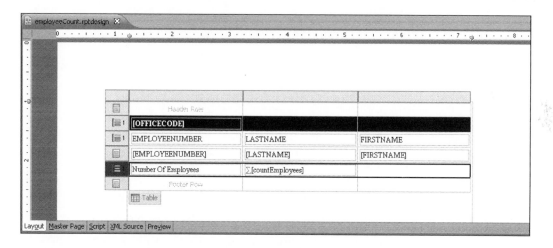

18. In the **Property Editor**, under the **General** tab, change the **Background color** to **Silver**.

19. **Save**, and **Preview** the Report.

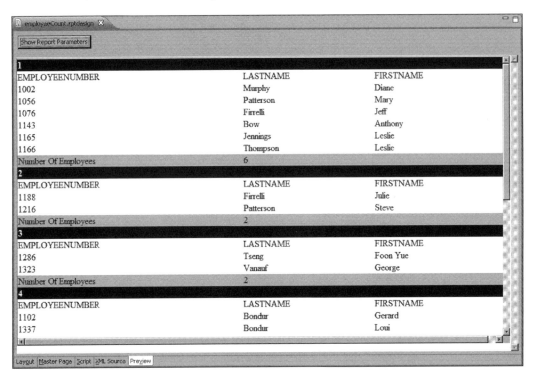

In the preview just shown, we can see that the Aggregate component (using the Count function) counts the number of Employees based on the Grouping of OFFICECODE. BIRT supports Aggregate functions such as Sum, Count, Min, Max, Running Sums and Counts, Average, Standard Deviation, and a number of others.

Table of Contents

Anytime you create a Group on a Table or List, it creates a Table of Contents. A Table of Contents is a convenient way to jump to a particular part of a report when using a Web Viewer. Using the previous example, you can view the report by going to **File | View Report | View Report in Web Viewer**.

When the Report Viewer is open, you can click on the TOC icon on the upper left corner to bring up the Table of Contents. This will list all the Groupings in the Table. When you click on **1**, it will bring you to that section of the report, and so on.

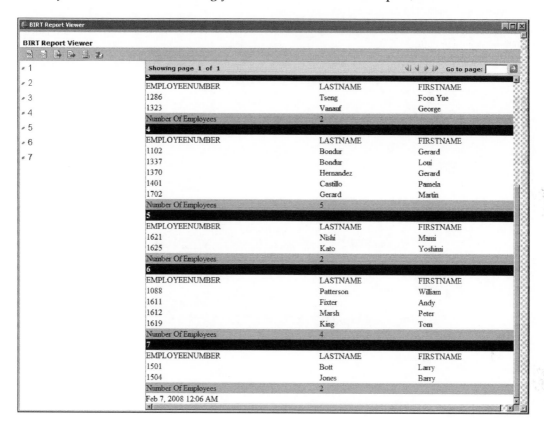

If you create other Groupings, they will appear as sub-groupings under the TOC. In the following screenshot, I added a Group by the Last Name; keep this in mind if you are designing reports for online consumption.

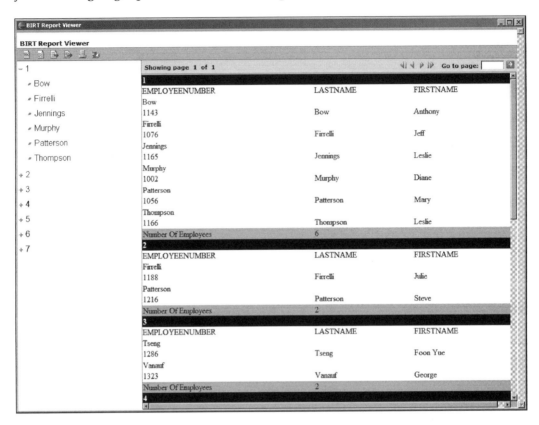

Crosstab

New to BIRT version 2.2 is the Crosstab component. A Crosstab is a type of report component that displays data in a row/column matrix, with summary information in the areas that cross. Crosstabs are useful for comparing two variables (for instance, number of BIRT users with some other variable such as number of users who like Muppets). The data would be laid out in a summary format that is similar to a Spreadsheet. The number of variables compared is not limited to two.

In the following example, we will create a simple Crosstab that displays the yearly and monthly sales figures compared to the employees who sold them.

1. Create a new report called **simpleCrosstab.rptDesign**, under the **Class_Cars_BIRT_Reports project**.

2. Create a new Data Source and use the **Classic Cars Inc. Sample Database**. Call this Data Source **classicCarsDataSource**.

3. In order to create the simple Crosstab, we need to bring in at least three variables—the Employee, the Price, and the Date—of an order. To calculate the Price, we need to take the individual price and multiply it with the quantity ordered. We will use the following query to bring in the required information:

    ```
    select
    CLASSICMODELS.EMPLOYEES.LASTNAME || ', ' || CLASSICMODELS.EMPLOYEES.
    FIRSTNAME employeeName,
    CLASSICMODELS.ORDERS.ORDERDATE,
    CLASSICMODELS.ORDERDETAILS.PRICEEACH * CLASSICMODELS.ORDERDETAILS.
    QUANTITYORDERED totalPrice
    from
    CLASSICMODELS.EMPLOYEES,
    CLASSICMODELS.CUSTOMERS,
    CLASSICMODELS.ORDERDETAILS,
    CLASSICMODELS.ORDERS
    where
    CLASSICMODELS.CUSTOMERS.SALESREPEMPLOYEENUMBER =
                        CLASSICMODELS.EMPLOYEES.EMPLOYEENUMBER
    and CLASSICMODELS.ORDERS.CUSTOMERNUMBER =
                        CLASSICMODELS.CUSTOMERS.CUSTOMERNUMBER
    and CLASSICMODELS.ORDERS.ORDERNUMBER =
                        CLASSICMODELS.ORDERDETAILS.ORDERNUMBER
    ```

4. In order to create a Crosstab, we have to create a Data Cube. In BIRT, a Data Cube is an implementation of an OLAP Cube built using Data Sets. In BIRT, Dimensions are called Groups, and Measures are called Summary Fields. We need to create Dimensions based on the Order Dates and Employee. Under the **Data Explorer**, right-click on the **Data Cubes** folder and choose **New Data Cube**.

5. Name the Cube **employeeSalesDataCube**, and choose **employeeSales** as the **Primary dataset**.

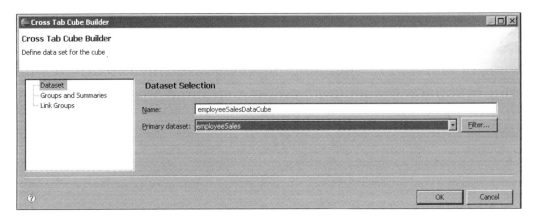

6. Under the **Groups and Summaries** screen, you can drag over the database fields that you want to summarize as your **Dimensions | Groups** and **Measures | Summary Fields**. Drag over the **EmployeeName** field as one of the **Dimensions**, and the **ORDERDATE** field as the other. Then drag over **TOTALPRICE** as the **Summary**.

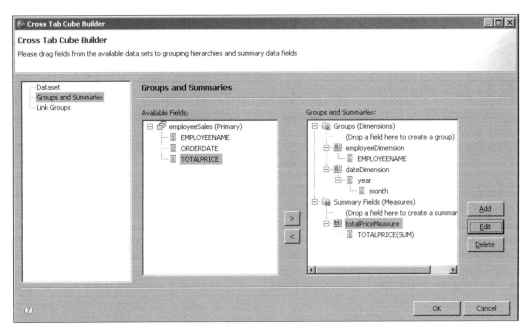

7. When you drag over the **ORDERDATE**, you will get a separate Dialog asking which levels of Grouping you want. As this is a DateTime field, you can filter this from the **year** all the way down to the **second**. Select **year** and **month**.

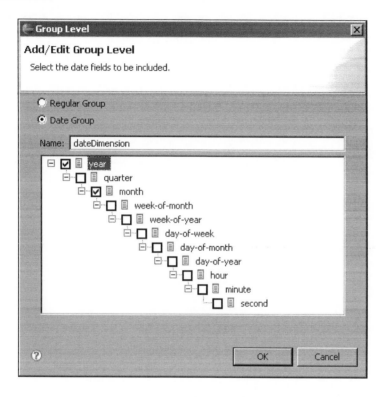

8. In the **Summary**, we can use any sort of Aggregation, such as Sum, Average, Min, Max, and Count. We will keep this as **SUM** for this example.

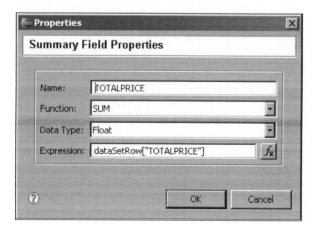

9. Now that our Cube is created, we can create the Crosstab. From the **Palette**, drag a **Cross Tab** component over to the Report Designer.

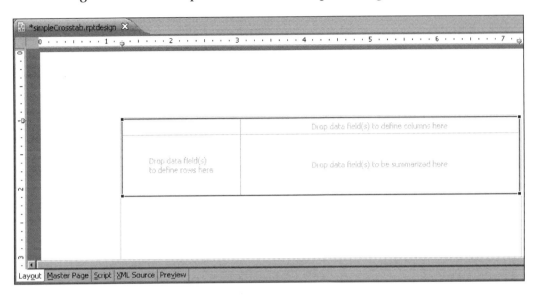

10. Using the **Data Explorer**, expand the area of the Cube to expose the **Groups** and **Summary Fields**.

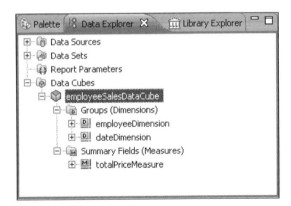

11. Drag the **employeeDimension** element over to the **Cross Tab** area that says **Drop data field(s) to define columns here**.

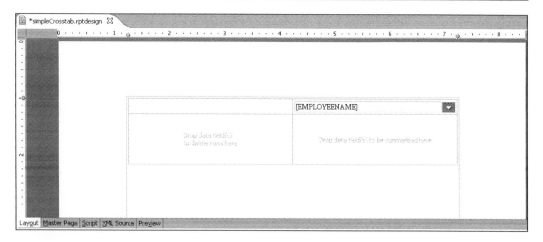

12. Drag **dateDimension** over to the **rows** section.

13. Currently the ORDERDATE Grouping just shows **year**. Because the month is another level of this Group, we need to show it as well. Click on the down arrow for the ORDERDATE grouping, and choose **Show | Hide Group Levels**.

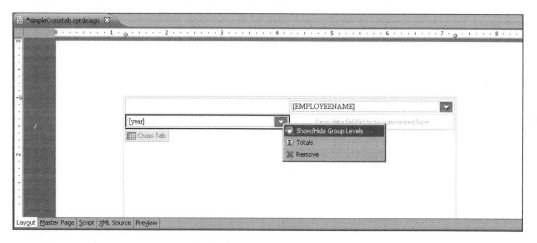

14. On the next screen, check the **month** check box, and click **OK**.

15. Now, drag the **totalPriceMeasure** field over to the area that says **Drop data field(s) to be summarized here**.

16. We want to change the format of the price to show as currency. Select the **[TotalPrice]** field with the drop-down arrow.

17. In the **Property Editor**, select **Format Number**.

18. Select **Currency** as the format type, check the **Use 1000s separator** check box, and choose the currency **Symbol** to be $.

19. **Save**, and **Preview** the report.

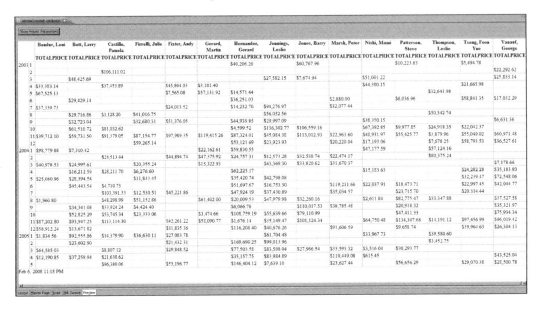

Of course, as we are working with Cubes, more complex reports can be developed. As I mentioned earlier, you can add any number of Dimensions to the Cube and the Crosstab. In the following screenshot, I have added **Country** as another Dimension, and color coded it just for good Measure.

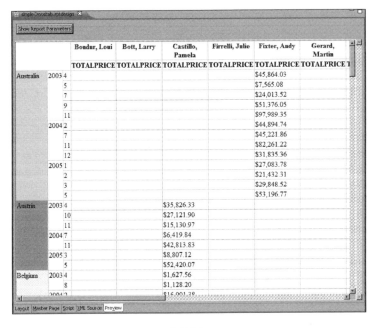

OLAP Cubes is a subject that is complex and outside of the scope of this book.

Summary

We covered a lot of ground in this chapter. We explored how to create all of the elements while connecting to different Data Sources in reports and Report Projects. We saw that BIRT supports different types of data, such as XML files, flat text files, and databases. We saw that for each type of Data Source there are different types of Dialogs to describe the data and create Data Sets. We saw how to bring in the different data-bound components. We also explored a few different methods of inserting visual components into a report layout, and how to change different properties of components. We saw how we could group related data based on the value of columns, how to create a calculated result using some basic expressions, and how to work with the Outline, the Property Editor, and the Layout Editor in greater depth.

Hopefully, at this point you are getting more comfortable with working in the BIRT environment. This is getting us ready to build some really interesting reports in later chapters. But there are still elements that we need to build fully functional reports. In the next chapter, we are going to learn how to get user input for reports, so that users can filter data in a manner that they need. We are also going to look at how Report Parameters are different from Data Set parameters, how they can be linked together, and how Report Parameters can be used in a data-independent way to affect layout of reports. We will also explore usage of Highlights and Maps. In later chapters, we will look at Charts and how to share report elements you build, using Libraries and Templates. However, with the understanding of how to connect data into your reports, you are well on your way.

6

Report Parameters

Up until now, the reports we have worked with have had one thing in common; they have been static reports. That is, they do not accept any sort of input from the user. Their output depends solely on the data present in a database. While we have demonstrated that a filter can be applied to the data coming back from a Data Source, we haven't discussed how a report user can specify what details they want to see.

In this chapter, we will look at the different types of parameters that BIRT offers. We will distinguish between parameters that can filter Data Sets, and parameters that can change the look and feel of reports. When it is completed, you will be able to take your reports one step further than the canned reports that we have developed so far. You will also be able to offer your users the ability to filter down large amounts of data to justify the information that is important to them.

Why Parameterize Reports?

This is a very important question to ask ourselves, and while the answer might seem obvious, it goes a little deeper: Imagine that you are a report developer for a large organization with several different departments. Now you create a report for a department that shows their costs for the fiscal quarter. That's great, and now a second department asks you to create the same report for them. Then a third department asks for a similar report; only they want to be able to see data for both last quarter and this quarter. By this time, you have created three similar reports, each representing the same set of data and running the same queries, only you have hard-coded the department information. Now, you have to maintain all three of those reports, and any changes or mistakes you find or an analyst finds, you will have to fix in all three reports.

The solution to this problem is to parameterize your report. In a simple scenario such as this, it becomes obvious that if you created a few parameters, such as one for department and a few to handle date ranges, you would then only have to maintain one report for all the departments and time frames that would be requested. By parameterizing, you are taking a larger number of reports needed to be maintained and verified and reducing it to a more manageable number. This becomes useful because, more often than not, report requests remain very similar.

Now, take a step back and let's look at something we haven't addressed up until now. Let's say that each department that runs the report wants its header or department logo to be displayed in the report. Now we are looking at something other than data-centric issues, and moving into the realm of layout-specific issues. With BIRT, we also have the ability to address these kinds of visual requirements. For example, if the manager from the accounting department wanted alternating row colors, but the other managers did not, we could easily create a Report Parameter that would ask the report user if he or she wanted to add alternating row colors. With the logo issue mentioned above, we can easily create some basic logic that is driven by Report Parameters to meet these requests. We will look at some examples in this chapter, and explore this more in depth in the chapter on *Scripting*.

Data Set Parameters and Report Parameters

In BIRT, there is a very important distinction between Data Set Parameters and Report Parameters. This distinction can be confusing at first, which is why I want to discuss it now. The difference is one of scope and function. A Report Parameter has a global scope and can be used in a number of different ways in reports. Report Parameters are user-facing variables that prompt the user for input. If you have ever worked with traditional reporting language, think of Report Parameters as a global variable combined with a standard input statement that will fill that variable with a value.

Data Set Parameters, on the other hand, are limited in scope to within the Data Set that they are declared in. Data Set Parameters work more like bind variables in a relational database management system, or a prepared query in a data-aware programming model, such as ADO or JDBC. Data Set Parameters are typically linked to Report Parameters to retrieve their values, but that is not always the case. They can be bound to a number of different sources.

This becomes a very important concept, especially when working with Data Sets that are not JDBC Data Sets. Data Set Parameters are limited to JDBC Data Sets only. With other types of Data Sets, Report Parameters will get linked to Filters, and not Data Set Parameters. This is something to keep in mind when working in BIRT, as the term parameter is used with both Report Parameters and Data Set Parameters, and gets even more confusing when taking into consideration that later versions of BIRT allow users to create Report Parameters directly from the Data Set Parameter Dialog. The difference will become clear throughout this chapter.

Getting Input from the User

Let's take a look at an example. In the following exercise, we are going to build a very simple query that will let us get the employee who has a particular Employee ID. The user will be prompted to enter an ID number, and the report will return the information relevant to that user.

1. Create a new report, and call it **Employee-Chapter6.rpDesign**.

2. Create a new Data Source from the Classic Cars Sample Database.

3. Create a new SQL statement Data Set called **dsetEmployeeInfo** based on the Classic Cars Data Source.

4. Use the following SQL statement as your query. Be sure to keep the question mark in the query, as it indicates to BIRT that a Data Set Parameter needs to be created and used in its place.

```
select
*
from
Employees
Where
EmployeeNumber = ?
```

5. When you click on **Finish**, you will be brought to the Data Set Editor screen. From here, click on the **Parameters** branch in the tree view on the left-hand side.

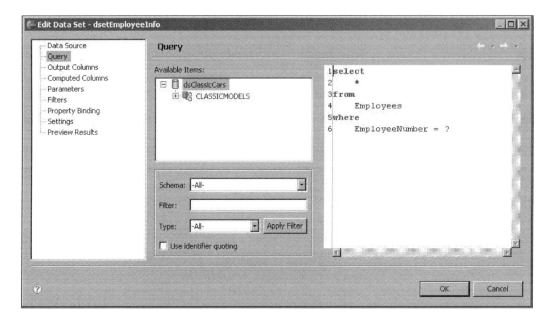

6. You will notice that there is a Data Set Parameter that has automatically been created for you, called **param_1**. It has automatically been assigned the type of the database type already; so we don't need to change anything. You should notice at the top of the screen that there is a red X with a comment about a default value. This is because if you do not have a default value in the parameter, BIRT will not have any sort of value in the parameter for report development. So we need to put one in there. Select **param_1** and click on the **Edit** button.

7. Change the **Name** to **dsprmEmployeeID**, and set the **Default Value** to **1002**. You will notice the drop-down box that says **Linked To Report Parameter**. Ignore this for now; we will come back to it. Click on **OK**.

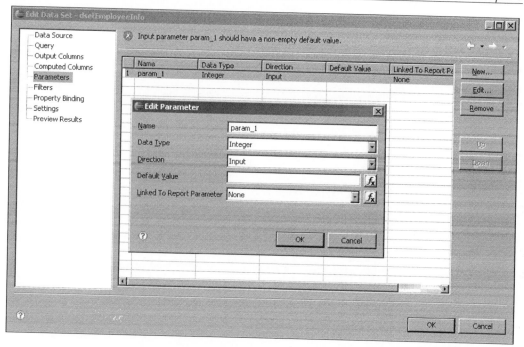

8. Now, if you go to **Preview Results** you can see you will retrieve one Employee. Click on **OK**.

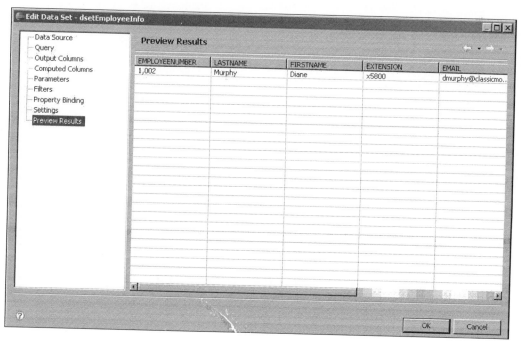

So, we have created a Data Set with a parameter, and assigned it a default value so that we can work with it. But we don't have a way to get user input and put that user input into the Data Set Parameter. Fear not! Because next we will create a Report Parameter and bind it to the Data Set for use in our report.

9. From the **Data Explorer**, go to **Report Parameters**, right-click on it, and choose **New Parameter** from the list.

10. On the next screen, you enter the properties for the Report Parameter. Here, we can set the Report Parameter as required for report execution. There are several options, such as:

     ◦ Hidden: which means the user will not see it in the parameter Dialog, although we can still pass values when calling the report with a URL.

     ◦ Is Required: which makes a value in the parameter mandatory.

     ◦ Do not echo input: which is useful for sensitive information.

11. Use the following values, and check the **Is Required** check box:

Field	Value
Name	rprmEmployeeID
Prompt text	Enter Employee ID
Data type	Integer
Display type	Text Box

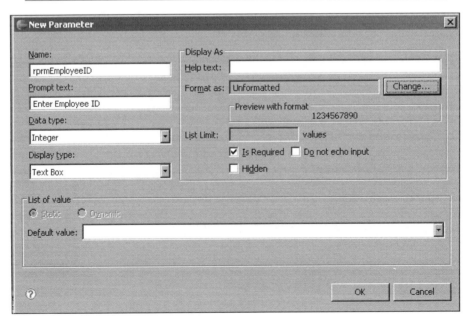

12. Click **OK**. At this point, there is no binding between the Data Set and the Report Parameter. To create the binding, start off by Double-clicking on **dsetEmployeeInfo** in the **Data Explorer** to open the **Edit Data Set** Dialog.

13. Go to the **Parameters** category. Double-click on **dsprmEmploeeID** or select it and click on the **Edit** button.

14. There are two different ways we can bind the parameter to the Data Set at this point. The easiest way is to select **rprmEmployeeID** from the **Linked To Report Parameter** drop-down box. This will work for versions of BIRT later than 2.1. Versions prior to BIRT 2.1 had to do it a different way. If you are using a later version of BIRT that has the drop-down box, go ahead and select **rprmEmployeeID** from the list. Otherwise, click on the function button (labled **fx** next to **Default Value**) to open up the Expression Editor. Under the **Categories** on the bottom: select **Report Parameters**, Sub Category ---**All**---, and double-click on **rprmEmployeeID**. Once finished, click on **OK**.

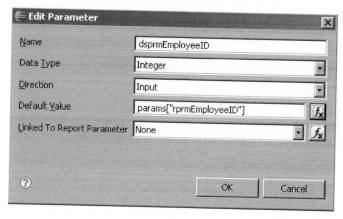

Here, we see the old fashioned way, using an Expression to link to the value of the Data Set Parameter to the Report Parameter.

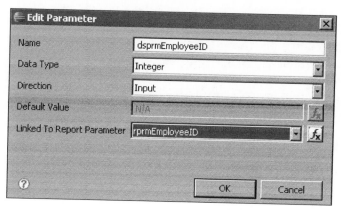

15. Under the **Data Explorer**, right-click on **dsetEmployeeInfo** and choose **Insert in Layout**, or "drag and drop" the **dsetEmployeeInfo** onto the Report Designer's **Layout** pane.

16. **Preview** the report.

The first time you preview the report with a Report Parameter, the BIRT Designer will bring up a Dialog box asking you to enter the Employee ID. Enter **1002** for the Employee ID to see the results of your report.

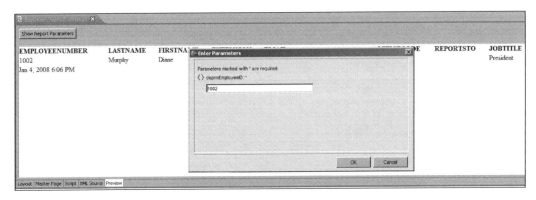

You can change the parameters to see other results after running the preview report, by clicking on the **Show Report Parameters** button in the **Preview** pane. The example just explained should demonstrate that there is a distinct difference between Report Parameters and Data Set Parameters. This will become an important distinction later on, when we start to use Report Parameters in ways that affect the layout and logic of a report that are separate from data.

Creating Parameter Binding the Easy Way

The last example was a good introduction to using parameters with data. In older versions of BIRT, it was the only way to create the binding between Data Set Parameters and Report Parameters. However, there are some tedious steps involved, which cause some confusion. Using the above method, you either need to know before you put your queries in what your Report Parameters are going to be and build them before you create your Data Set, or you need to double back as we did above. That seems a little counter-intuitive to typical Report Design. Fortunately there is an easier way to create Data Sets, Report Parameters, and bind them in one simple procedure. You might remember the button next to the **Linked to Report Parameter** text box that I said we would come back to. In the following example, we will revisit the process of creating a Data Set Parameter to show how much easier it is to do the linking of Report Parameters and Data Set Parameters in later versions of BIRT. In the next exercise we are going to go through the same steps as the previous exercise, except now we are going to use the quick method. Because we are going to use the same query as in the last example, you might want to go ahead and copy the existing one to the clipboard.

1. Under the **Data Explorer** or in the **Outline**, expand the **Report Parameters** branch, select **rprmEmployeeID**, and delete it. You can do this by either right-clicking and choosing **Delete**, going up to the **Edit** menu item and choosing **Delete**, or just hitting the *Delete* key on the keyboard.

2. Open up the **dsetEmployeeInfo** Data Set from either **Data Explorer** or **Outline**.

3. Under **Parameters**, select **dsprmEmployeeID** and click on the **Remove** button.

4. Click on the **New** button to create a new Data Set Parameter. At this point, we are basically at *Step 6* of the previous exercise. We have a new Data Set Parameter with no linking to any sort of values, and no default value.

5. From the **New Parameter** Dialog, use the same information as we did in the previous example.
   Name: **dsprmEmployeeID**
   Data Type: **Integer**
   Direction: **Input**

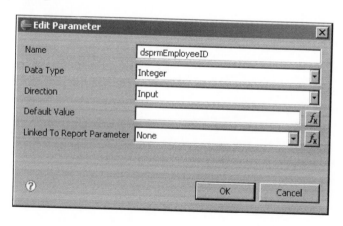

6. Click on the **fx** button next to the **Linked To Report Parameter** text box. This will bring up the Edit Dialog for the Report Parameter, with most of the relevant information filled in. You will notice the name is exactly the same as the Data Set Parameter. Fill in the prompt, and set the **Default Value** to **1002**.

Now, when you hit **OK** and go back to the Data Set Edit Dialog, click on **Preview Results**. You can see that the default value from the link Report Parameter is automatically filtered down to our Data Set. Use of this method is preferred, as it automatically creates that binding for you. It takes out the additional steps of creating the Report Parameter separately from Data Set Parameters.

Dynamic Report Parameters and Filters

We have seen how we can work with database-driven data and Report Parameters to filter data, using parameter binding between Report Parameters and Data Set Parameters. You may ask yourself, why did we go through the first exercise when the second exercise was so much easier? The reason is that this concept of binding through expressions is used a lot in BIRT. We will explain this in more detail in Chapter 12, when we discuss scripting. You may remember the Data component, which displayed text from a Data Set. The way it does that is by binding the data to the text element through an expression. In the next topic, we are going to see this expression binding again.

Report Parameters can require manual input from a user; you can also have pre-populated drop-down boxes for Report Parameters that are created at design time, or even populated from a database or other Data Set. This is useful for cases where the input needs to be exact; it is assumed that the user does not know all of the possible values, or exactly what information they are looking for.

While database data can be filtered through Data Set Parameters, the filtering done on the back-end database, other types of Data Sets, such as the XML, flat file, and scripted Data Sources do not have that capability. So how can you filter that data based on user input? The answer is by binding the Report Parameter to a Filter expression. You may recall that in the last chapter we were able to filter an XML Data Set by using a specialized expression, to only retrieve employees who had the job title of DEVELOPER. In this next example, we are going to create a simple Employee listing report using the Employees table, and instead of using a WHERE clause, we are going to use a Filter to limit the returned results. We are also going to bind this Filter to a Report Parameter that will have the possible job titles pre-populated from a database query. Please note, just as with the Report Parameter and Data set Parameter binding, there is a long way as well as an easy way to do it. I will only cover the easy way to do it, and leave it up to the reader to figure out the more difficult approach.

1. Create a new report called **EmployeeList-CH6.rptdesign**.

2. Create a new Data Source from the Classic Cars Sample Database.

3. Create a new Report Parameter, and call it **rprmEmployeeJobTitle**. Set the **Data type** to **String** and change the **Display Type** to **Combo Box**.

4. You will notice the Dialog box changes. You can set the **List of value** to **Static**, which means that you input this yourself at design time. If any new options need to be inputted, you will need to put them in yourself; or you can set it to **Dynamic**, which means it will be generated based on the results of a Data Set. The advantage of this is that you can have a back-end database someplace in which you can simply insert values and it will auto-populate this list. So it can be populated from an existing table in your database. The disadvantage is that you need a database, which can go offline, and you need to maintain it. Choose **Dynamic**.

5. The next screen shows all the options that you can set for dynamic generation. If you already have a Data Set, you can base the dynamic generation on that. In this example, we will create a new, dedicated Data Set—strictly for populating our parameters. Go ahead and click on the **Create New...** button.

6. Name the Data Set **dsEmployeeJobTitles**, and use the following SQL statement:

    ```
    select
    distinct
    CLASSICMODELS.EMPLOYEES.JOBTITLE
    from
    CLASSICMODELS.EMPLOYEES
    ```

7. Hit **OK** and exit out of the **Edit Data Set** Dialog. Once done, you will be back at the **Edit Parameter** Dialog with the Data Set already filled in to your new Data Set. From the two drop-down boxes, chose **JOBTITLE** for both the value and the display text. Why are they two? The reason is for Normalized databases. You can choose an ID for the value, and a string to be displayed to the user. For example, if you were choosing status codes for defect tracking: You would have things like Fixed, New, and In Process as possible statuses for an issue, and these would have ID numbers like 1, 2, and 3. You wouldn't expect the user to know the ID codes; so you would display the names instead.

Following is the screenshot of the Dialog with the values filled in and the Data Set created:

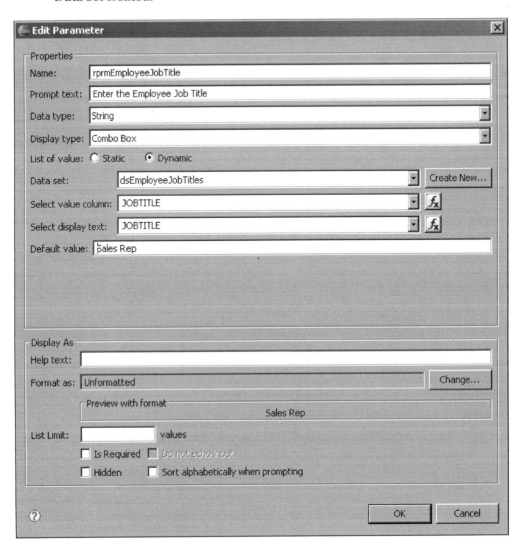

8.   For the **Default value**, use **Sales Rep**.

Create a new Data Set called **dsEmployeeList**. Use the following SQL statement:
```
select
*
from
CLASSICMODELS.EMPLOYEES
```

9. In the **Edit Data Set** Dialog, go to the **Filters** category. Create a new Filter.

10. Under **Expression**, select **JobTitle** from the drop-down list.

11. Under **Value 1**, select **Build Express** from the drop-down list.

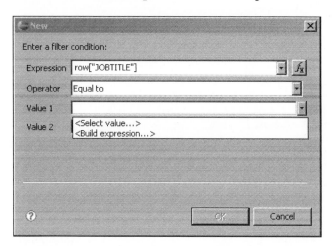

12. In the Expression Editor, under **Category**, select **Report Parameters**. Under Sub-Category, select **---All---**, and then select the Report Parameter as **rprmEmployeeJobTitle**. Double-click on it until it appears in the text box. Once it is there, click **OK**.

13. Click **OK**, and exit out of the Data Set Editor.

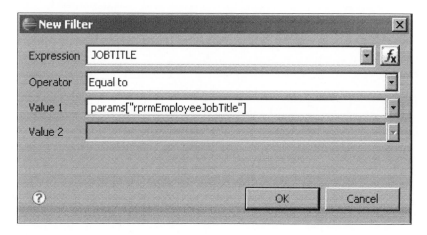

14. "Drag and Drop" the **dsEmployeeList** either from the **Data Explorer** or from the **Outline**.

15. **Preview** the Report.

Now, when you bring up the **Show Report Parameters** Dialog, you can see that you have a drop-down list with all the possible jobs for the employees. When you select one and hit **OK**, it will filter down to employees with that job.

The example just explained used a database Data Set instead of one of the static ones. In case of a database, you usually want to use a Data Set Parameter instead of a Filter. Using a "where" clause and a Data Set Parameter will always outperform a Filter, as the data is being filtered on the end of the DBMS. The DBMS is much more efficient at filtering data than BIRT would be. If you pulled a large Data Set, BIRT would have to retrieve that entire Data Set and apply the filter to it, wasting network bandwidth and processing time. Filters are useful in cases where you don't have a database to work with, such as a text file Data Source, or XML Data Source. In those cases, there is no DBMS to process a "where" clause and you have no choice but to use a Filter. However, in either case, we have seen how the user can influence the data that gets returned, as the last example will apply to the scripted Data Source, the flat file Data Source, and the XML Data Source.

Cascading Parameters

In some cases, it is desirable to have the user select a high-level category, in order to limit the number of parameter choices a user sees. For example, let's say we were looking at a report where a user needed to look at Products. In the case of a large company, there could be thousands of possible Products or Product Codes. It may be better to filter down based on a product line, to find the actual products you are looking for. Using the Classic Cars example, we have many different types of car models, such as the 1969 Harley Davidson Ultimate Chopper, Dodge Charger, and 1948 Porsche 356-A Roadster. If we want to limit what is displayed, we limit our parameter display by product lines, such as Classic Cars, Motorcycles, or Vintage Cars. Once a user selects one of those, they would only see the vehicles under each of those product lines. These are called Cascading Parameters.

Let's look at an example. In this report, we are going to modify the Employee-Chapter6.rptdesign report we created earlier to include a drop-down parameter list that allows a user to select a manager and list the employees that are under them, and then select an employee and get the report for that person.

1. Open **Employee-CH6.rptdesign**. Save the report as **Employee-Cascading-Chapter6**.

2. From the **Data Explorer**, delete the Report Parameter **dsprmEmployeeID. rptdesign**.

3. Create a new Data Set called **dsEmployeeManager**, and use the following query:

```
SELECT
        employeenumber,
        lastname || ', ' || firstname employeeName,
        (SELECT
                lastname || ', ' || firstname
        FROM
                EMPLOYEES managerEmployees
        WHERE
                employeenumber = currentemployee.REPORTSTO
        ) managerName
FROM
        EMPLOYEES currentemployee
union all
SELECT
        employeenumber,
        lastname || ', ' || firstname employeeName,
        'All' managerName
FROM
        EMPLOYEES currentemployee
```

4. In the **Data Explorer**, under **Report Parameters**, right-click on **Report Parameters** and choose **New Cascading Parameter**.

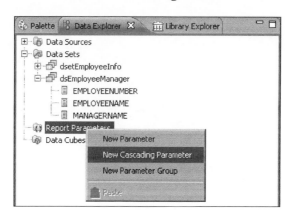

5. For the name use **rcprmEmployeeManagers** and enter the **Prompt text**.

6. Select **Single Data Set**.

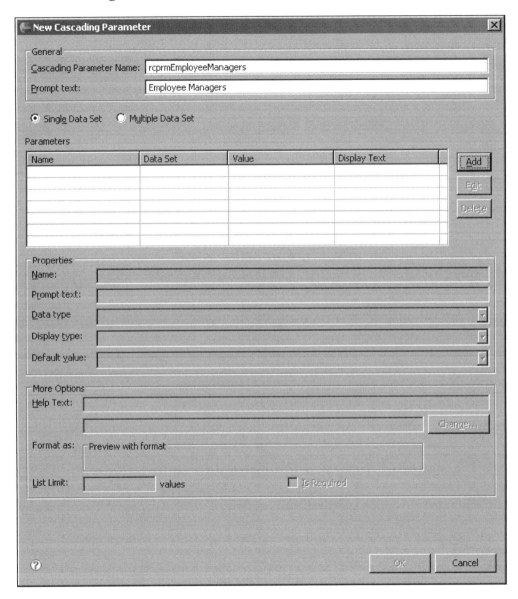

7. Click on the **Add** button. Enter the Dialog info as follows:

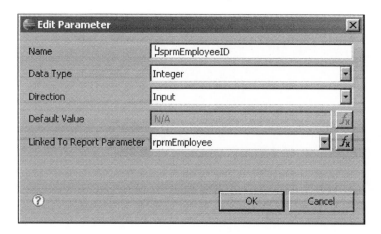

In versions of BIRT prior to 2.2, you would need to enter these values in the **Parameters** grid in the **New Cascading Parameter** Dialog.

8. Now, click **Add** again, and enter the following information for the Employee:

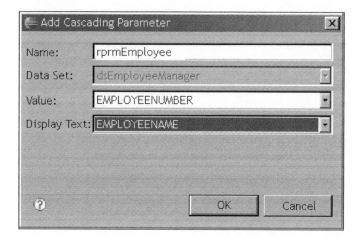

9. You can enter the **Prompt text** and **Default value** for each of these rows, just as you would do for regular parameters.

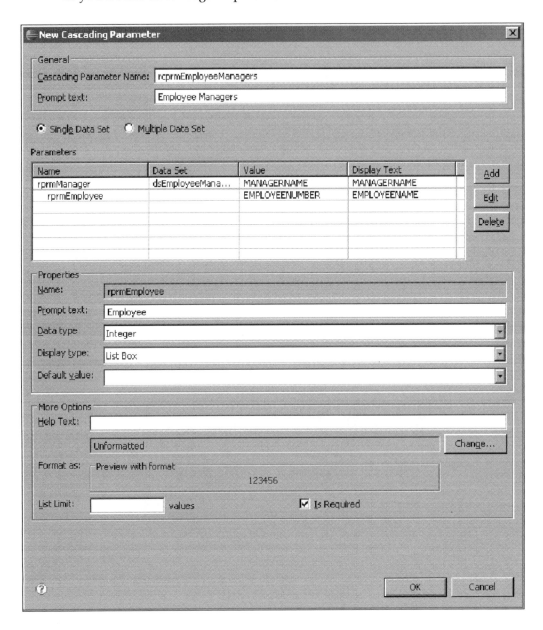

10. Hit **OK**. Under the **Data Explorer**, select **dsEmployeeInfo** and double-click to open the Data Set Editor.

11. Under **Parameters,** select **dsprmEmployeeID**, and click on the **Edit** button.

12. Set the **Linked to Report Parameter** to **rprmEmployee**.

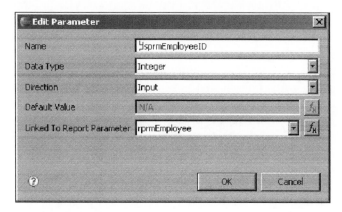

13. **Save** the report, and **Preview**.

Now, when you run the report, you will have two new parameters. When you select the Manager drop-down, the second list will get smaller. So if you select **All**, then all of the Employees will appear in the second drop-down list. Change the Manager drop-down to anyone else, and that list of Employees changes.

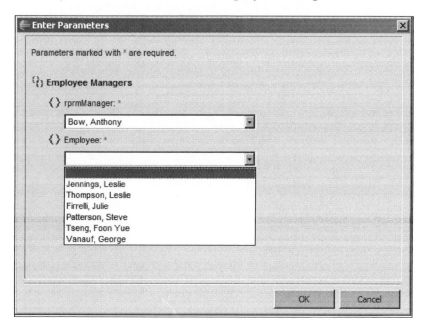

Parameter Grouping and Reports with Multiple Parameters

While we won't cover this here in detail, I would like to discuss it briefly. With reports you can create multiple Report Parameters, and bind them to a single Data Set or to multiple Data Sets. Just because a parameter has already been bound once, it does not mean it cannot be bound again. When you create a Report Parameter, that parameter becomes a global variable for your report that can be used anywhere else in the report. You can also use multiple parameters in a single Data Set—both as prepared parameters for queries and as filters. For example, let's say you have a query that pulls all orders for a particular market and a date range. In this query, you would have three parameters, one for the market, and two for the start date and end date. Each of these can be set to a Data Set Parameter and a Report Parameter.

So what happens when you start to have more parameters and need to manage them? The simple answer is that you can create a Parameter Group, and associate multiple parameters with that group. So in the last example, you can create a date range Parameter Group, and associate the start date and end date parameters with it. This is as simple as "dragging and dropping" existing parameters in the Data Explorer or Outline, or creating new parameters inside of an existing Parameter Group.

Summary

In this chapter, we have seen how we can interact with report users to help them retrieve specific information that they want to retrieve. Hopefully the distinct difference between Report Parameters and Data Set Parameters has been made clear. In later chapters, we will look at other ways in which Report Parameters can be used, and this concept is going to be used in more depth when we start to look at *Scripting* and changing visual components and properties. We have taken a look at how values can be bound to properties, which is going to be more important as we look at different report types and capabilities.

7
Report Projects and Libraries

Up until now, all the reports we built have been very simple reports. However, we have seen that all of these reports use very similar components between them, such as the Data Sources to the Classic Cars database, and the Data Sets that pull employee information. These are common elements between the reports we have built. In most project-based development environments there is a way to share common elements between components, and BIRT is no exception to this.

In the preceding chapters, we have worked with a single project. In this chapter, we are going to create a more structured reporting project, and work with Libraries to share the common report elements between reports. In most report development shops that I have come across, this is a great way to structure report development and can save developers lots of time, especially when more complex report components get developed. By grouping reports in projects, and reusing elements in libraries, common elements such as headers, Data Sources, and queries can be reused with minimal amount of development effort.

Report Projects

Way back early in the book, we created a Report Project that contains the examples we have built so far. However, we haven't really discussed the concept of what Report Projects are, and how to work with them.

A Report Project in Eclipse is simply a high-level container that will be used to store all files in a given project. In Eclipse, projects are simply folders, either contained within a workspace, or linked to an external file system folder or directory outside of the workspace. What differentiates projects from regular folders is a special file inside this folder, usually named `.project`, that defines various properties for the project. For your general purpose report development, you don't really need to know anything else about this file. Just know that projects are simply folders that contain all the files related to your project.

Project types are defined when you first create your project. In earlier versions of BIRT, there was only a **Report Project** type. In newer versions of BIRT, there are many different types of projects that are BIRT related. We have been working with the Report Project throughout the book. For the remainder of the book, we will continue using the BIRT Report Project; just keep in mind that there are other Report Project types as well. In BIRT 2.2, there are the BIRT ODA Designer Plug-in and the BIRT ODA Runtime Plug-in projects. You can build your own custom BIRT Open Data drivers for the BIRT Designer and BIRT Runtimes, respectively. There are also web-based development projects, such as the BIRT Charting Web Project (which will contain BIRT Chart Runtime components for a J2EE Web Project) and the BIRT Web Project (which will contain the BIRT Report Engine for a J2EE Web Project). So if you are building Java Servlets to handle report execution, you can do so using these pre-defined project types. The BIRT projects outside of the Report Project type are beyond the scope of this book, because they are for J2EE development.

Creating New Report Projects

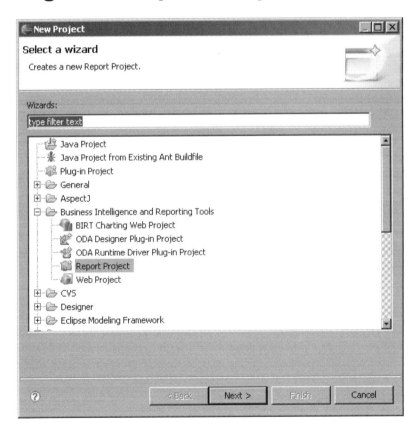

In the screenshot just shown, we can see the **New Project** wizard, with the different types of BIRT projects available.

As we have seen previously, Report Project creation is very simple. The general steps for creating a Report Project were illustrated in Chapter 3; so I will only touch on a few points, as there are a few different ways to create projects in Eclipse. Project creation is available from the **File** menu, and from the **Navigator**.

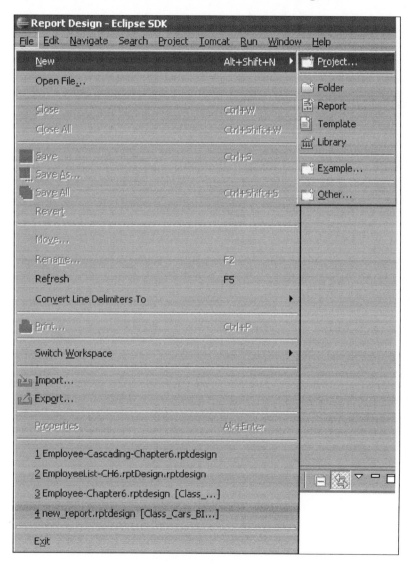

In the screenshot just shown, we can see the **File** menus, **New** options, with **Project...** highlighted.

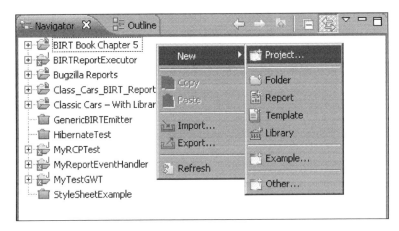

In the latest screenshot, we can see the **New** menu in the **Navigator**, accessed using the right-click context menu. Creating Report Projects from the Navigator is essentially the same as with the **File** menu, with the only difference being that when you create a project in the **File** menu, you will go to **File | New | Project** instead of right-clicking in the **Navigator** pane. If you are not in the BIRT perspective, you will have different options available under the **New** menu, as seen in the following screenshot when the **Java** perspective is open:

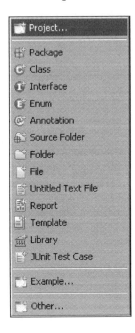

As you can see, in the **Java** perspective, the new **Report**, **Template**, and **Library** options for BIRT are also available. It is advisable to create new projects and reports from the BIRT perspective; however, most of the workbench sections—such as the Palette—do not open by default.

Importing and Exporting Report Projects

BIRT Report Projects are simply a collection of Report Design files, so the importing and exporting options available in Eclipse are not entirely useful. However, there are a few options that can be used for backup and restoration purposes. In the following examples, we will look at exporting a project to an archive file, and restoring it with the Import option.

Let's say that we need to archive the Classic Cars project that we have been building in this book. We will want to archive this as a ZIP file to C:\Temp\ClassicCars.zip. In order to do this, we need to right-click on the Project directory or the report file we want to archive and select the appropriate option. So in our case, we will use the Class_Cars_BIRT_Reports project. Then we will specify the archive file and the files to include in the archive.

1. From the **Navigator** pane, right-click on the **Class_Cars_BIRT_Reports** project and select the **Export...** option. You can also select the **Class_Cars_BIRT_ Reports** project, and then under the **File** menu, select the **Export...** option.

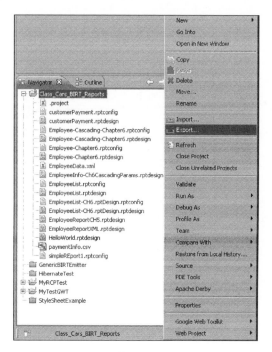

2. Under the **General** option, select **Archive File**.

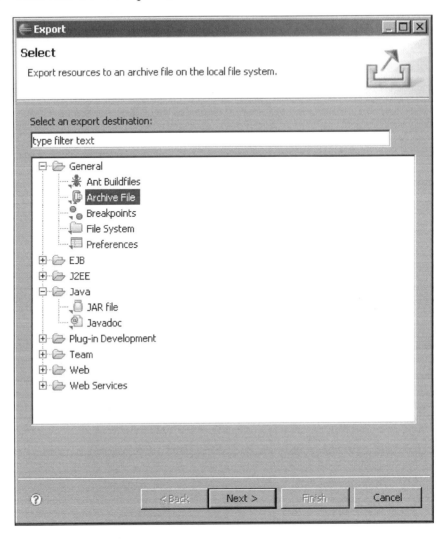

3. From the **Archive file** Editor, make sure the **Class_Cars_BIRT_Reports** project is checked. Make sure the files you want archived are also checked. In our case, this will be all of our files.

4. In the **To archive file** text box, enter the path. This can be done by using the **Browse...** button, or by manually entering the path. In my case, I will enter **C:\Temp\ClassicCars.zip**.

5. Make sure the **Save in zip format** and **Create directory structure for files** options are selected. ZIP is a format that is supported across multiple platforms; so I typically suggest this over Tar.

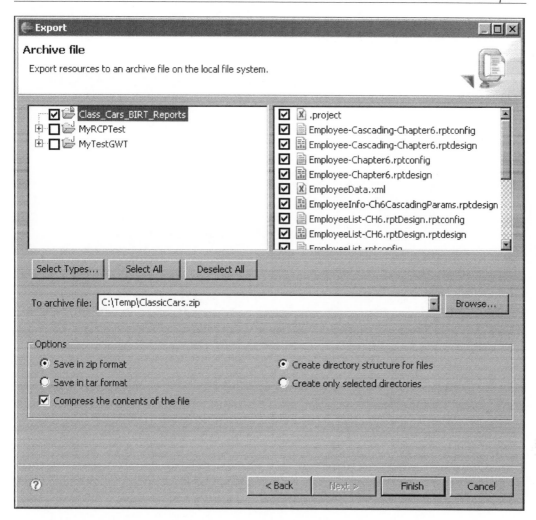

6. Click **Finish**.

So, we have made an exported archive of the project. Let's say that we received this archive and wanted to work with these report files. We would need to import the project into our Eclipse workspace. Fortunately, the process for doing so is very similar to exporting. This is the procedure:

1. Right-click on the **Navigator** and create a new **Report Project** called **Classic Cars Copy**.

2. Either from the **File** menu or by right-clicking in the **Navigator**, choose the **Import...** option.

3. From the **General** branch of the tree view, select **Archive File**.

4. In the Dialog that follows, enter the **From archive file** as **C:\Temp\ ClassicCars.zip**. You can also use the **Browse...** button to find the archive file.

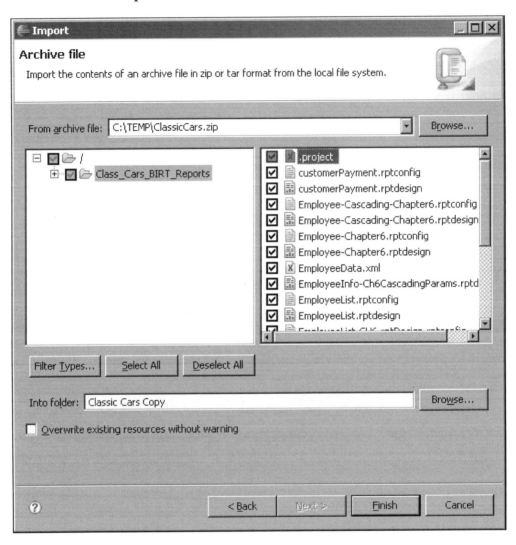

5. From the **Into folder** text box, make sure the **Classic Cars Copy** project is selected.

6. In the case of this archive, I want to deselect the **/** directory and the **Class_Cars_BIRT_Reports** folder. I just want to select the files that are under the **Class_Cars_BIRT_Reports** folder. This is due to the archive option that created the folder structure. I deselect both folders, and manually select the files under the file list box.

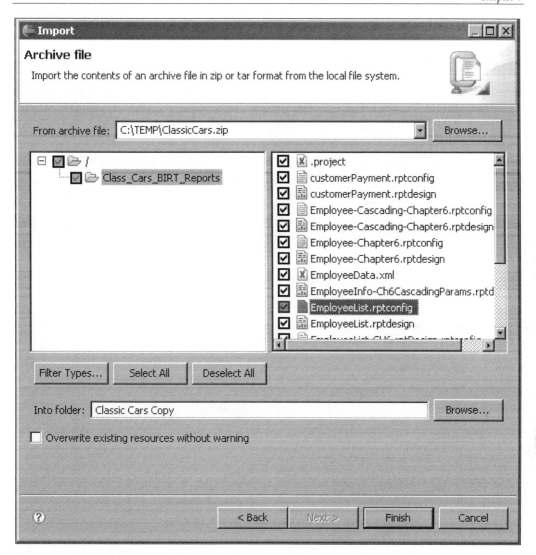

7.   Click **Finish**.

Other Project Options

In terms of reporting, there is very little else you will need to do with the vast number of options available for projects in Eclipse. If you are working with a lot of projects, often you might have projects open other than the one you are working in, in which case you may want to do a mass closing of projects. Eclipse offers a very nice option to close all projects unrelated to the selected one.

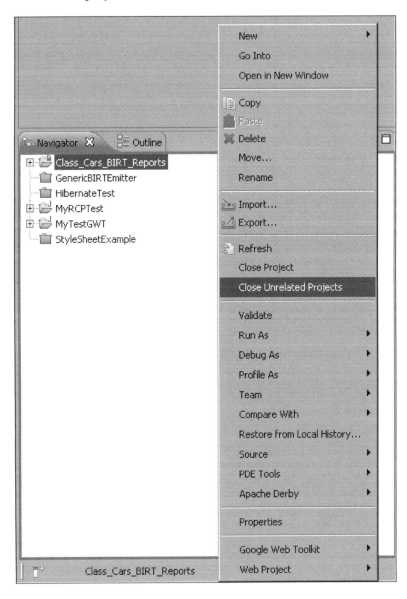

In the image just shown, you can see I have three projects opened—the **Class_ Cars_BIRT_Reports**, **MyRCPTest**, and **MyTestGWT**. I am only working with the **Class_Cars_BIRT_Reports** project, so it is the only project I want open. So I select it, right-click on it in the **Navigator**, and select **Close Unrelated Projects**. This will close all but the selected project.

If you need to focus a little more on a specific project, and closing projects isn't an attractive option, you have the option **Go Into** to go into a project or folder, and only its files will be visible in the Navigator. In the image just shown, I can right-click on **Class_Cars_BIRT_Reports** and select **Go Into** instead of **Close Unreleated Projects**. This will force the Navigator to only display the files and sub-folders under the Classic_Cars_BIRT_Reports project.

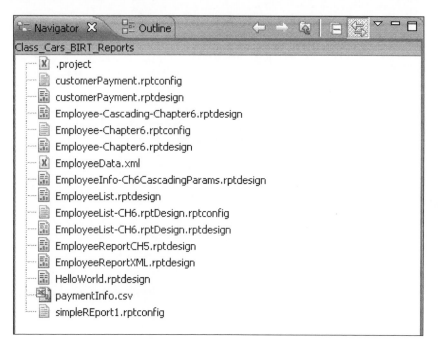

If you look at the latest figure, you can see the **Class_Cars_BIRT_Reports** project when **Go Into** has been executed on it. Notice, the yellow Left Arrow is available whereas the right one is not. The Left Arrow is the equivalent of a **Back** button. The Right Arrow is the same as the **Go Into** menu option. You also have the folder with an Up Arrow, which will bring you directly to the top level Workspace.

The final option we will look at—in the following example—is the Team option. This is useful when you have a versioning server, and you want to submit your files, or check out files from it. Eclipse—out-of-the-box—supports **CVS**; however, there are plug-ins available for Subversion and other versioning systems as well.

So, let's say that we have a CVS server at IP address 192.168.1.103. We want to be able to store our reports in this repository. Let's look at the steps on how to do so:

1. From the **Navigator**, right-click on the **Classic_Cars_BIRT_Reports** project, and choose **Team|Share Project...**.

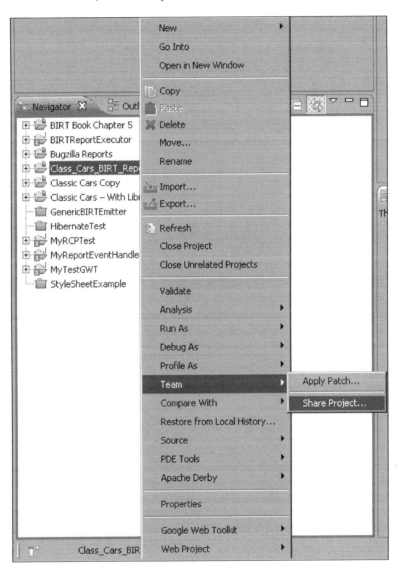

2. From the **repository type** screen, select **CVS**.

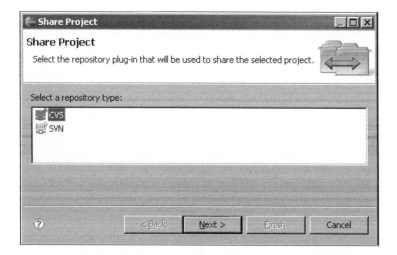

3. Input the necessary information to connect to the repository as follows:

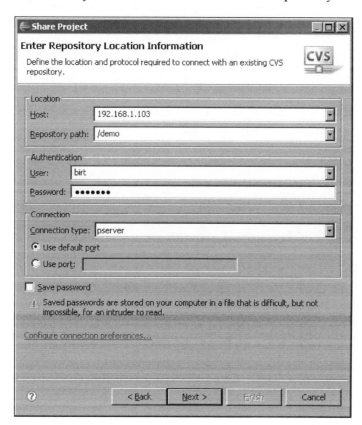

4. Specify a **Module Name**, or choose to use the Eclipse Project name as the repository project name.

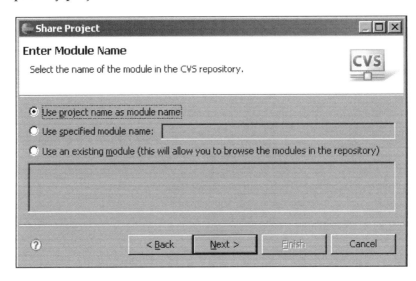

5. Click on **Finish**.

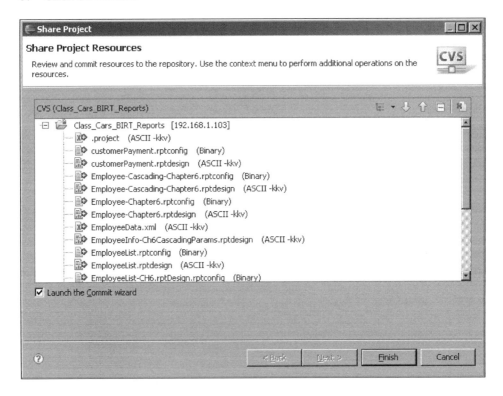

6. You will then be asked to enter a comment for the **Commit** of new files.

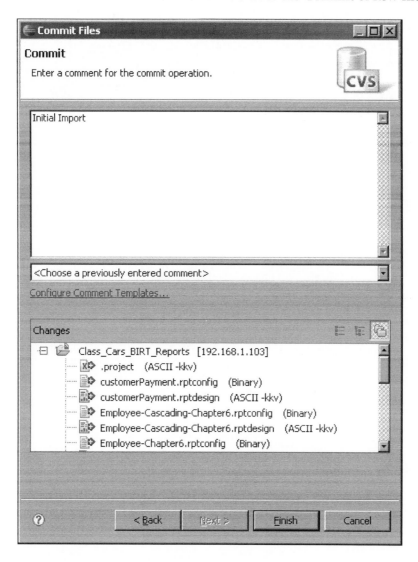

7. Now, your files have been stored in the repository. In the Navigator, a version number and type will appear next to each file. When you edit a file, it will only affect the local copy, and an indicator will appear next to the file indicating that a change has been made. In the following screenshot, the **HelloWorld.rptdesign** has been edited.

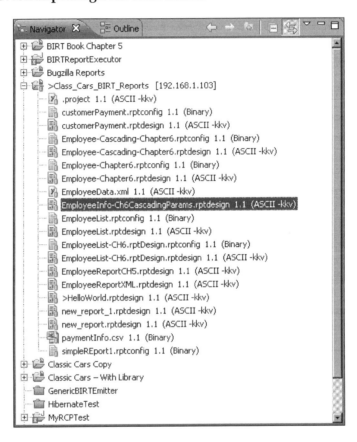

8. With a project shared, the Team menu will change and have additional options. You can **Synchronize with repository**, which will do a comparison between files to show which files are different on the repository, and which ones have been edited locally. You can **Commit** files to the repository, and you can **Update** your local files from the repository. You can also **Disconnect** from the repository, which will bring you back to the state where you can only edit your local files, and they will not be shared.

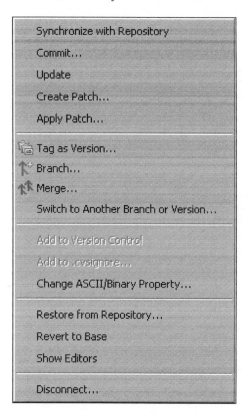

It is recommended that if you do use a repository then you should use the Synchronize option. From the Synchronize menu, you can see the differences between the local copy of files and the remote versions, see the revision history, and you have more control over the commit and update selections.

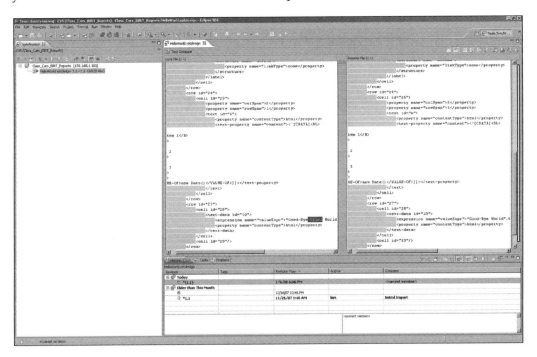

Libraries

Often, report development can lead to repetitive tasks. Things like report headers, commonly used Data Sets and Data Sources, formatting, and other elements are used in many different reports. This is where Libraries come into play. When using Libraries, report developers can store commonly used components for later reuse. It is also a useful tool when working in groups.

The concepts of reuse and group development are often overlooked in report development, and they seem to be all but entirely ignored with BIRT. However, if you have worked in a report development group, it is an all too often needed functionality. When I was working in a large report development group, the data that got pulled all too often was the same—or at least similar—to previous report requests, with modification to visual layouts, or modified parameters. Another scenario that was common was to develop reports only to find out that someone had done the same report several months ago. With BIRT's report libraries, these kinds of common tasks—from the same report queries, Data Sources, up to visual elements and output—can be stored in a central report Library and made accessible to other developers to reuse and share their components. This is even useful in single-developer situations to keep from having to rebuild commonly used objects in different reports.

In BIRT, Libraries are very similar in structure and design to a report document. The main difference is that Libraries can be referenced inside Report Designs, and the Visual editor for Libraries will be different. When there are changes to Library elements, these changes will trickle down into the Report Designs that are using them. The only exception is with Chart elements in versions of BIRT prior to 2.2.

Creating a New Library

As with Report Designs, a Library can be created using either the **New** option under the **Navigator** or the **File** menu. This is nice because it does not deviate from the expected behavior. In the following example, we are going to create a new Report Project called Classic Cars Library and create a new Library with it.

1. From either the **Navigator** or **File** menu, go to **New | Project...**. Name the project as **Classic Cars – With Library**.

2. In the **Navigator**, right-click on **Classic Cars – With Library**, and choose **New | Library**. Name the Library as **ClassicCarsLibrary.rptlibrary**.

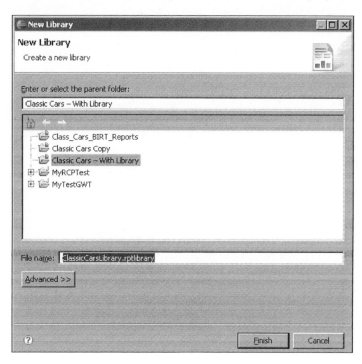

3. When you click on **Finish**, you will get a Dialog letting you know how to work with the visual designer. Click on **OK**.

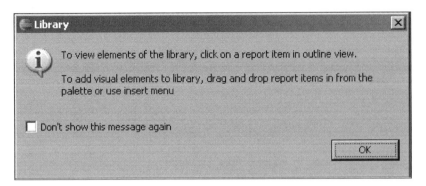

Adding Components to a Library

Now that we have a Library, we need to add a few components to it. With the reports that we have created throughout the book, we have used a consistent Data Source — the Classic Cars Sample Database. This would make a good candidate for a Library item. In the following example, we will add a Data Source to a Library, and a few components that we will use throughout our next few reports.

1. Open up the **ClassicCarsLibrary.rptlibrary**, if it is not already opened.

2. Open up the **Outline** Pane.

3. Open up the **Palette** Pane above the **Outline** pane, so that both panes are open at the same time.

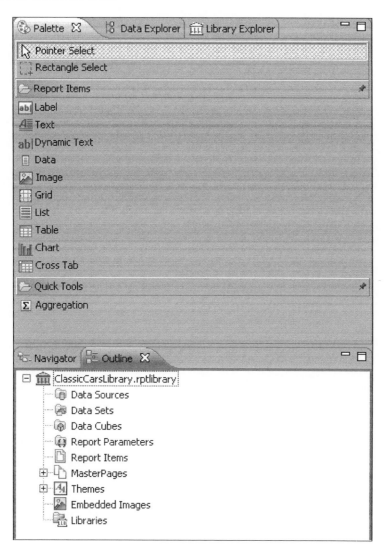

4. Right-click on the **Data Sources** icon under the **Outline**, and select **New Data Source**. Select the **Classic Models Inc. Samples Database**, and name the **Data Source** as **dsClassicCars**. Click **Next | Finish**.

So now we have a Data Source in a Library. This was easy to do.

Adding a Visual Element to a Library

So, what about visual elements? In our reports, we will want to add in simple report headers containing a logo for the Classic Cars Company—a company title line, and a report title line. The report title line will be populated by a Report Parameter so that the design of the header is consistent, but the title will be dynamic.

1. In the **Outline**, right-click on the **Report Parameters** icon. Select **New Parameter**.

2. Enter the following properties:
   Name: rprmReportTitle

   Prompt text: Enter the Report Title

   Change to a hidden parameter.

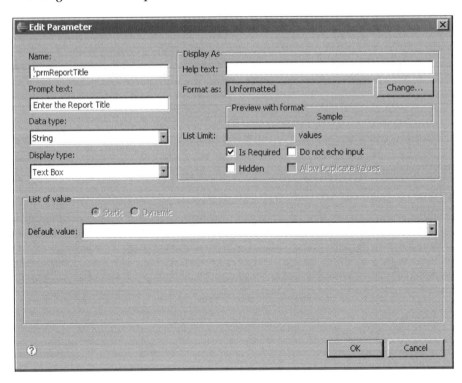

3. Drag a **Grid** item from the **Palette** to the **Outline**'s **Report Items** section.

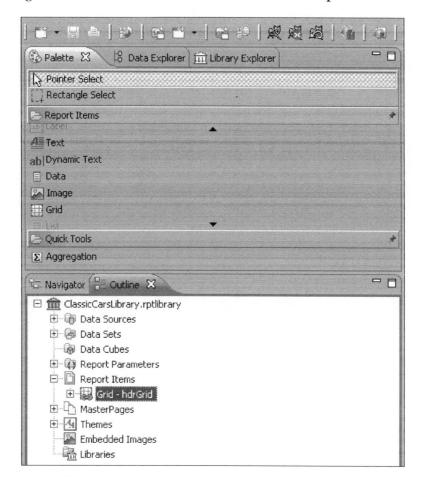

4. Set the **Number of columns** to 2, and the **Number of rows** to 3.

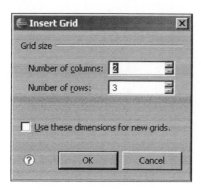

5. In the leftmost column, select all three rows, right-click on the selection, and choose **Merge Cells**. The **Merge Cells** option is also available from the **Element** menu.

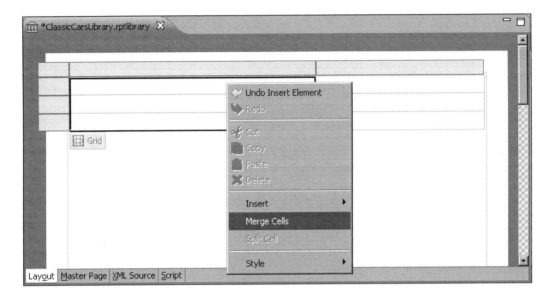

6. Change the **Name** of the Grid to hdrGrid under the **Property Editor — General** Tab.

7. Drag an **Image** object from the **Palette** over to the single, large cell.

8. In the Dialog that pops up, click on the Function button for the URL. We will borrow the Classic Cars logo from the Eclipse BIRT Website, so use the following URL: `http://www.eclipse.org/birt/phoenix/examples/solution/ClassicLogo.jpg`.

    Once the image has been added, change the name to **hdrLogo** under the **Property Editor — General** Tab.

9. Drag the column line over from the center as far as it will go to the left. This will eliminate the empty space from where the text and the image will go.

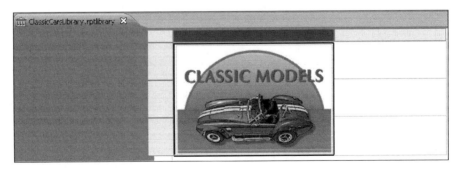

10. Drag a Label component over to the second column, first row cell.

11. For the text, enter **Classic Cars, Inc.**

12. Set the Label **Name** to **hdrHeaderLabel1**

13. Change the font properties as follows:

    Size: 24 points
    Weight: Bold

14. Drag a **Data** object to the second row. Set the name as **hdrHeaderLabel2**.

15. Enter the Expression Editor for the Data component. Navigate to **Report Parameters/All/rprmReportTitle** as the data expression. The final expression should be **params["rprmReportTitle"]** when done.

16. Enter the following font parameters:

    Size: 16 points
    Weight: Bold

17. Drag a **Text** object over to the third row. Set the name as **hdrHeaderLabel3**.

18. Change the value to **<VALUE-OF>new Date()</VALUE-OF>**

19. Select the **Grid** component, and change the **Background color** to **Silver**.

Using Components Stored in a Library

So now we have two components stored in a Library — a report header and a Data Source. How do we consume them? Well, that's what we are going to look at next. Using elements in a Library is fairly straightforward. You only need to use the Library in a Report Design that is stored in a project, and you are ready to go. We will look at how to do this in the next example.

1. Create a new Report Design under the **Classic Cars – With Library** report. Call it **Customer Order Form**. Make it a **Blank Report**.

2. Open up the **Outline** view for the new report. Open up the **Library Explorer** above the **Outline** view. You should see under the **Shared Libraries** section.

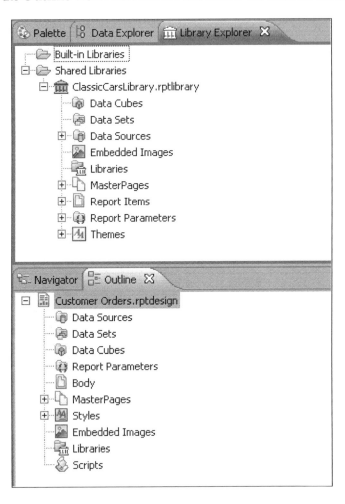

3. Drag the Data Source from under the **Library Explorer**'s **Data Sources** to under the **Data Sources** in the **Outline**. This will reference the Libraries' Data Source in the Report Design.

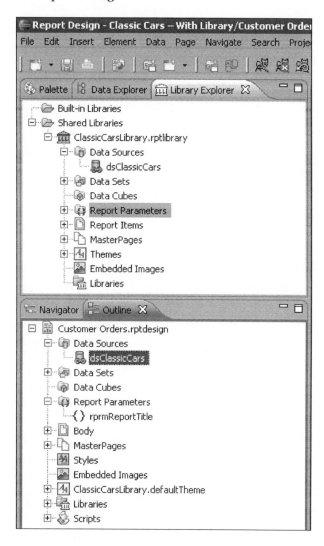

4. From under the **Report Parameters** section of the **Outline**, "drag and drop" the **rprmReportTitle** parameter over to the **Library Explorer**'s **Report Parameters** section.

5. Now, under the **Library Explorer**, expand the **Report Items** section. Right-click on the **hdrGrid** object. You will notice that the option **Add to Report** is grayed out. The reason is that the correct target location is not selected in the Report Design Outline. This is one caveat to adding through context menus that isn't an issue with "dragging and dropping."

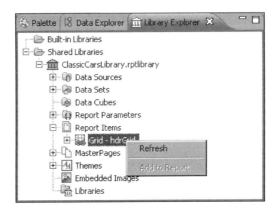

6. Expand the **MasterPages** section in the Report Design **Outline**, and select **Header**. Now, right-click on the **Libraries'** **Grid** object and choose **Add to Report**.

7. In the Report Design **Outline**, select the **rprmReportTitle** from **Report Parameters**, Right-click, and choose **Edit**. In the **Edit Parameter** Dialog, enter the **Default value** as **Customer Orders Report**.

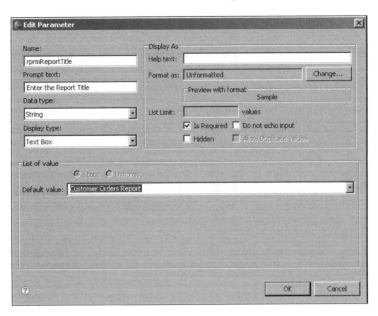

8. **Save** the report and **Preview**.

In the example just shown, as we are using a object that requires the Libraries' Report Parameter (the Data element for the Report Title), it is important to add that to the Report Design first, otherwise BIRT will throw an error. We will resolve the errors in the following screenshot in the next section.

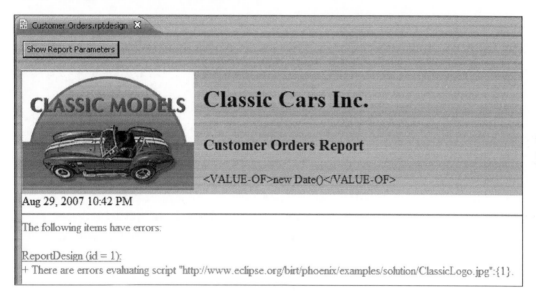

Updating Components in the Library to Update Reports

In the previous example, you will notice that when you preview the report, two errors are apparent. First, we have the error in bright red telling us that there were errors evaluating the tag for the URL to the Classic Models logo. The second error is that the current date is not showing up correctly in the third line of the header. This would be a problem with all reports that utilized this Library item. Now, we could fix these in the report themselves; however, the fix would be local to that report only. We don't want to do that. We would like this fix to trickle down to all reports that are using these items. In order for that to happen, we need to edit the Library itself.

1. Open **ClassicCarsLibrary.rptlibrary** from the **Library Explorer**.

2. Under the **Report Items**, select **hdrGrid**. It should become visible in the Report Design pane.

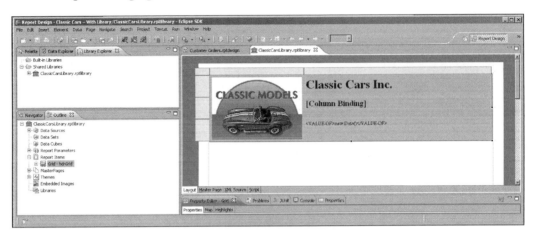

3. Double-click on the logo **hdrLogo** in the header to bring up the Editor.

4. Around the URL for the logo, put double quotes so it reads "**http://www. eclipse.org/birt/phoenix/examples/solution/ClassicLogo.jpg**", and hit **OK**.

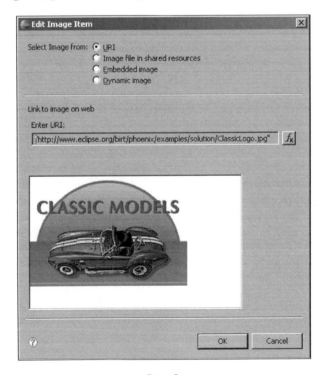

5. Double-click on **hdrHeaderLabel3** in the third row (second column) to open the Editor. Change the value of the mode from **Auto** to **HTML** Hit **OK**.

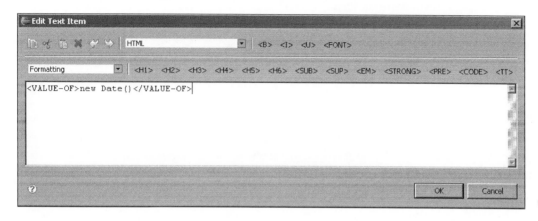

6. Save **ClassicCarsLibrary.rptlibrary**. Rerun the report. Now that the Library has been updated, when you run the report, you can see that the broken items have been fixed.

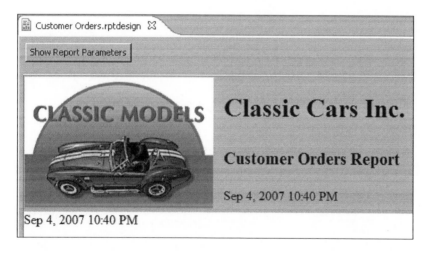

It should be noted that once you change a component in a report—such as its text—it then becomes part of the report and not of the Library. The reason is that technically, components consumed within a report become extensions of components in a Library. When you change something, you are changing it in the extension, not the original; however, unmodified components will still reflect changes. In the following example, we will demonstrate that changes made in the report will take precedence over the original Library item.

7. Open the **Master Page** section of the Report Designer. Double-click on the Label **hdrHeaderLine1** in the Report Design file. Change the text to read **Classic Cars Incorporated**.

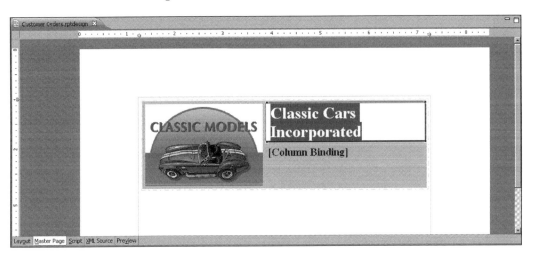

8. **Save** the report.

9. Open the **ClassicCarsLibrary.rptlibrary**. In the Outline, select **Report Items/ hdrGrid** to make the header visible in the Report Designer.

10. Delete the third line with the **<Value-Of>new Date()</Value-Of>** tag. **Save** the Library.

11. In the first line, remove the period from **Classic Cars Inc**.

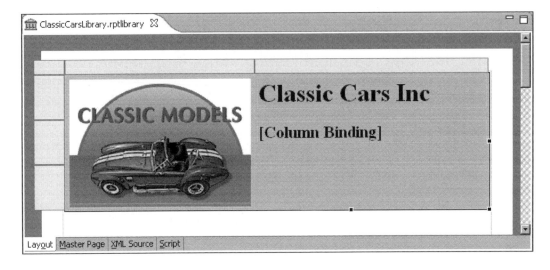

12. Save the Library, and run the report.

In the example just shown, the change made in the report will take precedence over the change made in the Library, while the deleted line will not be displayed in the report as the change will trickle down.

Adding Existing Components in Reports to Libraries

So far in this chapter, we have looked at developing and publishing components into a report Library from scratch. Then we looked at how reports could consume those Libraries and link in those components. Next, we looked at editing the Libraries and having them trickle down to reports.

So, what happens when we have a report we have developed and there are portions we want to share with others; how do we go about publishing these components to Libraries? There isn't really a way in the BIRT Report Designer to do this; so we will have to rely on more traditional methods to import existing report items into Libraries. In the following example, we will Cut and Paste elements from the Outline to a report Library.

In the next example, we will take a look at how to add report components from a report to a Library. You will see that this isn't the most intuitive process; however, it is one that does get requested. So, we will create a basic query to retrieve customer information, which we will use afterwards to combine with a second Data Set to have a master/detail type report.

1. Add a Data Set to the report called **getCustomerInformation**.

2. Use the following query:

```
select *
from CLASSICMODELS.CUSTOMERS
where CLASSICMODELS.CUSTOMERS.CUSTOMERNUMBER = ?
```

3. Create a report parameter called **rprmCustomerID** and link it to the Data Set. **Data type** will be **Integer** and set the **Prompt text** as **Enter the Customer ID**. Use the **Default value** of **148** to make developing a little easier so that we can debug and do not have to enter a value each time.

4. Save the report.

5. Open the **ClassicCarsLibrary.rptlibrary** file. Drag the tab for the Library in the Report Design file so that it is side by side with the Report Design file.

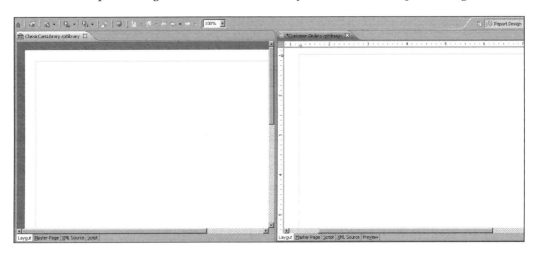

6. In the **Outline** for the Report Design, right-click on the **getCustomerInformation** Data Set and choose **Copy**.

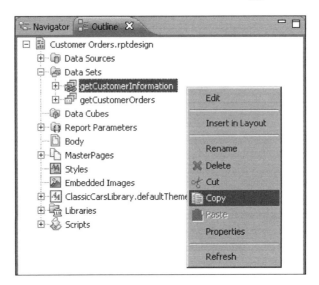

7. In the **Data Sets** branch of the Library's Outline, right-click and choose **paste**.

8. Repeat steps 6 and 7 for **rprmCustomerID**.

9. **Save** the Library.

> The problem with the above method is that the Data Set and the Report Parameter are both two separate instances from the Report Design files and the report Libraries. The way to link them is to delete the instances in the report and consume them using the steps shown earlier in this chapter.

10. In the Report Design file, delete both **getCustomerInformation** and **rprmCustomerID**.

11. Add both components from the Library back into the report. (Note: I encountered an issue here and had to close both the Library and the Report Design to accomplish this step.)

Summary

In this chapter, we looked at the aspects that are available to Report Projects and at creating a shared development environment using Libraries. There are other options we will look at in later chapters—such as Templates—that allow collaborative and consistent Report Designs across the enterprise.

We have seen how to create new Libraries, new Library components, and use those components in Report Designs. We have also seen how to add components from reports into Libraries, and how to edit Libraries.

We also saw some other elements that were new, such as the Master Page that is a common header and footer that will get placed on every page of a report in multi-page reports.

In the next chapter, we are going to expand on two themes: the concept of applying a consistent visual design to Report Designs using Styles, and how to apply overall styles in Libraries to reports using Themes.

8
Styles, Themes, and Templates

Up until now, we have worked with Report Designs using the formatting elements in a very specific way. We have looked at very specific elements of Report Design elements, such as how to change the font for a Data item, change the background color for a cell, etc.

This is fine if you don't mind formatting every element in a report manually, though, this can become bothersome in larger reports. Imagine having a large report with lots of elements, and having to settle on either the default visual properties (which are very plain as we have seen), or having to manually edit the properties for each component. This can become time consuming. Libraries can help by allowing a developer to store commonly used elements, such as headers (which are already formatted) for later use. However, there is a much more efficient way to format reports, by using Style Sheets.

The goal of this chapter is to look at how BIRT uses Style Sheets in Report Designs, and how Styles can be grouped in a Library to create Themes. This will allow you to have certain sets of Styles ready for use any time you develop a report, so that you (as a report developer) can focus strictly on the technical aspects of the report and do not have to worry about the tedious task of visual presentation.

We will also look at Templates in this chapter. Templates are existing report layouts that can be used as a starting point for new reports. This is useful if you use a similar layout in all your reports; you can create a Template and build from that for each new report.

Style Sheets

BIRT—being a web-based reporting environment—takes a leaf from general web development toolkits by importing Style Sheets. However, BIRT Style Sheets function just slightly differently from regular Style Sheets.

We are going to add on to the Customer Orders report we have been working with, and will create some Styles that will be used in this report.

1. Open **Customer Order.rptdesign**.

2. Right-click on the **getCustomerInformation** Data Set and choose **Insert in Layout**. Modify the Table visually to look like the following figure:

CUSTOMER NUMBER:	[CUSTOMERNUMBER]
CUSTOMER NAME:	[CUSTOMERNAME]
ADDRESS	[ADDRESSLINE1]
CITY	[CITY]
STATE	[STATE]
	[POSTALCODE]
COUNTRY	[COUNTRY]
PHONE	[PHONE]

3. Create a new Data Set called **getCustomerOrders**. Use the following query:

```
select
*
from
CLASSICMODELS.ORDERDETAILS,
CLASSICMODELS.ORDERS
where
CLASSICMODELS.ORDERS.ORDERNUMBER =
                       CLASSICMODELS.ORDERDETAILS.ORDERNUMBER
And CLASSICMODELS.ORDERS.CUSTOMERNUMBER = ?
```

4. Link the Data Set Parameter to **rprmCustomerID**.

5. Save the Data Set, then right-click on it in the Data Explorer and choose **Insert in Layout**.

6. On the first column for **ORDERNUMBER**, select the column.

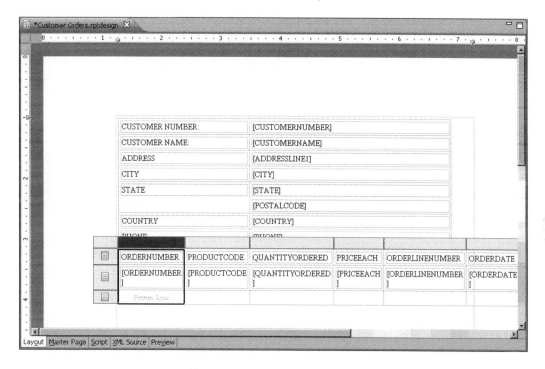

7. Under the **Property Editor**, select **Advanced**. Go to the **Suppress duplicates** option and change it to **true**.

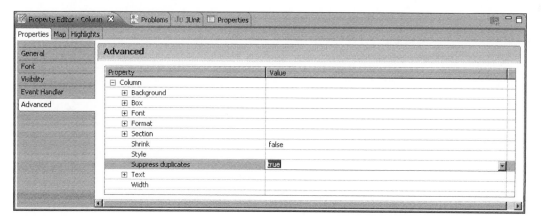

8. In the **Outline**, right-click on **Styles** and choose **New Style...**. In the Dialog that follows, choose **table-header** from the **Predefined Style** drop-down box.

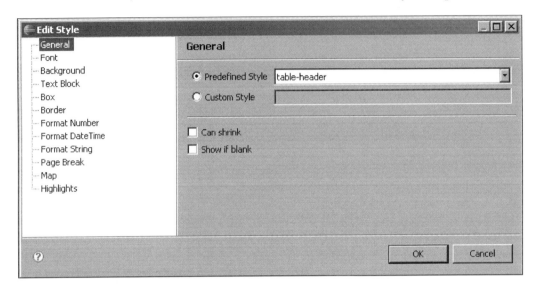

9. Under the **Font** section, use the following settings:

    Font: **Sans Serif**

    Color: **White**

    Size: **Large**

    Weight: **Bold**

10. Under the **Background** section, use the following settings:

    Background color: **Black**

11. Hit **OK**.

Now, when we run the report, we can see that the header line is formatted with a black background and white font.

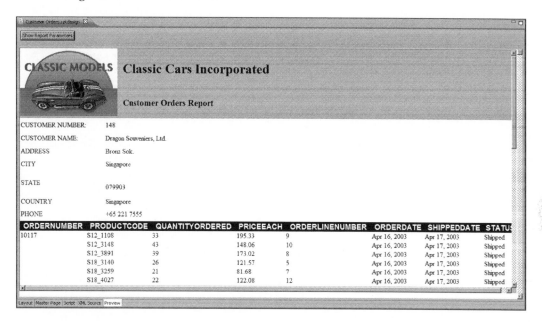

Custom Style Sheets

In the previous example, we can see that we didn't even need to apply this Style to any elements; it was automatically set to the header of the order details Table. This would be the case for any Table that had the detail row populated with something. This is the case with any of the predefined Styles in BIRT. So next, let's look at a Custom-defined Style, and apply it to our customer information table.

1. Right-click on the **Styles** section of the outline, and create a new Style.
2. Under the **Custom Style** text box, enter **CustomerHeaderInfo**.

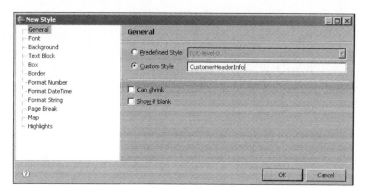

3. Under the **Font** section, enter the following information:

    Font: **Sans Serif**

    Color: **White**

    Size: **Large**

    Weight: **Bold**

4. Under the **Background** section, enter the following information:

    Background color: **Gray**

5. Under the **Box** section, enter **1 | points** for all sections. Under the **Border** section, enter the following info:

    Style (All): **Solid**

    Color (All): **White**

    Width (All): **Thin**

6. Hit **OK** and **Save**. Now, select the Table with the Customer Information, and select the first column:

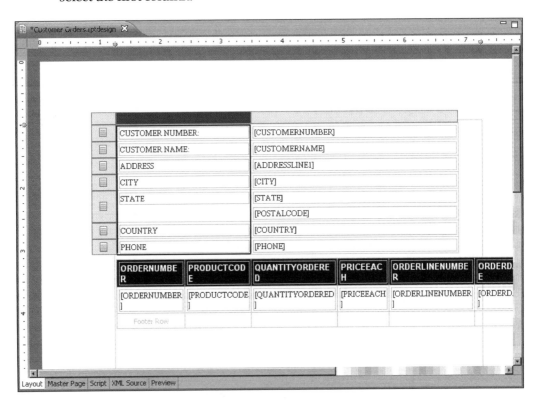

7. Under the **Property Editor | Styles**, select **CustomerHeaderInfo**. The preview report will look like the following screenshot:

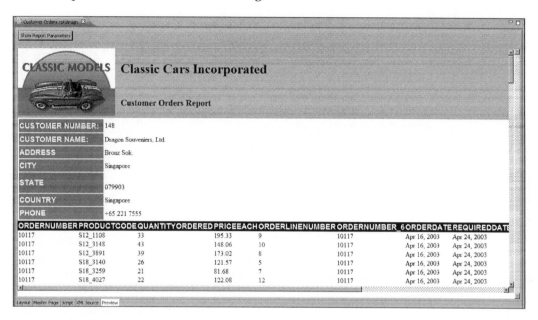

8. Right-click on the **Styles** section in the **Property Editor**, and create a new Custom Style called **CustomerHeaderData**.

9. Under **Box**, insert **1 | points** for all fields. Under **Border**, enter the following information:

    Style (Top) : Solid

    Style (Bottom) : Solid

    Color (All): Gray

10. Hit **OK**. Select the Customer Information Table, and select the second column.

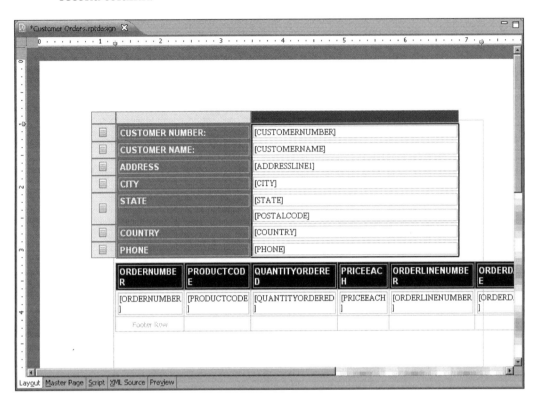

11. Under the **General** Tab in the **Property Editor**, change the **Style** property to **CustomerHeaderData**.

12. The finished report will look like following screenshot:

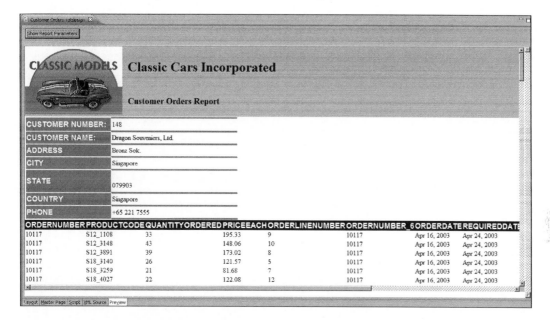

Editing Style Sheets

So far, we have two Custom Styles and one predefined Style used in our report. However, we need to make a change. If you look at the previous example, the gray lines in the Data section of our header do not match the white lines of the Label section. Normally, such tedious visual elements are concerns for graphic designers; however, in our case this provides us the perfect excuse to look at editing Style Sheets.

In the following example, we will take a look at editing the column of our header information so that the lines are gray instead of white. Editing Style Sheets is a fairly trivial task; simply double-clicking on existing Styles will bring up the Style Editor.

1. In the **Outline**, under the **Styles** section, double-click on the **CustomHeaderInfo** Style.

2. Select the **Border** Section. Under the **Top** and **Bottom** colors, select **Gray**.

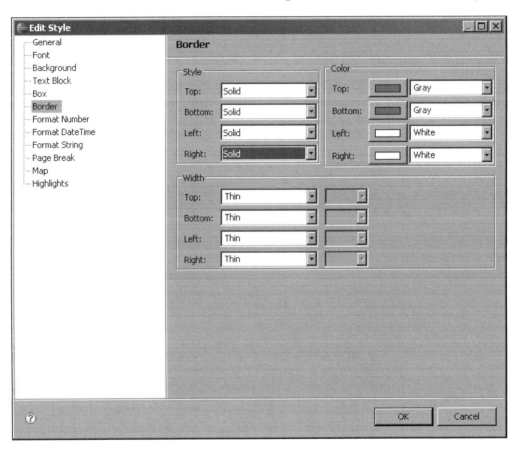

That was easy enough. But now, there is a small (few pixels) gap between the Label column and the Data column. Let's remove it.

3. Select **CustomHeaderInfo | Border**. Change the **Left** and **Right** line **Style** to **No line style**.

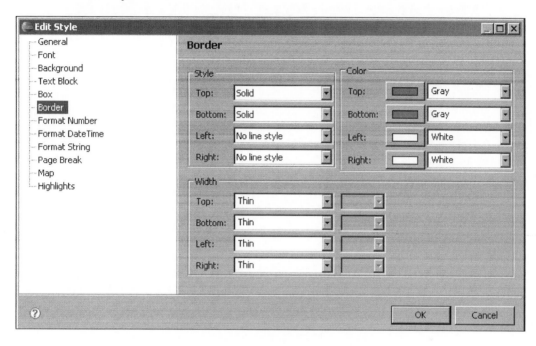

4. Repeat steps 1 through 3 for **CustomHeaderData**.

Alternating Row Colors Using Highlights

So far, our report is coming along nicely. However, the detail section leaves a little to be desired visually. It is hard to distinguish lines from each other, and it would be nice to have the first line of a new order to be of different color to distinguish it. Well, we are in luck. BIRT provides a very nice capability called a Highlight, which allows us to change formatting options based on a particular condition.

Highlighting can be applied in one of two ways: it can be applied either to an element directly, or in a Style. There is really no difference in editing a Style between the two. I will cover both methods.

First, let's look at applying the alternating row color through a Style.

1. Create a new Style called **Detail Alternating Row Color**. Select **Highlights** from the list of categories.

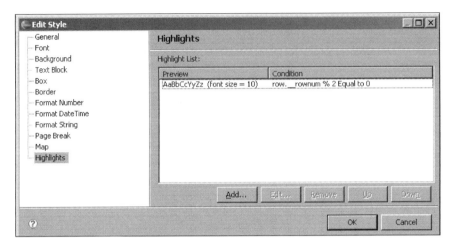

2. Click **Add**. Use the following condition: **row.__rownum % 2**. This is an Expression that will select every other row. We will discuss Expressions in more detail in the chapter on *Scripting*. Set the operand to **Equal to** and value to **0**. Also set the **Background Color** to **Silver**.

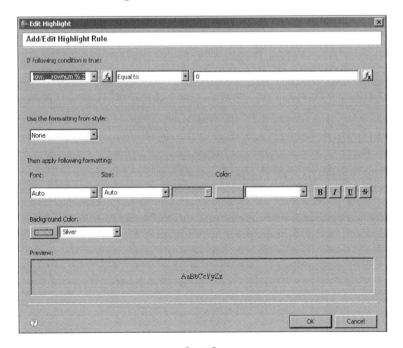

3. Hit **OK** and exit out of the Style Editor.

4. Select the Detail row for the **getCustomerOrders** Table either from the Visual Designer or from the **Outline**.

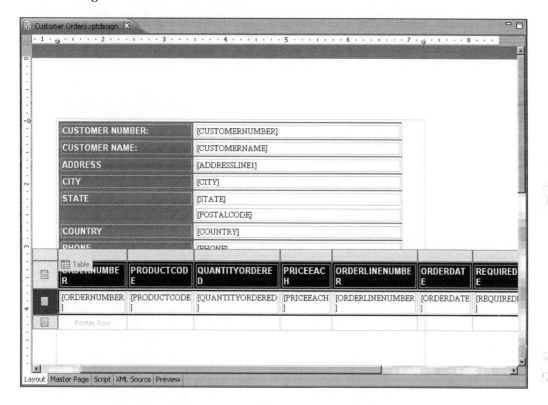

5. In the **Property Editor**, Select **General**. Under **Styles**, select **Detail Alternating Row Color**.

Now, when we run the report, we can see that the Detail row has the alternating colors we were looking for. We can easily apply this to any of the detail rows in our report.

Classic Cars Incorporated

Customer Orders Report

CUSTOMER NUMBER:	148
CUSTOMER NAME:	Dragon Souveniers, Ltd.
ADDRESS	Bronz Sok.
CITY	Singapore
STATE	
	079903
COUNTRY	Singapore
PHONE	+65 221 7555

ORDERNUMBER	PRODUCTCODE	QUANTITYORDERED	PRICEEACH
10117	S12_1108	33	195.33
	S12_3148	43	148.06
	S12_3891	39	173.02
	S18_3140	26	121.57
	S18_3259	21	81.68
	S18_4027	22	122.08
	S18_4522	23	73.73
	S24_2011	41	119.2
	S50_1514	21	55.65
	S700_1938	38	75.35
	S700_3962	45	89.38
	S72_3212	50	52.42
10150	S10_1949	45	182.16
	S10_4962	20	121.15
	S12_1666	30	135.3
	S18_1097	34	95.67
	S18_2949	47	93.21
	S18_2957	30	56.21
	S18_3136	26	97.39

Creating Themes

Using the power of Style Sheets and Libraries, we have the ability to apply general formatting to an entire Report Design using Themes. Themes provide a simple mechanism to apply a wide range of Styles to an entire Report Design, without the need to manually apply them.

In the following example, we will move the Styles we have created into our Library, and apply them to our report using a Theme.

1. Following the instructions from the last chapter, copy and paste all of the Styles in this report into the **ClassicCarsLibrary.rptlibrary** file. All of the Styles will reside under the **defaultTheme** (under the **Themes** section).

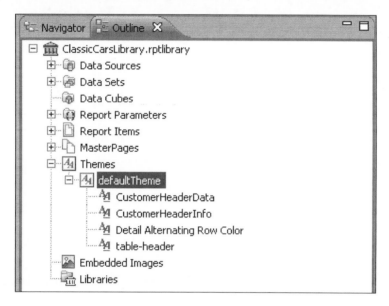

2. **Delete** all of the Styles stored in the **Customer Orders.rptdesign** file. Right-click on **Customer Orders.rptdesign** under the **Outline,** and choose **Refresh Library**.

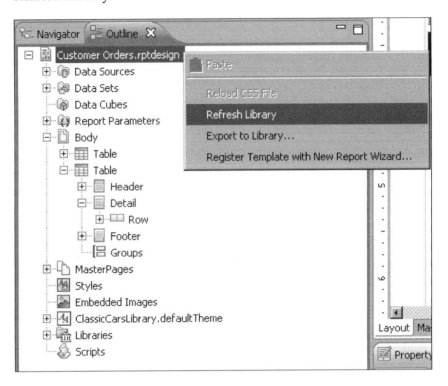

3. In the **Library Explorer**, right-click on **ClassicCarsLibrary.rptlibrary**, and choose **Refresh**.

4. Under the **Property Editor**, change the **Themes** drop-down to **defaultTheme**.

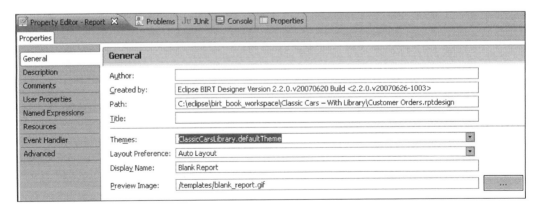

5. When you apply the Theme, you will see that the Detail Table header automatically applies the Style for the Table header.

6. Apply the remaining Custom Styles.

Now, you can create several different Themes by grouping Styles together in Libraries. Now, when developing reports, you can create several different overall looks that can be applied to reports by simply applying Themes using Libraries.

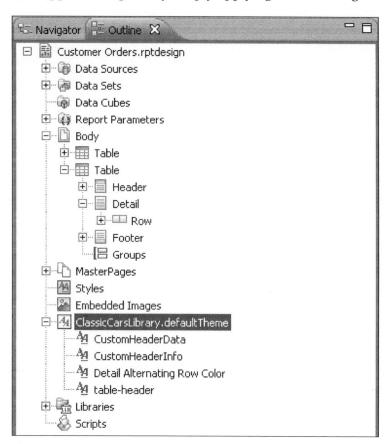

Using External CSS Style Sheets

A new feature in BIRT 2.2 is the ability to use external Style Sheets and simply link to them. This works out very well when report documents are embedded into existing Web Portals, by using the portal Style Sheets to keep a consistent look and feel. This creates a sense of uniformity in the overall site.

Let's say for instance, your graphics designer gives you a CSS file, and asks you to design your reports around it. There are two ways you can use CSS files in BIRT:

- Importing CSS files
- Using CSS as a resource

In the following examples, we are going to illustrate both scenarios. The following is the CSS Style Sheet we are going to use:

```
.page {
    background-color: #FFFFFF;
    font-family: Verdana, Arial, Helvetica, sans-serif;
    font-size: 12px;
    line-height: 24px;
    color: #336699;
}
.table-group-footer-1 {
    font-family: Verdana, Arial, Helvetica, sans-serif;
    font-size: 12px;
    line-height: 24px;
    color: #333333;
    background-color: #FFFFCC;
}
.title {
    font-family: Verdana, Arial, Helvetica, sans-serif;
    font-size: 24px;
    line-height: 40px;
    background-color: #99CC00;
    color: #003333;
    font-weight: bolder;
}
.table-header {
    font-family: Verdana, Arial, Helvetica, sans-serif;
    font-size: 20px;
    background-color: #669900;
 color: #FFFF33;
}
.table-footer {
  font-family: Arial, Helvetica, sans-serif;
    font-size: 14px;
    font-weight: bold;
    line-height: 22px;
    color: #333333;
    background-color: #CCFF99;
}
```

Importing CSS Files

I will import this Style for use in a new BIRT report called Top Employees that will display the Employees based on associated customer sales. In the following example, I will show how to import an external CSS file into a BIRT Report Project.

1. Create a new report called **Top Employees** under the **Classic Cars – With Library** project.

2. Import the **dsClassicCars** Data Source from the **ClassicCarsLibrary. rptlibrary**.

3. Create a new Data Set called **topEmployees** using the following query:

```
select
EMPLOYEES.EMPLOYEENUMBER,
EMPLOYEES.LASTNAME,
EMPLOYEES.FIRSTNAME,
ORDERDETAILS.PRICEEACH
from
EMPLOYEES,
CUSTOMERS,
ORDERS,
ORDERDETAILS
where
CUSTOMERS.CUSTOMERNUMBER = ORDERS.CUSTOMERNUMBER
and CUSTOMERS.SALESREPEMPLOYEENUMBER = EMPLOYEES.EMPLOYEENUMBER
and ORDERDETAILS.ORDERNUMBER = ORDERS.ORDERNUMBER
and ORDERS.ORDERDATE between ? and ?
```

4. Create two date parameters—**startDate** and **endDate**—and link them to the two Data Set Parameters in **topEmployees**.

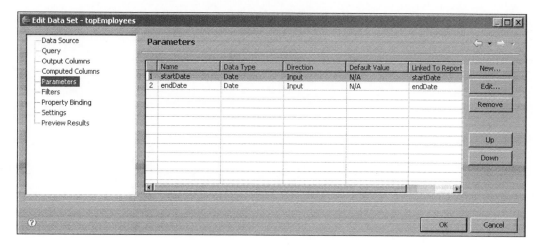

5. Insert the **topEmployees** Data Set into the Report Design by right-clicking on it and choosing **Insert in Layout** under the **Data Explorer**.

6. Create a Grouping on **EmployeeNumber** in the Table, and call it **employeeNumberGrouping**. The following screenshot is the Table after the Grouping has been created.

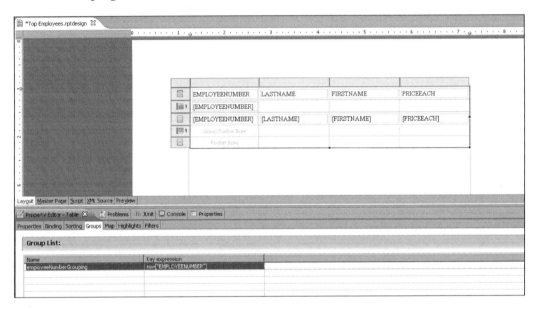

7. In the **Table Properties**, click on the **Binding** tab, and then click on the **Add Aggregation...** button.

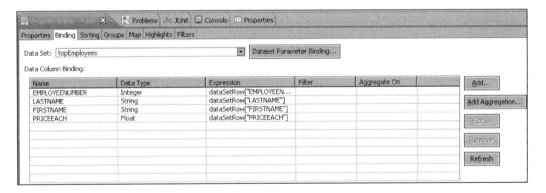

8. Create an aggregation on the **PRICEEACH** field and set it on the **employeeNumberGrouping**. We are going to sum the **PRICEEACH** field into a new field called **totalEmployeeSales**.

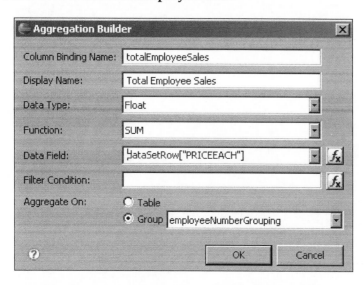

9. Hit **OK**. Create a second aggregation called **totalSales**. This is just like the **totalEmployeeSales**, except that it is on the **Table** instead of on the **employeeNumberGrouping**.

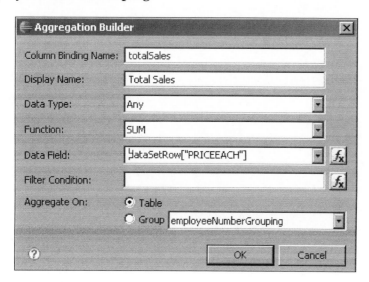

10. In the **Outline, Delete** the **Row** under **Groups | Header**.

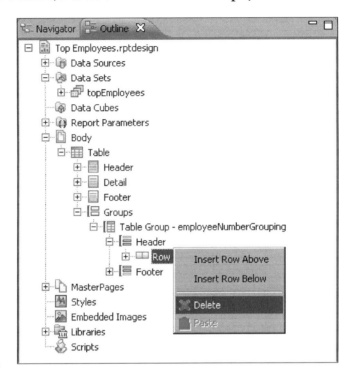

11. "Drag and drop" all of the data elements from the **Table | Detail | Row | Cells** into the **Table | Group | Footers | Cells**.

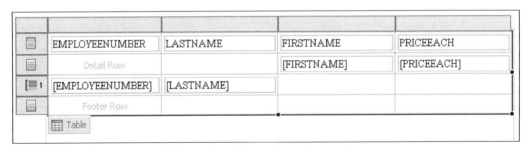

12. Delete the **Detail Row** from the **Table**. Double-click on the **PRICEEACH** field to enter the edit Dialog. Enter the function Dialog and change the **Expression** to **Available Column Binding | Table | totalEmployeeSales**.

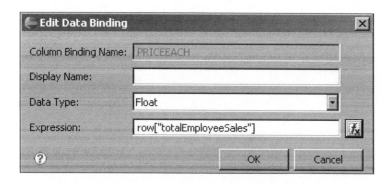

13. Insert a new data element into the cell in the **Table Footer Row** (last column), and set the **Expression** to **row["totalSales"]**. This will display the total overall sales as specified in the aggregation in the report.

14. Click on the **Table Header Row**, and change the text alignment to **Left**.

15. Click on the **Header Label** for PRICEEACH and change it to **Employee Sales**.

16. Click on the last column and change the text alignment to **Right**. As this is a currency field, we want this to be right justified, which is normal for accounting-related reporting.

17. In the data elements for **totalEmployeeSales** and **totalSales**, change the **Format Number | Format As** value to **Currency**.

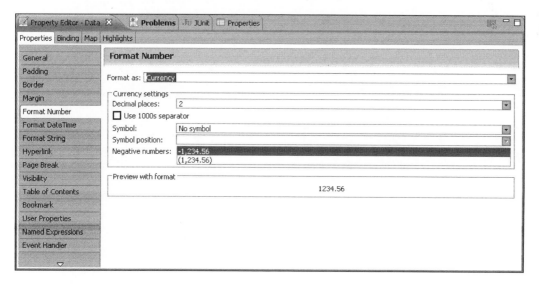

18. Select the **Master Page** tab in the Report Designer. Drag a **Label** over to the **Header**, and enter **Top Employees**.

Top Employees			
EMPLOYEENUMBER	**LASTNAME**	**FIRSTNAME**	**EMPLOYEE SALES**
1165	Jennings	Leslie	9137.12
1166	Thompson	Leslie	1171.38
1188	Firrelli	Julie	1013.86
1216	Patterson	Steve	2069.89
1286	Tseng	Foon Yue	946.47
1323	Vanauf	George	1649.76
1337	Bondur	Loui	2119.26
1370	Hernandez	Gerard	11149.47
1401	Castillo	Pamela	3974.08
1501	Bott	Larry	4099.64
1504	Jones	Barry	747.53
1611	Fixter	Andy	3765.23
1612	Marsh	Peter	3167.06
			45010.75

Oct 11, 2007 9:54 PM

19. Now, we need to import the Style Sheet. I have it saved as **topEmployees.css**. From the **Outline**, right-click on **Styles** and choose **Import CSS Style....**

20. From the Dialog, navigate to where the CSS file is saved and select it. For the list of Styles to be imported, click on **Select All**.

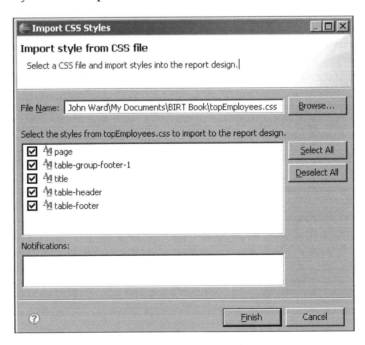

21. Hit **OK**. You will see that all of the predefined Styles get applied automatically.

22. TITLE—which is one of the Styles defined in the CSS—is a Custom Style and will not automatically be applied. We need to apply it manually to the Label in the Master Page. Select the **Label** under **Master Page**, and in the **Property Editor**, under **styles**, select **title**.

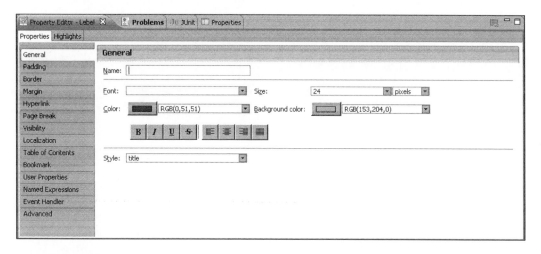

23. **Preview** the Report.

Top Employees			
EMPLOYEE NUM	**LASTNAME**	**FIRSTNAME**	**EMPLOYEE SALES**
1165	Jennings	Leslie	9137.12
1166	Thompson	Leslie	1171.38
1188	Firrelli	Julie	1013.86
1216	Patterson	Steve	2069.89
1286	Tseng	Foon Yue	946.47
1323	Vanauf	George	1649.76
1337	Bondur	Loui	2119.26
1370	Hernandez	Gerard	11149.47
1401	Castillo	Pamela	3974.08
1501	Bott	Larry	4099.64
1504	Jones	Barry	747.53
1611	Fixter	Andy	3765.23
1612	Marsh	Peter	3167.06
			45010.75
Oct 11, 2007 10:08 PM			

It is important to note: when creating External Style Sheets, as long as the Style name corresponds to the BIRT element name and preceeds it with a dot, it will be applied automatically. In the previous example, everything except TITLE was applied automatically because there is no BIRT element called TITLE. A list of BIRT predefined Style elements is available in the BIRT Style Editor, under the Pre-Defined drop-down list. It is a matter of preference whether you choose to use the predefined Styles. If you choose to use predefined Styles, the Style will apply to all elements in a report unless explicitly overridden.

Using CSS as a Resource

Another option is to import the CSS Style as a Report Project resource, and use the file in your `resource` folder.

1. Delete the Styles in the **Top Employees** report.

2. From either the **File** menu or the **Navigator**, right-click and select **Import...**. In the **Import** Dialog, select **General | File System**.

3. Navigate to the directory containing the CSS file. Then, from the file selection list, select the CSS file.

4. Make sure the **Into folder** option contains your project name.

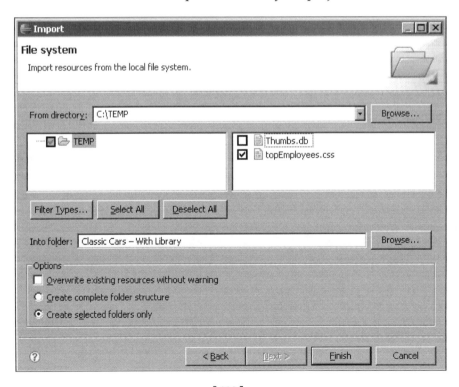

5. The CSS file is now part of your project resources. From the **Outline**, right-click on **Styles**, and choose **Use CSS File....** From the **Use CSS** Dialog, click on the **Browse...** button for **File Name**.

6. You will see two Tree View nodes, with the **Resource Folder** able to be expanded. Expand the **Resource Folder** and select the **topEmployees.css** file.

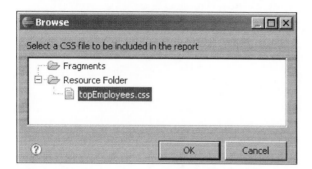

7. A list of Styles will show up under the **Available styles**. Just click **OK** as there is no option to select individual styles.

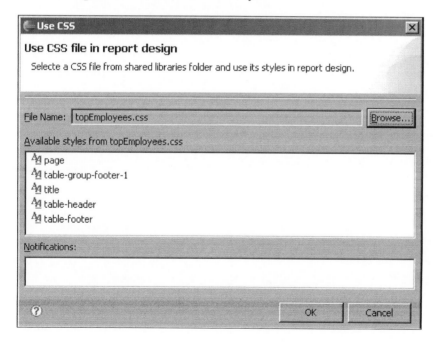

8. The styles that are pre-defined BIRT element names get automatically applied. Go ahead and apply the Custom Style of title to the Master Page Header section.

You might notice that the **Styles** section of the **Outline** is a little different. Rather than displaying the Styles themselves—when using a resource—it shows the CSS file name, and when you right-click on the file name, you have the option to **Reload**. This allows users to make changes to the external CSS file and reload them into the BIRT report without having to re-import.

Templates

Templates are pre-designed report layouts. We have been using Templates throughout the entire book, when we create the Blank report. We will expand out and take a look at using Templates to set up for the detail reports we will build in the next chapter.

Building a Report from a Template

Templates, for the most part, take the nasty work out of having to re-create the same layout over and over again. For instance, in this book, we have constantly dragged over a single Data Set into the Report Designer to create a single listing report. With Templates, we could either use the existing, canned Listing Report Template or build our own and save the effort for more complex tasks. It's as simple as creating a new report, using a Template, and following the Cheat Sheets.

In this example, we are going to use a Grouped Listing Report Template to create a simple Employee Sales Detail Report that we will use as a target for a Drill-Down report, which will be explained in the next chapter.

1. Create a new report called **Employee Sales Details Report.rptdesign**. In the **New Report** Template screen, choose **Grouped Listing Report**.

2. When the Report Design opens, the **Cheat Sheet** is open on the right-hand side. It lays out a series of steps for creating a basic report. As we already have the Data Source created in our Library, go ahead and add the Data Source from the Library, and click on the **Click to skip** option for the Data Source hint.

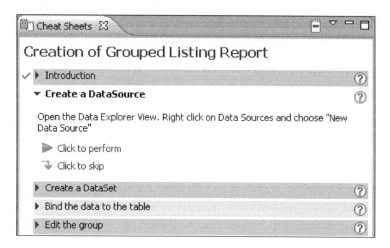

3. For the Data Set, click on the **Click to Perform** option. Call the Data Set **Get Employee Sales**, and use the following query:

```
select
    EMPLOYEES.EMPLOYEENUMBER,
    EMPLOYEES.LASTNAME || ', ' || EMPLOYEES.FIRSTNAME name,
    ORDERDETAILS.PRICEEACH sales,
    ORDERS.ORDERDATE
from
    EMPLOYEES,
    CUSTOMERS,
    ORDERS,
    ORDERDETAILS
where
    ORDERS.ORDERNUMBER = ORDERDETAILS.ORDERNUMBER
    and EMPLOYEES.EMPLOYEENUMBER = CUSTOMERS.SALESREPEMPLOYEENUMBER
    and ORDERS.CUSTOMERNUMBER = CUSTOMERS.CUSTOMERNUMBER
    and ORDERS.ORDERDATE between ? and ?
```

4. Create two Report Parameters called **startDate** and **endDate**, and bind them to the Data Set Parameters. For **startDate**, use the **Default value** of **2005-01-01**, and for **endDate**, use the **Default value** of **2005-04-01**.

5. When back at the **Cheat Sheet**, click on **Click to Complete** for the Data Set.

6. For the **Edit Date Binding Cheat Sheet**, drag the fields over as in the following figure. Make the **Group Header Row** have a **Silver Background**, and bold the text.

Report Header		
Header Row		
[EMPLOYEENUMBER]	[NAME]	
Detail Row	[ORDERDATE]	[SALES]
Group Footer Row		
Footer Row		

7. Group by **EmployeeNumber**. Select the column with the **Name/[OrderDate]** fields, and choose **Suppress duplicates**. Select the **Group Header Row**, and under the **Property Editor**, choose the **Bookmark** tab. Use the following expression:

```
row["EMPLOYEENUMBER"]
```

Now we have built a report from a Template. Using other Templates is very similar, where a Cheat Sheet can be used.

Creating a Template

Creating Templates can be done in two different ways. One is to create a Template from the **New** option under the **File** menu; the other is to convert an existing report into a Template.

1. Open any existing report file.

2. Go to **File | Register Template with New Report Wizard...**.

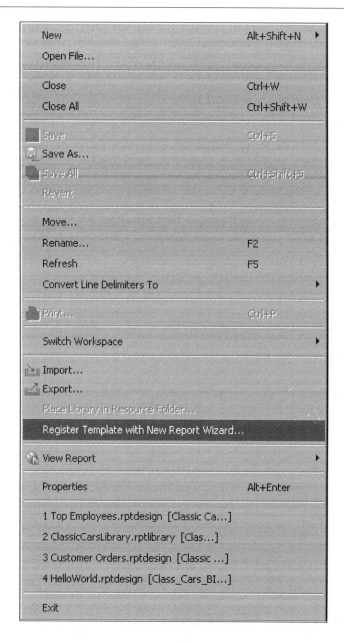

3. Follow the Wizard to create a new Template.

   Not much to it! Now, let's take a look at creating a new Template from scratch.

4. Go to **File | New | Template**. Call the Template **myNewTemplate. rpttemplate**.

5. Under **Display Name**, use **My First Template**. Under **Description**, type **Testing a Template**.

6. If you have an image, associate one with your Template.

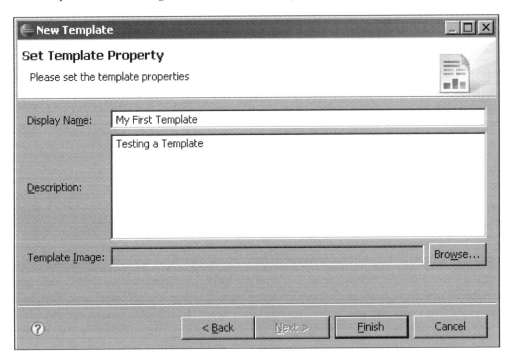

Now we have a new Template to create reports from. Create any sort of layout you would like, and save. When you want to use this Template, simply open it and save it as a Report Design. If you'd like this to show up in the New Report Wizard, do the same thing as done previously with an existing report, and go to **File | Register Template with New Report Wizard...**.

So, what about the Cheat Sheets we saw in the canned Templates? Well, Cheat Sheets are simply XML files that explain the steps that are installed as Eclipse Plug-ins. Describing how to do so is beyond the scope of this book; however, it is possible to create new Cheat Sheets if you are familiar with the process. So, let's say we wanted to associate the My First Report Template Cheat Sheet with the Template we just created. Under the Report Properties, we would put in the plug-in class under the **Cheat sheet** Property. The **Dev2Dev** article **Building Cheat Sheets in Eclipse** provides a good tutorial on building Cheat Sheets at `http://dev2dev.bea.com/ pub/a/2006/08/eclipse-cheat-sheets.html`.

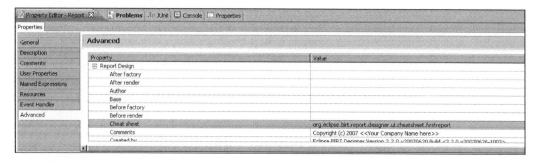

Summary

In this chapter, we have seen how to create Styles and Themes that can be used to create a consistent appearance for your Reporting Projects. This becomes important later on when you have large Report Projects with a large number of reports, and you do not want to spend a whole lot of development time on formatting.

We have also seen how to work with external CSS files in Report Projects. This is useful if your Reporting Project will be part of a larger Web Portal and you want to maintain a uniform look and feel with the overall site.

This chapter showed us a slightly different way to work with and create Report Designs. Report Designs can be promoted to Templates to reduce the amount of redundant work in large Reporting Projects. In the next chapter, we are going to look at Charts and Drill-Downs. We will use the Employee Sales report that we built in this chapter as a detail for a summary Chart report.

9
Charts, Hyperlinks, and Drill-Downs

It has been said that a picture is worth a thousand words. In the world of reporting, this is especially true, where we call these pictures Charts. Charts can present a large amount of data with relative ease in comparison to large amounts of data output. Charts are useful when used with raw data to really drive home points, such as percentages, or used with other Charts to build dashboards.

BIRT has an exceptional Charting Engine. BIRT can create a number of different Chart types, including the tried-and-true Pie Chart, Bar Chart, and Line Charts. In addition, there are several other Chart types that were extras to BIRT's commercial counterpart, such as the Meter Chart and Gantt Chart.

In this chapter, we are going to look at building a few different Charts centered around employee sales performance. First, we will build a Pie Chart that will illustrate the top employees based on sales. Then, we will create a Gauge Chart that will show how close an employee is with respect to meeting a quota. Finally, we will create a Bar Chart that will show sales performance for employees during a particular time period.

Pie Chart

In the following exercise, we are going to look at how to build a Pie Chart. A Pie Chart is a very common report type used in business to display percentages.

1. Create a new report called **Employee_Sales_Percentage.rptdesign** for the **Classic Cars - With Library** project.

2. From the **ClassicCarsLibrary.rptlibrary** under **Library Explorer**, right-click on **dsClassicCars** Data Source, and select **Add to Report**.

3. Create a new Data Set called **totalSales** using the following query:

```
select
    CLASSICMODELS.EMPLOYEES.EMPLOYEENUMBER,
    CLASSICMODELS.EMPLOYEES.LASTNAME || ', ' ||
    CLASSICMODELS.EMPLOYEES.FIRSTNAME name,
    sum(CLASSICMODELS.ORDERDETAILS.PRICEEACH) sales
from
    CLASSICMODELS.EMPLOYEES,
    CLASSICMODELS.ORDERS,
    CLASSICMODELS.ORDERDETAILS,
    CLASSICMODELS.CUSTOMERS
where
    CLASSICMODELS.CUSTOMERS.SALESREPEMPLOYEENUMBER =
        CLASSICMODELS.EMPLOYEES.EMPLOYEENUMBER
    and CLASSICMODELS.ORDERS.CUSTOMERNUMBER =
        CLASSICMODELS.CUSTOMERS.CUSTOMERNUMBER
    and CLASSICMODELS.ORDERDETAILS.ORDERNUMBER =
        CLASSICMODELS.ORDERS.ORDERNUMBER
    and CLASSICMODELS.ORDERS.ORDERDATE between ? and ?
group by
    CLASSICMODELS.EMPLOYEES.EMPLOYEENUMBER,
    CLASSICMODELS.EMPLOYEES.LASTNAME,
    CLASSICMODELS.EMPLOYEES.FIRSTNAME
```

4. Create two Report Parameters called **startDate** and **endDate** as **Date** types, and link them to the two Report Parameters. Use **2005-01-01** as the **startDate Default value**, and **2005-05-01** as the **endDate Default value**.

5. Drag a **Chart** component from the **Palette** to the Report Designer.

6. In the Chart Dialog, select **Pie** Chart. Change the **Output Format** from **SVG** to **PNG**. Typically, I use either PNG or JPEG because SVG is not a universally supported format. However, SVG does have a distinct advantage over both PNG and JPEG in that it is of significantly smaller size due to its vector nature.

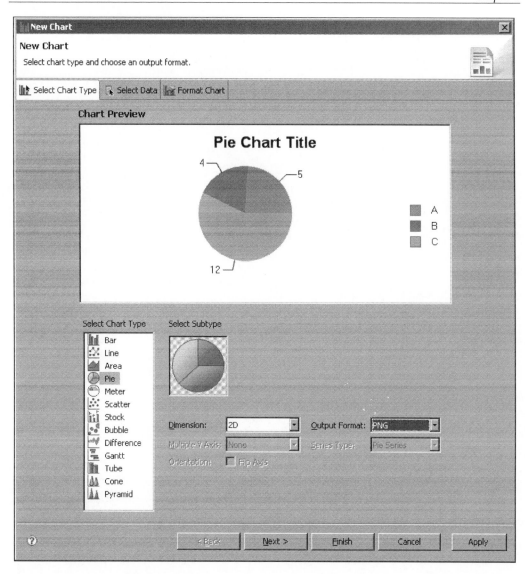

7. Open the **Select Data** tab. Under the **Select Data** section, select **Use Data Set**, and choose the **totalSales** Data Set.

8. You can drag the column headers from the Data Set to the slice definitions. Drag the **Sales** column to the **Slice Size Definition**, and the **Name** column to the **Category Definition**.

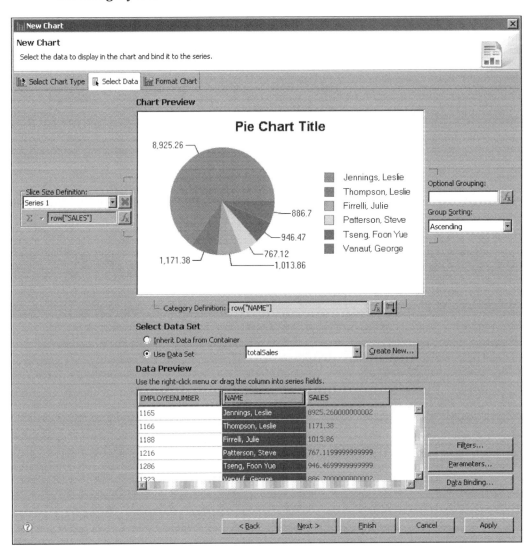

9. Select the **Format Chart** tab. Under the **Chart Area | Title** section, enter **Employee Sales Percentages** as the **Chart Title**.

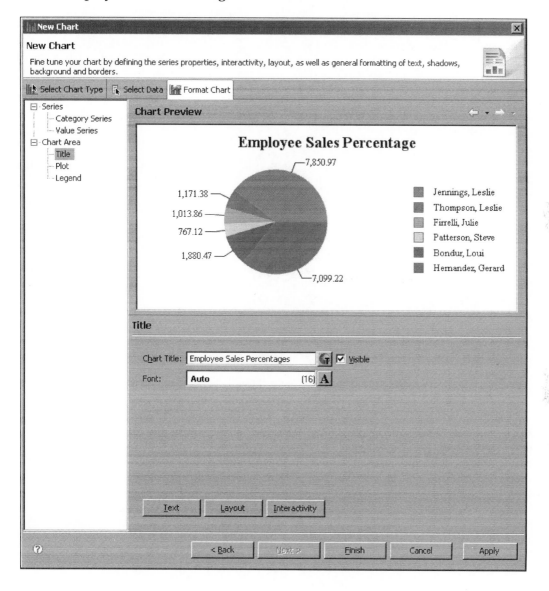

10. Click on **Finish**. Resize the Chart to take up the report page.

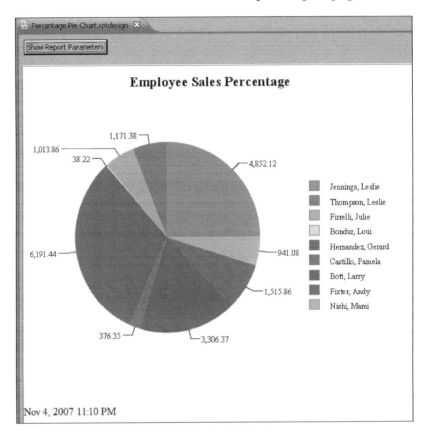

Modifying Chart Properties

So, we have built a fairly simple report so far. This report is a Pie Chart with a Legend that shows us the employees' color code, with an excerpt that shows us the value of that slice. However, it would be a little easier visually to view if the slices were exploded, and if the slices had an Outline. Let's take a look at how to modify some of the Chart properties to do this:

1. Double-click on the **Chart** in the Report Design. This will re-open the Chart Dialog. Open the **Format Chart** tab.

2. Open the **Series | Value Series** section. Under the **Slice** section, change the **By Distance** value to **6**.

3. For **Slice Outline**, choose the color Black from the color palette.

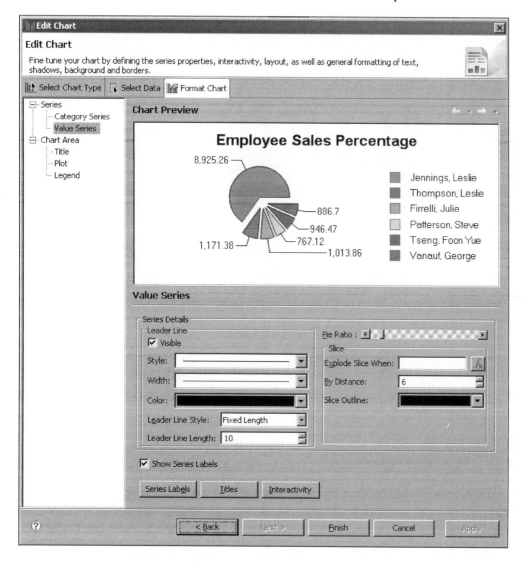

The following screenshot shows the result, which is using numbers for display:

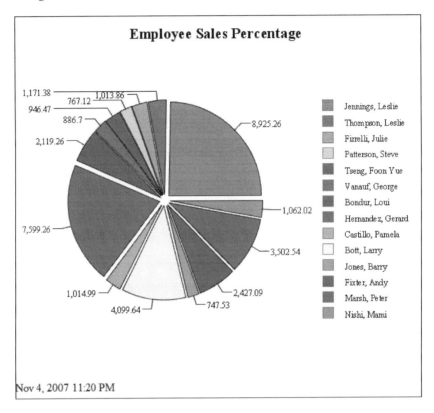

Using Percentages

Let's say we want to change the Chart to display percentages instead of numbers, and add a little interactivity to the Chart to display the sales number when clicked on.

1. Double-click on the **Chart**. Select the **Value Series** section, and click on the **Labels** button.

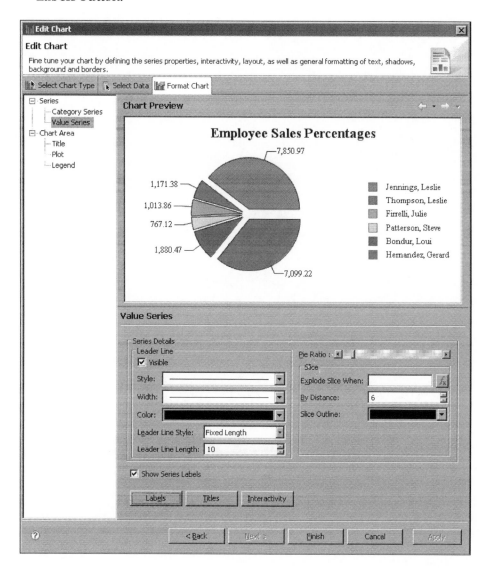

2. Under **Values**, **Remove** the **Value Data** option, and **Add Percentile Value Data**.

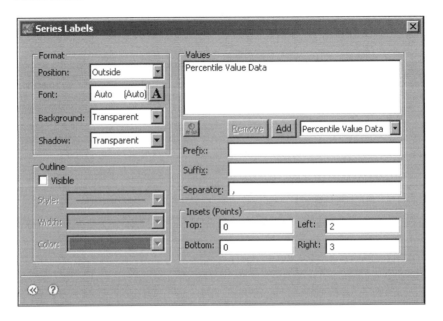

3. Close the **Series Labels** Dialog. In the **Edit Chart** Dialog, click on the **Interactivity** button. Choose **Mouse Click** as the **Event** and **Hyperlink** as the **Action**.

4. Use the following **Hyperlink**, and set the **Target** to **Self**:

```
"javascript:alert('" + row["SALES"] + "');"
```

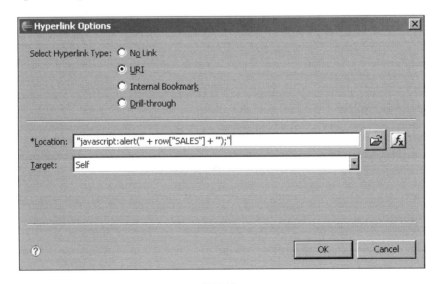

When we go back to preview the report, we can click on any of the slices, and have our pop-up alert telling us the actual values behind the percentages. We can also see that our values have changed to percentages, and our pie chart slices have been exploded.

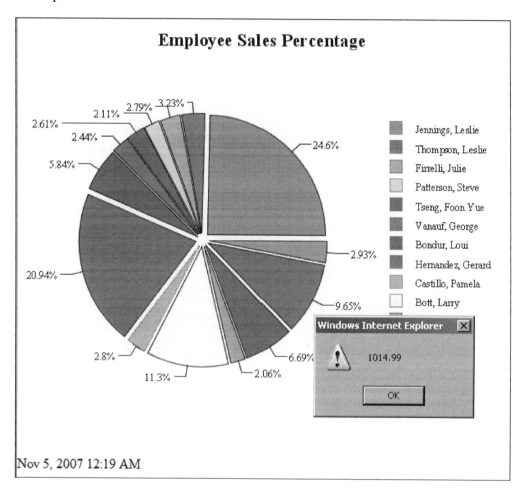

Gauge Chart

With the next Chart—the Gauge Chart—we will expand on the interactivity a bit, and demonstrate how Drill-Downs work. We want the user to be able to click on a Chart, and have it pull up an external report with the details for a particular user. This is called a Drill-Down.

The following Chart will demonstrate an employee's sales versus a target amount per month—let's say 3000, on a 5000 dollar scale. This will be broken up and grouped monthly in the query statement. When the user clicks on the chart, it will bring them to the detail report that we created in the last chapter for Employee sales.

1. Create a new report called **Employee_Sales_Gauge.rptdesign** for the **Classic Cars - With Library** project.

2. From the **ClassicCarsLibrary.rptlibrary**, drag the Data Source **dsClassicCars** over to the Report Design.

3. Create a new Data Set called **employeeSales** using the following query:

```
select
CLASSICMODELS.EMPLOYEES.EMPLOYEENUMBER,
CLASSICMODELS.EMPLOYEES.LASTNAME || ', ' ||
CLASSICMODELS.EMPLOYEES.FIRSTNAME name,
sum(CLASSICMODELS.ORDERDETAILS.PRICEEACH) sales,
CLASSICMODELS.ORDERS.ORDERDATE
from
CLASSICMODELS.EMPLOYEES,
CLASSICMODELS.CUSTOMERS,
CLASSICMODELS.ORDERS,
CLASSICMODELS.ORDERDETAILS
where
CLASSICMODELS.ORDERS.ORDERNUMBER =
CLASSICMODELS.ORDERDETAILS.ORDERNUMBER
and CLASSICMODELS.EMPLOYEES.EMPLOYEENUMBER =
CLASSICMODELS.CUSTOMERS.SALESREPEMPLOYEENUMBER
and CLASSICMODELS.ORDERS.CUSTOMERNUMBER =
CLASSICMODELS.CUSTOMERS.CUSTOMERNUMBER
and CLASSICMODELS.ORDERS.ORDERDATE between ? and ?
group by
CLASSICMODELS.ORDERS.ORDERDATE,
CLASSICMODELS.EMPLOYEES.EMPLOYEENUMBER,
CLASSICMODELS.EMPLOYEES.LASTNAME,
CLASSICMODELS.EMPLOYEES.FIRSTNAME
```

4. Link the two Data Set Parameters to two Report Parameters, called **startDate** and **endDate** respectively.

5. We need to create a new Computed Column to have the **OrderDate** column with just the year and month. Click on the **Computed Columns**. Create a new Computed Column called **orderDateShort**, and use the following **Expression**:

```
var combinedDate = row["ORDERDATE"].getFullYear() + "-";
if ((row["ORDERDATE"].getMonth() + 1) < 10)
{
combinedDate += "0" + (row["ORDERDATE"].getMonth() + 1);
}
else
{
combinedDate += (row["ORDERDATE"].getMonth() + 1);
}
combinedDate;
```

This expression will take the OrderDate column, and create a string containing the 4-digit year, and append the month (leaving off the day). We will discuss expressions more in depth in the next chapter.

6. Create a Table element in the report, and bind it to the **employeeSales** Data Set. Do this either by dragging over from the **Data Explorer**, or using the **Palette**. Delete the **OrderDate** column.

7. Create a Group in the Table called **GroupByEmployee**, and set it to group on the **EmployeeNumber**. Create another group below **GroupByEmployee**, and call it **groupByDate**. Set it to group on the **orderDateShort** field.

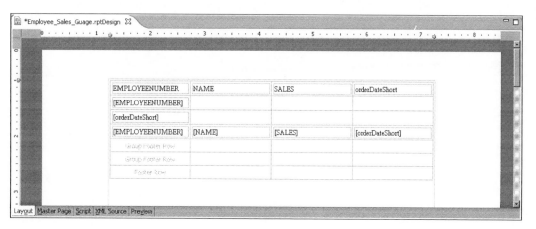

8. Merge all of the cells in the **orderDateShort Detail Row** into one large cell.

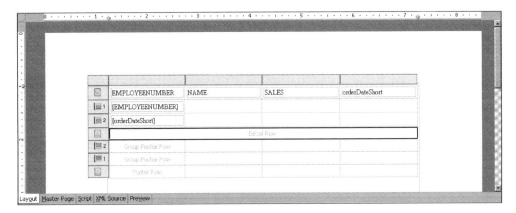

9. In the new large cell, create a **Chart** element.

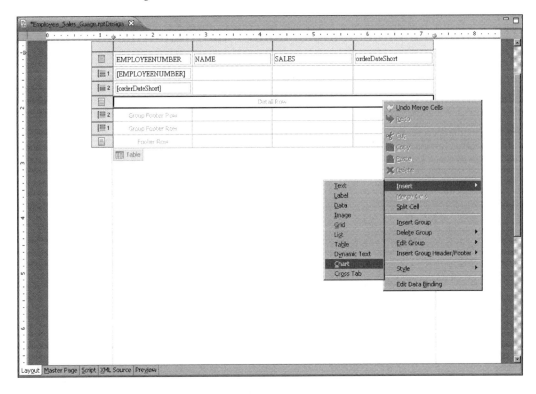

10. Select **Meter** as the type, and select the **Super imposed Meter** as the Chart subtype. Change the **Output Format** to **PNG**.

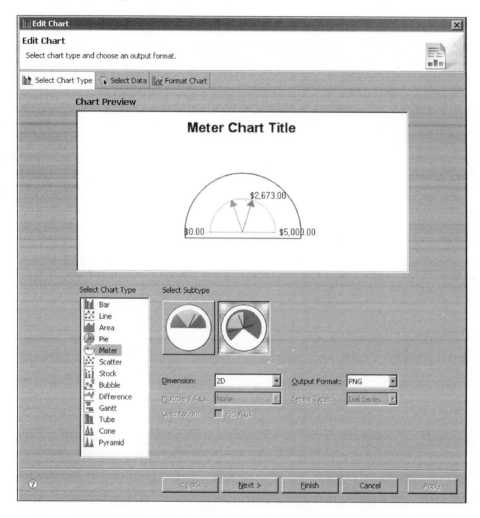

11. In the **Select Data** tab, create another **Dial** by selecting **<New Series...>** from the **Meter Value Definition** drop-down list.

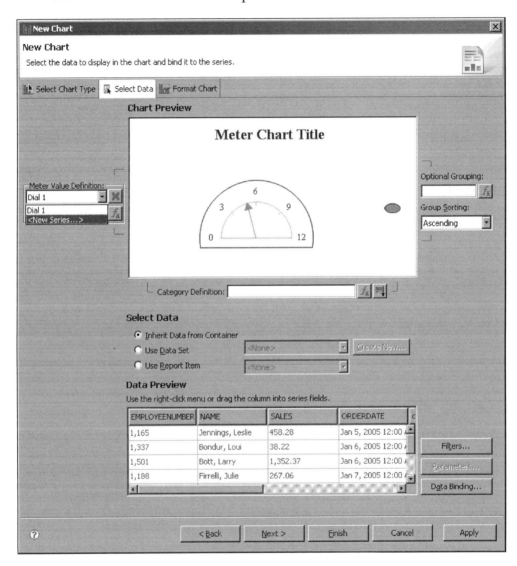

12. For the expression for Dial 1, select **row["SALES"]** by either dragging the column over from the **Data Preview** pane, or by using the **Expression Builder**. The value for **Dial 2** should be set to **3000**.

13. For **Category Definition**, use **row["NAME"]** by either dragging the column over from the **Data Preview** section, or using the **Expression Builder**.

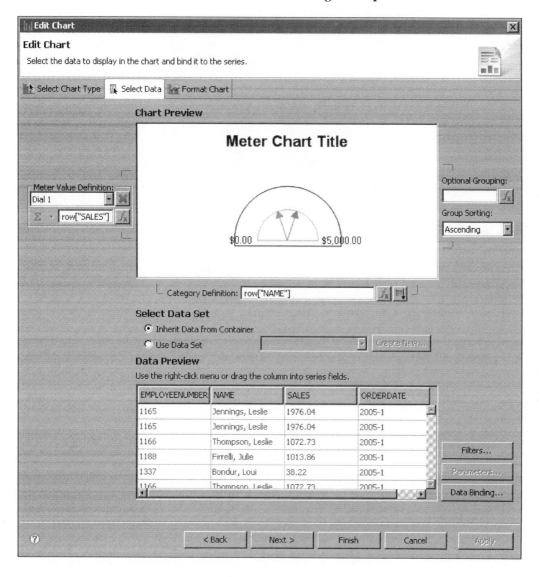

14. Under the **Format Chart**, select the **Series | Value Series**. Click on the **Scale** button. For the **Min**, put in **0**. For the **Max** put in **5000**. We have now set up the scale.

15. Under **Chart Area | Legend**, uncheck the **Visible** checkbox.

16. Select **Chart Area**, and click on the **Interactivity** button. For **Event**, select **Mouse Click**; for **Action**, select **Hyperlink**.

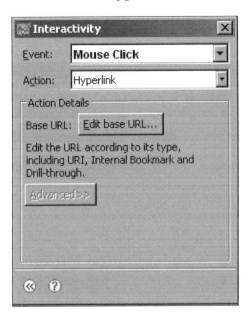

17. Click on the **Edit base URL...** button. For the **Hyperlink Type**, select **Drill- through**. For the Report Design, navigate and select the **Employee_Sales_Details_Report.rptdesign**.

18. Select the **startDate** and **endDate** parameters under the **parameters** drop-down, which selects the parameters in the target report. For the **Values**, enter **params["startDate"]** and **params["endDate"]**, or whatever names you used for the current reports for startDate and endDate parameters.

19. Under **Step 2**, select **Target Bookmark**. Under the drop-down, select **row["EmployeeNumber"]**. For **Step 4**, select **New Window**.

20. We can skip **Step 5** as we are outputting to the default format, HTML. We could have the target report open in any format that we have an emitter registered for. An emitter is a plug-in to BIRT that handles the rendering to an output format.

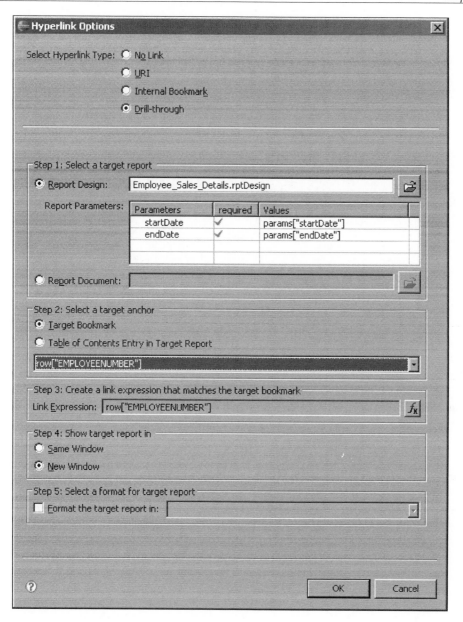

21. Click on **OK** to exit the Dialog, and **Save** the report. View the report by going to **File | View Report | View Report in Web Viewer**. When you click on any of the Charts, a detail report will open and automatically jump to the employees section, as specified in the Bookmark in the target report.

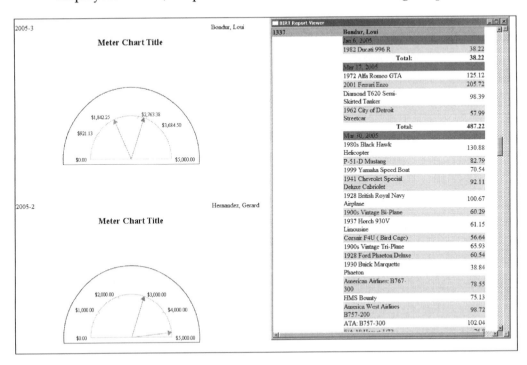

Of course, this example can be heavily modified to simplify things. The Charts could be consolidated into a single Chart with more needles for each month instead of separate Charts for each month. It can be done by moving the Chart into the EmployeeNumber Group's header or footer row, and adding a group by date in the Chart Editor Dialog under the Select Data tab. It is also possible to set the needles to have interactivity, and to filter down to the specific user and date range by modifying the bookmarks in the target report; but I will leave that up to the reader to discover.

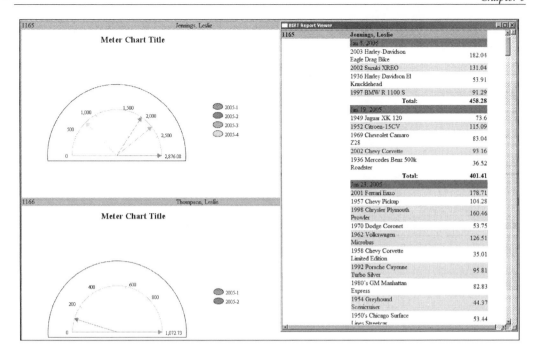

Bar Chart

The previous example demonstrates some of the power that Charting can have with reports, by adding both the graphical representation of data and the interactivity for users to see the details of that data in a separate report. It also demonstrates how to pass data through to the target report by using an expression. In the following report, the Hyperlink will take us to an internal bookmark, which means it will jump us to a location inside of the same report containing the details for our report. We will also look at aggregating values inside of the Chart so that we can just provide a query that gives the details and let BIRT handle the tricky stuff for us, and write a query that just retrieves data.

1. Create a new report called **EmployeeSalesPerformanceReport.rptdesign**. Use the **dsClassicCars** Data Source in the Library.

2. Create a new Data Set called **employeeSales**, and use the following query:

```
select
CLASSICMODELS.EMPLOYEES.EMPLOYEENUMBER,
CLASSICMODELS.EMPLOYEES.LASTNAME || ', ' ||
  CLASSICMODELS.EMPLOYEES.FIRSTNAME name,
CLASSICMODELS.ORDERDETAILS.PRICEEACH,
CLASSICMODELS.ORDERS.ORDERDATE,
CLASSICMODELS.PRODUCTS.PRODUCTNAME
from
```

```
CLASSICMODELS.EMPLOYEES,
CLASSICMODELS.CUSTOMERS,
CLASSICMODELS.ORDERS,
CLASSICMODELS.ORDERDETAILS,
CLASSICMODELS.PRODUCTS
where
CLASSICMODELS.ORDERS.ORDERNUMBER =
CLASSICMODELS.ORDERDETAILS.ORDERNUMBER
and CLASSICMODELS.EMPLOYEES.EMPLOYEENUMBER =
CLASSICMODELS.CUSTOMERS.SALESREPEMPLOYEENUMBER
and CLASSICMODELS.ORDERS.CUSTOMERNUMBER =
CLASSICMODELS.CUSTOMERS.CUSTOMERNUMBER
and CLASSICMODELS.PRODUCTS.PRODUCTCODE =
CLASSICMODELS.ORDERDETAILS.PRODUCTCODE
and CLASSICMODELS.ORDERS.ORDERDATE between ? and ?
```

3. Map the Data Set Parameters to Report Parameters **startDate** and **endDate**.

4. Drag a Table element over from the **Palette**, with **3** columns, **1** Detail Row, and map it to the **employeeSales** Data Set.

5. In the **Header Row**, insert a new row.

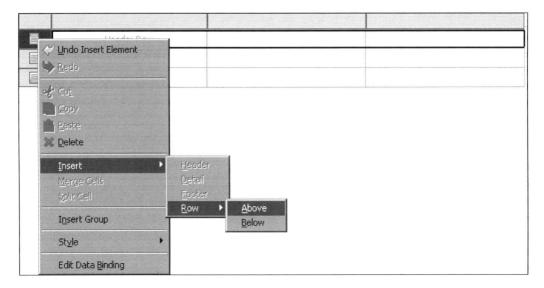

6. We want to create a space in the report header for our Chart. This will serve as a summary of the sales data before displaying the details. In the top most part of the header, merge all the cells into one large cell.

🔳	Header Row		
🔳	Header Row		
🔳	Detail Row		
🔳	Footer Row		

7. Insert a **Chart** element into the large cell. Select **Bar** Chart as the type. Select the **Stacked Bar Chart** as the subtype. Change the **Output Format** to **PNG**.

8. Go to the **Select Data** tab. For the series value, drag in the **PriceEach** column.

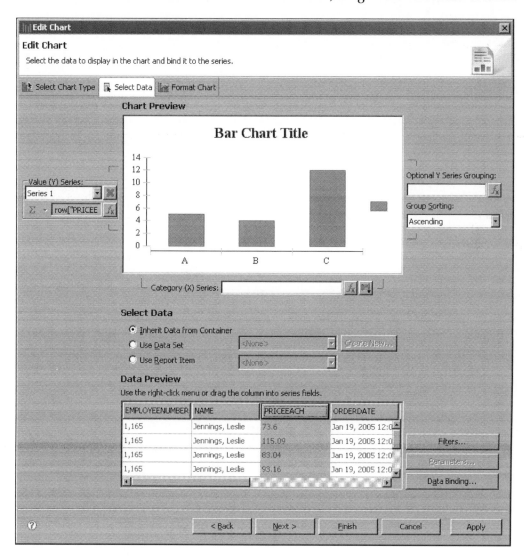

9. For the **Category (X) Series**, use the following expression:

```
importPackage(java.text);
var dateFormater = new SimpleDateFormat("yyyy-MM");
dateFormater.format(row["ORDERDATE"]);
```

The above is a BIRT Expression using JavaScript to take the date field and format it as a YYYY-MM format. This is similar to the formatting we did for the computed column in the last exercise, except we are using Java objects to format the date. We will discuss this more in depth in the next chapter.

10. At this point you may get an error depending on the version of BIRT you are using. If you do not get an error as shown in the following screenshot, skip to step 13.

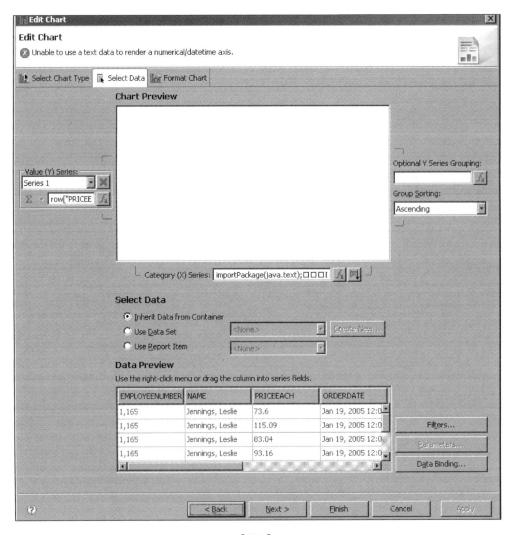

11. To fix the error, go to the **Format Chart** tab. Under **Chart Area**, expand the **Axis** branch and click on the **X-Axis** item.

12. Change the **Type** to **Text**. The error is caused by BIRT changing the axis data type to the data type of the column used by default. In our case, it automatically changed to **DateTime**. Go back to the **Select Data** tab when this is done.

13. For the Optional **(Y) Series** Grouping, drag in the **Name** column.

14. Next to the **Category (X) Series** expression editor button is a button to edit Group and Sorting. Click on that button. In the following screenshot, you can see the **Edit group and sorting** hint next to the button.

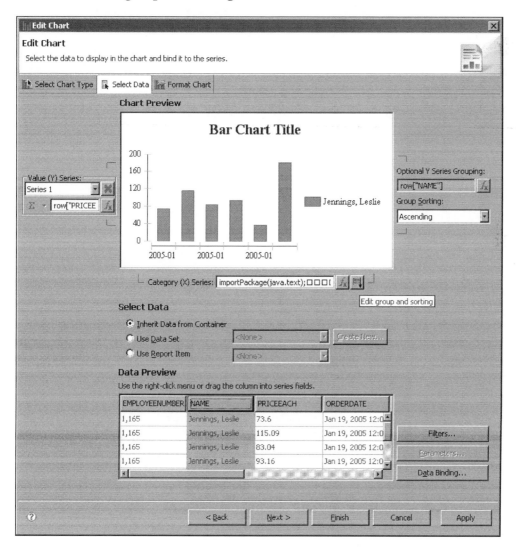

15. For **Data Sorting**, enter **Ascending**. Click on the **Enabled** checkbox under **Grouping**. Set the Interval to 0 and click **OK**. This will set the interval in which items are grouped in the chart. If you do not set this to 0, items in the total aggregation will be skipped and not reflected in the chart.

16. Click **Finish** and **Save** the report.

17. Select the Table, and create a Group on **EmployeeNumber**.

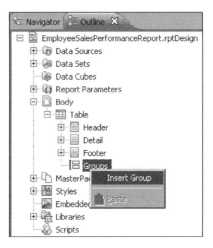

18. Create second Group on **OrderDate** called **SalesDateGroup**. For the **Detail Row**, drag over the **ProductName** into the second column, and **PriceEach** into the third column.

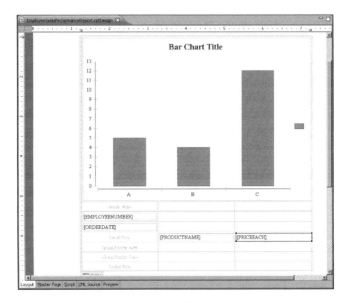

19. From the **Palette**, drag over an **Aggregation** element into the **Group Footer Row** (third column) for the **OrderDate** Grouping.

20. Create the aggregation on the **PriceEach** field for the **salesDateGroup**.

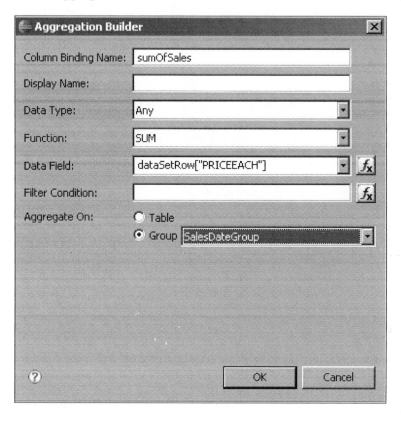

21. Add in any formatting that you feel might spruce up the look of your report. We discussed various formatting options in Chapter 8.

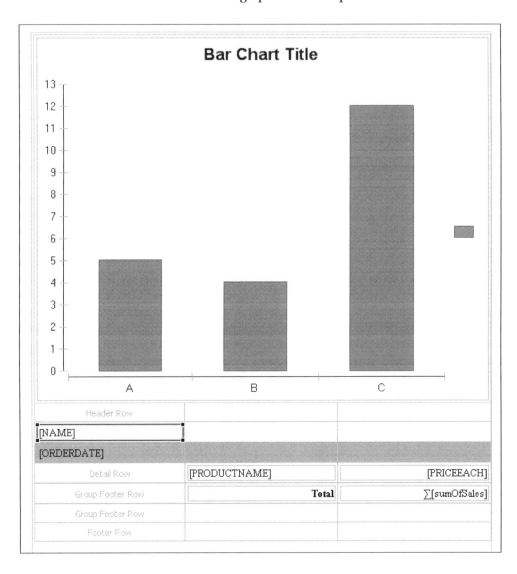

22. Select the **OrderDate** Grouping's **Header Row**. It is the one with the **OrderDate** in silver in the previous figure. Select the **Bookmark** tab under the **Property Editor**. Use the following expression for the bookmark:

```
importPackage(java.text);
var dateFormater = new SimpleDateFormat("yyyy-MM");
row["EMPLOYEENUMBER"] + dateFormater.format(row["ORDERDATE"]);
```

23. Double-click on the Chart to enter the Chart Editor. Select the **Format Chart** tab.

24. Select **Series | Value (Y) Series**, and click on the **Interactivity** button. Select **Mouse Click** as **Event**, and **Hyperlink** as **Action**.

25. Click on the **Edit base URL...** button. In the **Hyperlink** Dialog, select **Internal Bookmark** as the type. Select the following from the drop-down:

```
importPackage(java.text);
var dateFormater = new SimpleDateFormat("yyyy-MM");
row["EMPLOYEENUMBER"] + dateFormater.format(row["ORDERDATE"]);
```

26. Click **OK, Save**, and **Run** the report.

Now, when you click on any of the different colored sections of the Bar Chart, it will bring you to the detail section within your own report with the grouped date section.

Summary

In this chapter, we have seen how to create several different Chart types. We have seen how we can create Interactivity both within a single report and Drill-Down into a separate report using Charts and passing through parameters. We have seen how to aggregate data within a Chart to serve as a summary for the more detailed data. We have opened the Dialog to edit properties of Charts, and seen how a few of the properties affect the look and feel of Charts as well as the behavior.

Knowing how to navigate through the property Dialogs of the Chart Editor is useful as Charts share many similar properties. Now, if you need to adjust the data properties of your Chart, you should know that you can go into the Select Data tab in the Chart Editor to make adjustments. If you need to make adjustments to the visual elements, such as the legend, or if you want to change the font used within a Chart, you should know that you can go into the Format Chart tab.

The concept of Interactivity is similar between Charts and regular text elements as well as Hyperlinks in regular text or data elements, which are accessible through the Hyperlink tab in the Property Editor (use the same Dialog as the Hyperlink Options Dialog that we used in the Chart Editor to add in our jumps to our internal bookmarks and our external drill-through report.)

In this chapter, we had a good introduction to some basic concepts of scripting in the BIRT environment, when we worked with formatting our Date types. In the next chapter, we are going to expand on the concept of scripting.

10
Scripting and Event Handling

We have come a long way since we started this book. We have seen all the different aspects of the BIRT Report Development environment. We have seen how to "drag and drop" reports with the Palette and the Report Designer, how to work with the Outline and the Navigator, and how to set properties for each of the report components.

Now, we are going to look at the aspect of BIRT that make it really powerful, Scripting. Scripting is a complex topic, but once you understand it, you will be able to make BIRT do some really amazing things. It is possible to modify data as it comes through, using Scripting. It is possible to build Data Sources of Java objects with Scripting. And it is even possible to build reports from the ground up using Scripting.

BIRT utilizes the Mozilla Rhino Engine to handle its Scripting capabilities. What this means is that inside of BIRT reports, Report Designers have full access to all primitive types, objects, methods, and Libraries accessible to JavaScript. As an added bonus, Report Developers even have full access to all Java classes that are in the Classpath. In the BIRT Report Designer, this means you have full access to all the Java objects in the Eclipse environment. You can even use custom Java objects in your report to handle certain aspects of processing.

In this chapter, we are going to look at the two different types of Scripting that BIRT has to offer, Expressions and Event Handling. We are going to look at how to access different types of BIRT properties using Expressions. Then we are going to look at how to handle report generation events using BIRT's implementation of the Rhino engine, and also how to handle those same events using Java objects. Although a prior knowledge of Java or JavaScript isn't necessary, it will greatly enhance the understanding of the topics covered in this chapter. But to follow along effectively, the reader should understand:

- Variables
    - Types
    - Creation
    - Assignment

- Operators
    - Arithmetic
    - Logical
    - Comparison

- Functions
- Objects

    - Properties
    - Methods

Types of Scripting

In BIRT, there are two different types of scripting: Expressions and Event Handling. Expressions are simple bits of Script (usually ranging from one to less than ten lines of code) that return a single value for use in a BIRT report. Event Handlers are usually a bit larger than Expressions, and are meant to accomplish some sort of task, such as retrieve a row from a Data Set, manipulate data before output, or handle preparations for rendering.

Expressions

Expressions make up the bulk of the Scripting used in BIRT. In fact, we have used Expressions multiple times already in this book. Expressions are usually single line statements that return a single result. Tasks such as retrieving a value from a row and outputting it in a Data element, retrieving parameter values, and the Highlight Expressions used in the last chapter are all examples of Expressions. Any time we use the Expression Editor in BIRT, we are working with Expressions.

In the last chapter, we used a few Expressions to format Date types to YYYY-MM format. Let's look at these again and understand what they are doing. Following is the first Expression we used to format the dates:

```
var combinedDate = row["ORDERDATE"].getFullYear() + "-";
if ((row["ORDERDATE"].getMonth() + 1) < 10)
{
combinedDate += "0" + (row["ORDERDATE"].getMonth() + 1);
}
else
{
combinedDate += (row["ORDERDATE"].getMonth() + 1);
}
combinedDate;
```

In the line

```
var combinedDate = row["ORDERDATE"].getFullYear() + "-";
```

we are creating a new variable called `combinedDate`. In BIRT Script, you do not need to set the variable type of a variable; BIRT will take care of this for you. `row["ORDERDATE"]` is a means of accessing the value of the column ORDERDATE using array index notation. In this case, it uses the name ORDERDATE to correctly identify which value to use. This is similar to a Map in Java. This returns a Date type. As it is returning a Date type, we have access to all properties and methods that are accessible to a Date type. In this case, we are using the method `getFullYear()` to return the 4 digit year as an Integer type. Then we use the `+ "-"` to concatenate a character String of `"-"` to the 4 digit date. This will automatically convert the 4 digit date to a String, and concatenate the dash to the end; then we assign the whole thing to the `combinedDate` variable. The result of this statement (assuming the ORDERDATE value is "2005-JAN-01") is "2005-".

Next, we use conditional logic—in this case an IF statement—to test if the month value of the `ORDERDATE.getMonth()` is less than 10. If it is, we need to prefix the numeric month with a 0; otherwise it will just add the 2 digit month to our String. In the case of "2005-JAN-01", the returned value will be a 0, with the +1 correcting the offset month value. The IF statement will return true, and use the following line:

```
combinedDate += "0" + (row["ORDERDATE"].getMonth() + 1);
```

This will ensure that we have a 0 preceding our month value. The resulting value of `combinedDate` is now "2005-01".

The final statement will just return the value of `combinedDate`. The thing to take into account is that this is a very simple few lines of code that return a single value. Expressions return single values; in our case, the result of `combinedData`. We want to use it to assign a value used in some element in our report. In the above example, we used it in a Computed Column to set the value of that Computed Column.

Using Expressions in Data Elements

Expressions don't need to be as complicated as our last example. In fact, we commonly use Expressions to set very simple values, such as setting a Data element to the value of our current row. Let's take a look at where the Expression is most commonly used in the Data element. Open up the **Customer Orders** report that we used in the last chapter, and double-click on the **CUSTOMERNUMBER** field.

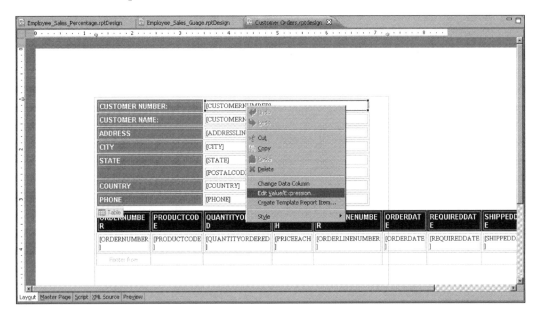

Here, we have a finished report with numerous Expressions used throughout. Let's take a look at what one of these Expressions looks like.

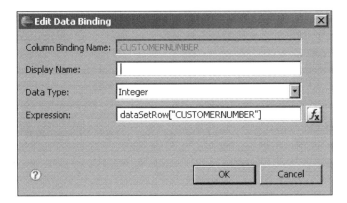

The previous image shows us a very simple Expression that retrieves the value of the column CUSTOMERNUMBER from the current row. `dataSetRow` is an array that represents the current row in the detail band, and CUSTOMERNUMBER is a named value that points to the column where CUSTOMERNUMBER resides. It is also possible to use numeric offsets to reference columns. The above Expression illustrates that a single value is returned with a very simple line of code.

In the following example, we are going to add a line number to the order detail Table.

1. Open the **Customer Orders** report from Chapter 8.

2. Insert a column to the left of the **CustomerNumber** column.

3. Insert a **Data** element in the cell for the detail band.

4. For the Expression, enter the following:

    ```
    row.__rownum + 1
    ```

5. Hit **OK** and **Preview** the report.

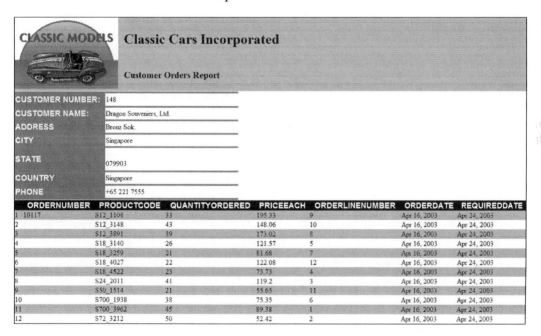

There is now a column with the current line number for the report. While not exactly the most attractive addition, the Expression works. We have seen Expressions such as these throughout the book. In the *Customer Orders* report, the Report Title is pulled from the `rprmReportTitle` parameter using the expression `params["rprmReportTitle"]`.

As we saw with the *Bar Chart* example, Expressions are simply JavaScript. Expressions also have access to JavaScript methods, operators, and objects. In the line number example just explained, we used the addition operator, and in the *Bar Chart* example, we used the `toString()`, `getMonth()`, and `getYear()` methods. All assignment operators—math, comparison, and logical—available in JavaScript are included. Let's look at the following example, which shows the JavaScript String methods being used to return the length of a String.

1. Create a new report called **String Length.rptdesign**.

2. Drop a **Data** element anywhere on the Report Design.

3. Use the following Expression:

   ```
   "This is a test".length
   ```

4. Hit **OK**, and **Preview** the report.

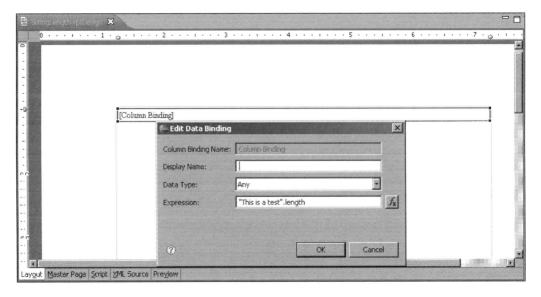

A simple report with the number 14 should be displayed. The above Expression can also be replaced with the following Expression:

```
var testString = "This is a test";
testString.length;
```

In the above example, we are breaking from the one line Expression and using multiple lines and a variable. The key is that the last line is returning a single value. All sorts of computations can take place, as long as a single value is returned. If we change the Expression to the following:

```
var testString = "This is a test";
var splitString = testString.split(" ", 5);
splitString[3].toUpperCase();
```

the report will only return the word TEST. Again, while multiple things are being done in this Expression, such as the assignment of the String, splitting the String, and converting the 3 element to upper case, only a single result is returned.

Calling Java Objects in Expressions

In the *Bar Chart* example from the last chapter, we used another method to retrieve a formatted date. Let's look at the following code sample:

```
importPackage(java.text);
var dateFormater = new SimpleDateFormat("yyyy-MM");
dateFormater.format(row["ORDERDATE"]);
```

In this example, we are using the Java `SimpleDateFormat` object to format our date object instead of the straight JavaScript method we used in the *Gauge Chart* example. The reason this is possible is that any object that is available in the Classpath for the BIRT Runtime Environment is available for use in your reports. So by default, any of the intrinsic Java objects are usable, such as the `SimpleDateFormat` object. The caveat is that you need to import the object using the `importPackage()` method.

Looking at the first line of code above, we are including the `java.text` package, of which the `SimpleDataFormat` object is a part. This method is part of the Mozilla Rhino JavaScript Engine, which BIRT uses for its Script processing. In the next line, we are creating a `dataFormater` variable and assigning it a new implementation of the `SimpleDateFormat` object, and assigning the format the default of YYYY-MM. The third line returns the formatted result as a String because the `SimpleDataFormat` method returns a String. Keep in mind when building Expressions that you can use any Java object in your report that is available in the Java Classpath.

Event Handling

So, if Expressions are simple lines of code that return a single value, how do Event Handlers fit into the Scripting world in BIRT? Simple! They do exactly what they say they do; they handle events.

Well, to understand what that means, we need to look at how BIRT reports are generated. BIRT Reports are generated in phases, as explained in the BIRT Report Object Model Scripting Specification at `http://www.eclipse.org/birt/phoenix/ref/ROM_Scripting_SPEC.pdf`. There are 5 phases in the report generation life cycle:

- Startup
- Data Transform
- Factory
- Presentation
- Shutdown

Let's take two of these phases and look at them graphically:

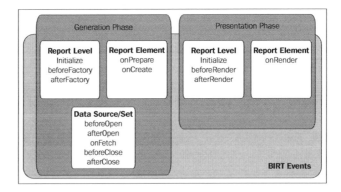

In each of these Phases, particular events are triggered so that the report developer can override the default behavior of the report generation. This allows us to do all sorts of advanced things with BIRT, such as custom filtering of Data, dynamically adding or removing BIRT objects in the report, or even building an entire BIRT report through Script. So, in the **Generation Phase**, at the report Level (globally for the entire report) we have a few sample events in the previous figure—**Initialize**, **beforeFactory**, and **afterFactory**. If we look at the **Data Set** element, we have five different events associated with it:

- **beforeOpen**—executed before opening the Data Set for processing
- **beforeClose**—executed before closing the Data Set
- **onFetch**—executed each time a row is retrieved from a Data Set
- **afterOpen**—executed after the Data Set is open
- **afterClose**—executed after the Data Set is closed

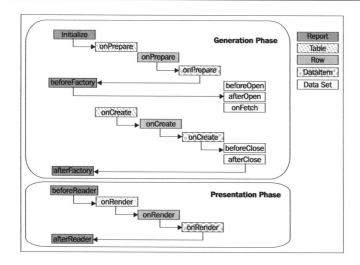

These Events are called in a particular order. So, we would be in the Startup phase first; then we would retrieve and transform the data. Then, we would generate the report with the values of our data. Then, we would render the report in the presentation phase. And finally, we would shut down the Engine. The Events that are called (and in what order) for the **Generation Phase** and **Presentation Phase** are illustrated in the previous figure.

Let's say for example, we have two things that we need to do with the Data Set. First, we need to initialize a counter variable to 0 for the number of rows that are going to be processed. Next, we need to add to the counter each time a row is retrieved. So, where we do these things is important. The order in which these Events take place is **beforeOpen**, **afterOpen**, **onFetch**, **beforeClose**, and **afterClose**. So, in either the **beforeOpen** or **afterOpen**, we need to set our variable to 0. Then, in the **onFetch** event, we need to add 1 to our counter. Let's look at an example for how to do this:

1. Open **Customer Orders.rptdesign**.

2. First, we need to define the global variable that we will use for our count. In the Report Designer, open the **Script** tab.

3. Using the **Outline**, select the Root element **Customer Orders.rptdesign**.

4. In the Event drop-down, select **initialize**.

5. Use the following code to define our global variable:

    ```
    var globalCount;
    ```

6. Select **getCustomerOrders** from the **Outline**. From the Event drop-down, select **beforeOpen**. Use the following code to initialize the `globalCount` variable:

    ```
    globalCount = 0;
    ```

7. From the Event drop-down, select **onFetch**. Use the following code to increment the counter:

```
globalCount++;
```

8. Open the Report Designer **Layout** tab. Drag a **Data** element to the bottom of the Report Design. Use the following Expression:

```
globalCount
```

9. **Run** the report.

Understanding the order of execution is important. The report's initialize method will get executed before any of the other methods. Next, the data set gets generated in the data transform phase. And finally, the value of globalCount gets inserted into the data element we dropped into the report design in the factory phase.

Contexts

From any of the Report Generation Phases, you have access to various Contexts. For the most part, each of the five Phases has its own context; in addition, there are also a few extra Contexts—one for the Data Row, and one for displaying an element.

In BIRT, Contexts are used to access objects within the Scripting environment. At a very high level, you have access to the Report Context. The Report Context is a mapping in the BIRT Scripting environment to the Java object `IReportContext`, inside of the `org.eclipse.birt.report.engine.api.script` package. This object allows Script developers access to the design object, report parameters, and various other aspects of the report, although many of these objects are shorthanded by other, easier-to-use references, such as using the `params` array to access Report Parameters. Let's take a look at how to access parameters:

1. Open the **String Length.rptdesign** file.

2. Create a new Report Parameter called **accessMe** as a String, and assign it the **Default value** of "Test Parameter".

3. Drag a Data component over to the Report Designer, and for the **Expression**, enter **valueFromScript**.

4. In the report designer, open the **Script** tab.

5. Open the **Outline** pane.

6. In the **Outline**, select the Root element **String Length.rptdesign**.

7. Open the **Palette** view.

8. When the **Script** tab is open, the **Palette** view changes to allow quick access to different objects and methods in the same way the Expression Editor does.

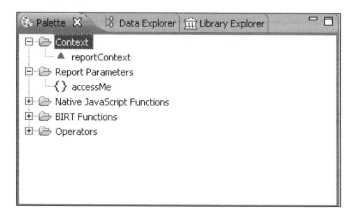

9. In the **Script** Editor, under the **initialize** Event, put in the following code:

```
valueFromScript = params["accessMe"];
```

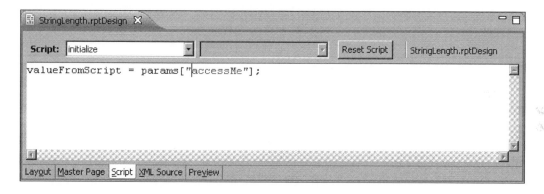

10. Take a moment to play around with the **Palette**. You can see that if you double-click on the **reportContext** under the **Context** folder, it will automatically put that into the **Script** Editor. Also, when you are typing, you may notice that a drop-down box appears that allows you to see all of the objects and properties associated with the **reportContext** object.

11. **Run** the report. The Data element that was bound to **valueFromScript** will show whatever you put in as your parameter value.

12. After running the report, modify the **initialize** method as follows:

```
valueFromScript = reportContext.getParameterValue("accessMe");
```

13. **Run** the report.

In the last modification, we didn't use a local Context. Instead, we used the global `reportContext` to access the Reports Parameters. The `reportContext` is accessible in all of the Event Handlers, and can be used to set and get global variables, access the `HTTPServletRequest` object, and access Report Engine variables (such as the Output Format, the Application Context, Render Options, and the Report Design Object).

Adding Elements to Reports

Next, let's look at using the `reportContext` to add a new element to the report. In order to do this, we only need to change the `initialize` method from the last example with the following code:

```
valueFromScript = reportContext.getParameterValue("accessMe") + "
modified";
//import the needed packages from the Java API
importPackage(Packages.org.eclipse.birt.report.model.api);
importPackage(Packages.org.eclipse.birt.report.model.api.elements);
//using the report context, get the design handle
design = reportContext.getReportRunnable().designHandle;
//get the element factory to create the new label
elementFactory = design.getElementFactory();
dataElement = elementFactory.newLabel("testElement");
//set the text from the valueFromScript variable and add
//to the report designs body
dataElement.setText(valueFromScript);
design.getDesignHandle().getBody().add(dataElement);
```

So let's take a look at this example. The `valueFromScript` variable is assigned from the Report Parameter (retrieved from the `reportContext`, same as the previous example). The next two lines are not really necessary, but they do illustrate that we will be using objects retrieved from the BIRT API packages. This is the same as using the intrinsic Java objects in our Expressions earlier, except we are using the BIRT API packages.

The next step is to retrieve the Design Handle from the `reportContext`. First, we use `getReportRunnable`, which is a reference to the open Report Design. Then we use the `designHandle` reference to get the Report Design Handle.

The next two lines retrieve the report element factory, which is a convenient way to create Report Design elements (from the Design Handle), then use that element factory to create a new Label element called `testElement`. Then we set the text of that label to `valueFromScript`.

The last part of the Script needs to reference the `getBody` method in order to get a slot in the report to add a new element to. Then we add the new element to the report.

Now, where we add elements is important. Remember the Phases from earlier examples. Well, you cannot add new elements after the factory phase. So that means if we look at the Report Root, we can only use the code in the initialize Event from the previous example (or in the beforeRender and the beforeFactory Events). The afterFactory and afterRender Events will not work. If we move the code to those elements, then the element will not get added.

One other thing to notice: if you look in the beforeFactory Event, you will notice that the Context that points to the `IReportDesign` object is available, but it is not available in any of the other Events. When working with reports through Scripting, remember that objects are not always going to be available, depending on what point of the report creation cycle we are at.

Removing Elements from a Report

The easiest way to drop elements from reports is to find the element using the Design Handle's `findElement` method. This method will return a reference to a `DesignElementHandle`, referencing the item whose name is used. Let's say we were to change the name of the Data element with the test String Expression used earlier in this chapter to `dataElementToRemove`. The following code will search the Report Design, find the matching element, and remove it from the report. It is run from the report's `initialize` method.

```
reportContext.getReportRunnable().designHandle.getDesignHandle().findE
lement("dataElementToRemove").drop();
```

Adding Sorting Conditions

In addition to adding report elements, it is also possible to add conditions, such as Highlights, Maps, and Sorting conditions. The following example will show how to dynamically add Sorting conditions to a report based on the value of a Report Parameter checkbox.

1. Create a new report in a BIRT Reporting Project. Call this new report **customerPaymentDynamicSort.rptdesign**. Bring in the **dsClassicCars** Data Source from the Library. Create a new Data Set using the following query:

```
select
  *
from
  CUSTOMERS,
```

```
PAYMENTS
where
CUSTOMERS.CUSTOMERNUMBER = PAYMENTS.CUSTOMERNUMBER
and customers.customernumber = ?
```

Name the parameter as **dsprmCustomerID**.

2. Under the Dialog for the Data Set Parameter, create and link to a report parameter called **rptprmCustomerID**. Set it as a **Text Box** entry.

3. "Drag and drop" the newly created Data Set over to the Report Design pane. Delete all columns except for the following:

    - **CustomerNumber**
    - **CustomerName**
    - **PaymentDate**
    - **Amount**

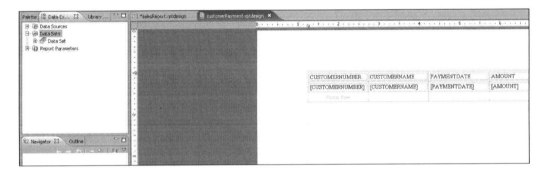

4. Create a new Report Parameter called **rptprmSortOrder**. Set it to allow null values and hidden.

5. Add the following Script to the OnPrepare Event of the Table:

```
//We only want to add this into our code when the value is not null
  for the parameter sort
if ( params["paramSortOrder"].value != null )
{
//Bring in the BIRT Report Model API and for CONSTANTS
  importPackage( Packages.org.eclipse.birt
  .report.engine.api.script.element );
//Create a dynamic sort condition
  var sortCondition = StructureScriptAPIFactory.
  createSortCondition();
//Based on the value of the sort parameter, set the appropriate key
  value for sorting
  switch (params["paramSortOrder"].value)
  {
```

```
//Remember that for the key, we need to use the fully qualified
  row and field name as a string, not as a value
case "date" :
sortCondition.setKey("row[\"PAYMENTDATE\"]");
break;
case "price" :
sortCondition.setKey("row[\"AMOUNT\"]");
break;
}
//set condition to ascending order
 sortCondition.setDirection("asc");
//Add to the table
 this.addSortCondition(sortCondition);
}
```

6. In the Header Row, we need to create Hyperlinks that will call this report, and pass in parameters to tell which column to sort by. So, save the report as it is; otherwise, the parameters will not show up in the Drill-Down Dialog. Select the **PaymentDate** column header, and create a Hyperlink like the following:

    °   Select **Drill-Down**.
    °   Link to the **customerPayment.rptdesign** file.
    °   Select the **rptprmCustomerID** field, and set the value to **para ms["rptprmCustomerID"]**.
    °   Select the **rptprmSortOrder** parameter, and set the value to **"date"** with the quotation marks.
    °   Set to open in the same window.

7. Do the same thing for the Amount column, except set the value of **rptprmSortorder** to **"price"**.

With that done, now you can reorder the report in time view, when the user clicks on the date or the amount columns. With a little more logic developed in, you can have the report do both ascending and descending sorts, and even have it refresh the report without having to refresh the viewing page.

Scripted Data Source

One of the other things we can do with BIRT Scripting is to create a Data Source. In the following example, we will create a simple report that will return 1 through 10 using a Scripted Data Source.

1. Create a new report called **countOneToTen.rptdesign**.

2. Right-click on the **Data Sources** section under the **Data Explorer**, and choose **Scripted Data Source** as the type.

3. Create a new Data Set called **dsCount**.

4. A Dialog will pop up for the columns to return. Add one column called **cnt** as type **Integer**.

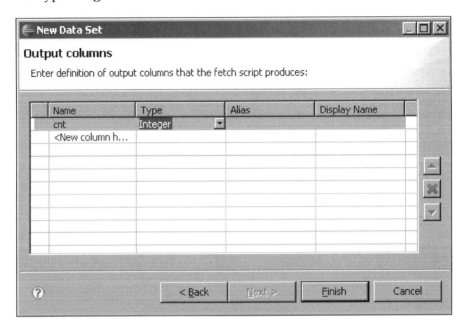

5. The **Script** Editor will open up. In the **Open** Event, add the following code:

```
reportContext.setGlobalVariable("currentCount", 0);
```

6. In the **fetch** method, use the following code:

```
var currentCount = reportContext.getGlobalVariable("currentCount"
);
if (currentCount < 10)
{
currentCount++;
row["cnt"] = currentCount;
reportContext.setGlobalVariable("currentCount", currentCount);
return true;
}
return false;
```

7. In the Report Designer, drag over the **dsCount** Data Source to the Report Designer.

8. **Run** the report.

In the example just shown, we did a few things interestingly. First, we created the Scripted Data source. The way this works is that the `fetch` method needs to return true when data is returned and false when data is not returned, to get data into the returned row into the **cnt** column. Then we are using the `reportContexts.setGlobal` variable to keep track of the running count.

Using Java Objects as Event Handlers

The last thing we are going to look at in this chapter is using Java objects as Event Handlers instead of JavaScript in the Script Editor. In order to implement Java-based Event handlers, the designer needs to extend the appropriate Event Handler object. For example, if we are going to implement the last example as a Java object, we will need to extend the `org.eclipse.birt.report.engine.api.script.eventadapter.ScriptedDataSetEventAdapter` class. So, to do this, I created a separate Java project in Eclipse. I created a class like the following:

```
package com.birtbook.eventHandler;
import org.eclipse.birt.report.engine.api.script.IUpdatableDataSetRow;
import org.eclipse.birt.report.engine.api.script.ScriptException;
import org.eclipse.birt.report.engine.api.script.eventadapter.
ScriptedDataSetEventAdapter;
import org.eclipse.birt.report.engine.api.script.instance.
IDataSetInstance;
public class ScriptedDataSetHandler extends
ScriptedDataSetEventAdapter {
private int currentCount;
@Override
public boolean fetch(IDataSetInstance dataSet, IUpdatableDataSetRow
row) {
//increment the counter
currentCount++;
if (currentCount < 11)
{
//set the rows value
try {
row.setColumnValue("cnt", currentCount);
} catch (ScriptException e) {
e.printStackTrace();
}
return true;
}
return false;
}
@Override
```

```
public void open(IDataSetInstance dataSet) {
super.open(dataSet);
//initialize the count
currentCount = 0;
}
}
```

Now, I have to restart Eclipse in order for it to recognize the class in my Report Design. Then, once I restart Eclipse, I am able to use my class and debug in Eclipse when I run the report. Next, I go into the Report Design, select my **dsCount** Data Source, and clear all of the Script out of the Events. Then, under the **Event Handler** tab, I click on the **browse** button, and select my class. When I run the report, it will use my new class as the Event Handler.

The benefit to this approach is that it is much easier to debug during development. Plus, I have full access to the Eclipse IDE, code completion, and a much cleaner IDE to develop Event Handlers. The drawback is that I would need to deploy the classes with the reports and make sure they are visible in the Classpath for my runtime environments.

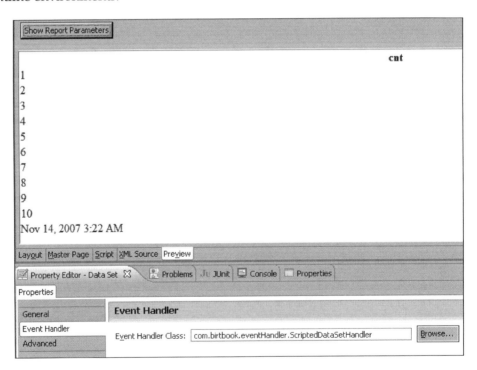

Summary

In this chapter, we looked at some of the Scripting capabilities that BIRT has to offer with Expressions and Event Handlers. We have looked at the different Report Contexts that are available for accessing properties and methods in BIRT Report Designs, adding and removing report elements dynamically, and finally we have looked at how to use Java objects as Event Handlers.

This touches on the BIRT API, which is a large topic and outside of the scope of this book. But it gets the reader familiar with some of the things that are possible with the Scripting and API environments that BIRT provides. More information can be gathered on the Eclipse Website and Newsgroups, the BirtWorld blog, and on my website.

The final part of this book will look at deploying BIRT reports.

11
Deployment

So, you've developed a bunch of reports by now. While some of these reports may be for your own use, some may be for others. How do you get these reports to these users? That's the question that Deployment seeks to answer.

Within BIRT, Deployment is a large topic. Some people consider the BIRT Viewer (that comes with the BIRT Runtime) as the Deployment endpoint. But in fact, BIRT Deployment is a much larger topic due to the fact that the BIRT Report Engine API is available to embed into Java applications.

In this chapter, we are going to look at two of the different Deployment options available. We will look at the BIRT Viewer for J2EE that comes with the BIRT Runtime and is embedded into the BIRT Eclipse IDE, and we are also going to look at a basic Java application that implements the Report Engine API to run reports. We are also going to look at the command-line tools that come with the BIRT Runtime for executing reports.

Everything in this chapter uses utilities from the BIRT Runtime installation package, available from the BIRT homepage at `http://www.eclipse.org/birt`.

BIRT Viewer

The BIRT Viewer is a J2EE application that is designed to demonstrate how to implement the Report Engine API to execute reports in an online web application. For most basic uses—such as for small to medium size Intranet applications—this is an appropriate approach. The point to keep in mind about the BIRT Web Viewer is that it is an example application. It can be used as a baseline for more sophisticated web applications that will implement the BIRT Report Engine API.

Installation of the BIRT Viewer is documented at a number of places. The Eclipse BIRT website has some great tutorials at:

`http://www.eclipse.org/birt/phoenix/deploy/viewerSetup.php`

`http://wiki.eclipse.org/BIRT/FAQ/Deployment`

This is also documented on my website in a series of articles introducing people to BIRT:

`http://digiassn.blogspot.com/2005/10/birt-report-server-pt-2.html`

I won't go into the details about installing Apache Tomcat as this is covered in depth in other locations, but I will cover how to install the Viewer in a Tomcat environment. For the most part these instructions can be used in other J2EE containers, such as WebSphere. In some cases a WAR package is used instead. I prefer Tomcat because it is a widely used open-source J2EE environment.

Under the BIRT Runtime package is a folder containing an example Web Viewer application. The Web Viewer is a useful application as you require basic report viewing capabilities, such as parameter passing, pagination, and export capabilities to formats such as Word, Excel, RTF, and CSV.

Name	Size	Type	Date Modified
about_files		File Folder	11/1/2007 4:08 PM
ReportEngine		File Folder	2/3/2008 7:40 PM
WebViewerExample		File Folder	2/3/2008 7:40 PM
about.html	5 KB	Firefox Document	11/1/2007 4:08 PM
birt.war	34,772 KB	WAR File	11/1/2007 5:29 PM
epl-v10.html	17 KB	Firefox Document	11/1/2007 4:08 PM
notice.html	7 KB	Firefox Document	11/1/2007 4:08 PM
readme.txt	5 KB	Text Document	11/1/2007 5:29 PM

For this example, I have Apache Tomcat 5.5 installed into a folder at `C:\apache-tomcat-5.5.25`. To install the Web Viewer, I simply need to copy the **WebViewerExample** folder from the BIRT Runtime to the web application folder at `C:\apache-tomcat-5.5.25\webapps`.

Name	Size	Type	Date Modified
balancer		File Folder	2/3/2008 7:49 PM
jsp-examples		File Folder	2/3/2008 7:49 PM
ROOT		File Folder	2/3/2008 7:49 PM
servlets-examples		File Folder	2/3/2008 7:49 PM
tomcat-docs		File Folder	2/3/2008 7:49 PM
webdav		File Folder	2/3/2008 7:49 PM
WebViewerExample		File Folder	2/3/2008 8:22 PM

Accessing the BIRT Web Viewer is as simple as calling the **WebViewerExample** Context.

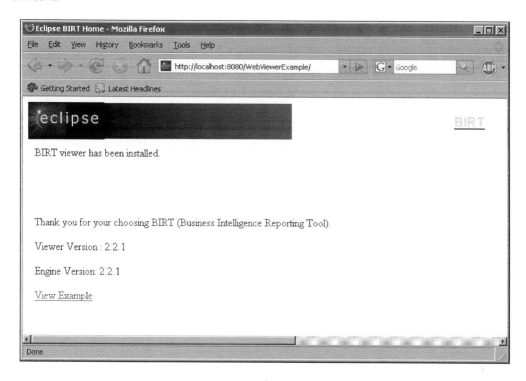

When copying the `WebViewerExample` folder, you can rename this folder to anything you want. Obviously `WebViewerExample` is not a good name for an online web application. So in the following screenshot, I renamed the `WebViewerExample` folder to **birtViewer**, and am accessing the BIRT Web Viewer test report.

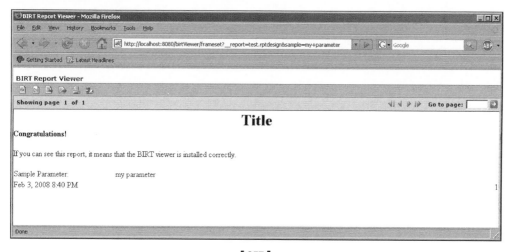

Installing Reports into the Web Viewer

Once the BIRT Viewer is set up, Deploying reports is as simple as copying the report design files, Libraries, or report documents into the application's Context, and calling it with the appropriate URL parameters.

For example, we will install the reports from the `Classic Cars – With Library` folder into the BIRT Web Viewer at `birtViewer`. In order for these reports to work, all dependent Libraries need to be installed with the reports. In the case of the example application, we currently have the report folder set to the Root of the web application folder.

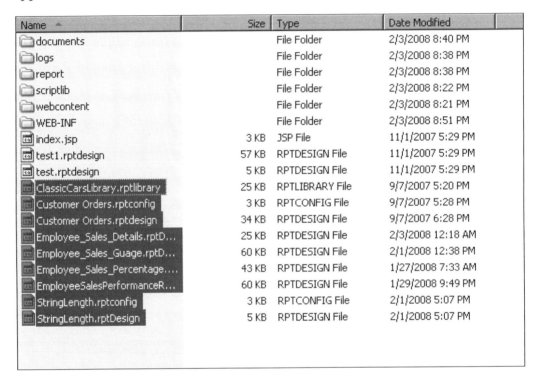

Name ▲	Size	Type	Date Modified
documents		File Folder	2/3/2008 8:40 PM
logs		File Folder	2/3/2008 8:38 PM
report		File Folder	2/3/2008 8:38 PM
scriptlib		File Folder	2/3/2008 8:22 PM
webcontent		File Folder	2/3/2008 8:21 PM
WEB-INF		File Folder	2/3/2008 8:51 PM
index.jsp	3 KB	JSP File	11/1/2007 5:29 PM
test1.rptdesign	57 KB	RPTDESIGN File	11/1/2007 5:29 PM
test.rptdesign	5 KB	RPTDESIGN File	11/1/2007 5:29 PM
ClassicCarsLibrary.rptlibrary	25 KB	RPTLIBRARY File	9/7/2007 5:20 PM
Customer Orders.rptconfig	3 KB	RPTCONFIG File	9/7/2007 5:28 PM
Customer Orders.rptdesign	34 KB	RPTDESIGN File	9/7/2007 6:28 PM
Employee_Sales_Details.rptD...	25 KB	RPTDESIGN File	2/3/2008 12:18 AM
Employee_Sales_Guage.rptD...	60 KB	RPTDESIGN File	2/1/2008 12:38 PM
Employee_Sales_Percentage....	43 KB	RPTDESIGN File	1/27/2008 7:33 AM
EmployeeSalesPerformanceR...	60 KB	RPTDESIGN File	1/29/2008 9:49 PM
StringLength.rptconfig	3 KB	RPTCONFIG File	2/1/2008 5:07 PM
StringLength.rptDesign	5 KB	RPTDESIGN File	2/1/2008 5:07 PM

Accessing Reports in the Web Viewer

Accessing reports is as simple as passing the correct parameters to the Web Viewer. In the BIRT Web Viewer, there are seven servlets that you can call to run reports, which are as follows:

- frameset
- run
- preview

- download
- parameter
- document
- output

Out of these, you will only need *frameset* and *run* as the other servlets are for Engine-related purposes, such as the preview for the Eclipse designer, the parameter Dialog, and the download of report documents.

Out of the these two servlets, *frameset* is the one that is typically used for user interaction with reports, as it provides the pagination options, parameter Dialogs, table of contents viewing, and export and print Dialogs. The *run* servlet only provides report output.

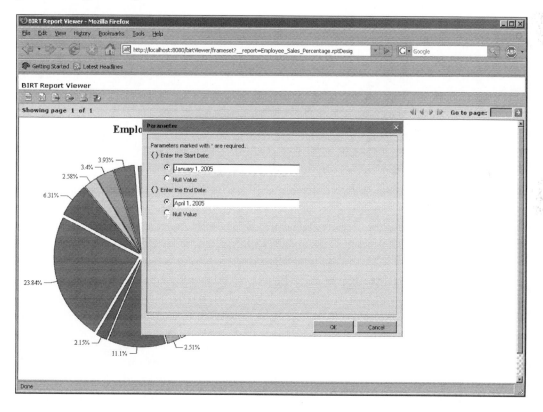

There are a few URL parameters for the BIRT Web Viewer, such as:

- __format : which is the output format, either HTML or PDF.
- __isnull: which sets a Report Parameter to null, parameter name as a value.

- __locale: which is the reports locale.
- __report: which is the report design file to run.
- __document: which is the report document file to open.

Any remaining URL parameter will be treated as a Report Parameter. In the following image, I am running the **Employee_Sales_Percentage.rptdesign** file with the **startDate** and **endDate** parameters set.

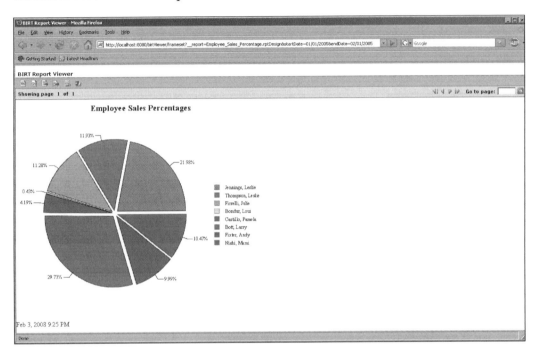

Command-Line Tools

The command-line tools that come with the BIRT Runtime make a useful tool for scheduled report execution. Under Windows, calling a batch file using the Windows Scheduler or the AT utility makes unattended report execution very simple. In the case of the UNIX world, there are tons of Cron daemons available schedule the report execution without the need to interact with a GUI application, which is very convenient.

In the Runtime folder, the batch or script files are located under the `ReportEngine` folder. The prerequisites are that you must have a Java implementation greater than version 1.4, and preset the `BIRT_HOME` environment variable to the location of the `birt-runtime Root` folder.

More information can be found in the ReadMe file, and on my website at http://digiassn.blogspot.com/2006/07/birt-birt-report-scheduling-without.html.

First, I am going to create a batch file called runReport.bat. The file will be simple and only have the following lines:

```
Set BIRT_HOME=C:\birt_runtime\birt-runtime-2_1_0\
C:\birt_runtime\birt-runtime-2_1_0\ReportEngine\genReport.bat -runrender
-output "c:\birt_runtime\birt-runtime-2_1_0\ReportEngine\sameples\output.
html" -format html "C:\birt_runtime\birt-runtime-2_1_0\ReportEngine\
samples\Hello_World.rptDesign"
```

To Schedule this file to run, I go to the **Control Panel | Scheduled Tasks**, and create a new Scheduled Task. I set the command to run as **C:\birt_runtime\birt-runtime-2_1_0\ReportEngine\runReport.bat**. I set up the appropriate time, and set the directory to start in as **C:\birt_runtime\birt-runtime-2_1_0\ReportEngine**. I also set this to run as a dedicated report user. The following figure illustrates the values I use under Scheduler.

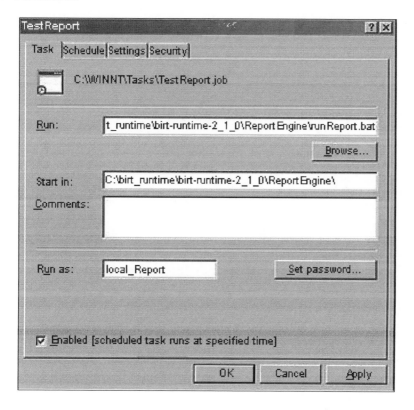

Now, I can schedule BIRT reports to run without needing Apache. This cuts down on system overhead. There are a few caveats to take into consideration. If your BIRT report hits a database, the appropriate drivers will need to be included in the ReportEngine\plugins folders. For example, if the report uses JDBC to connect, the JDBC drivers will need to be installed under the ReportEngine\plugins\org. eclipse.birt.report.data.oda.jdbc_<version> folder. Also, you will need to copy the iText.jar file (as indicated in the BIRT Runtime installation instructions) to the appropriate plug-ins directory.

From this exercise, I learned a few interesting things. I was unaware that Java classes could be invoked from the command line. For example, if I set an environment variable called BIRTClassPath like the following:

```
SET BIRTCLASSPATH=%BIRT_HOME%\ReportEngine\lib\commons-cli-1.0.jar;%BIRT_
HOME%\ReportEngine\lib\commons-codec-1.3.jar;%BIRT_HOME%\ReportEngine\
lib\com.ibm.icu_3.4.4.1.jar;%BIRT_HOME%\ReportEngine\lib\coreapi.
jar;%BIRT_HOME%\ReportEngine\lib\dteapi.jar;%BIRT_HOME%\ReportEngine\
lib\engineapi.jar;%BIRT_HOME%\ReportEngine\lib\js.jar;%BIRT_HOME%\
ReportEngine\lib\modelapi.jar;%BIRT_HOME%\ReportEngine\flute.jar;%BIRT_
HOME%\ReportEngine\lib\sac.jar;
```

I can run the following command from the DOS prompt and get the parameters that the ReportEngine class is expecting:

```
java -cp "%BIRTCLASSPATH%" org.eclipse.birt.report.engine.api.
ReportRunner
org.eclipse.birt.report.engine.impl.ReportRunner
--mode/-m [ run | render | runrender] the default is runrender
\\For runrender mode: we should add it in the end<design file>
--format/-f [ HTML | PDF ]
--output/-o <target file>
--htmlType/-t < HTML | ReportletNoCSS >
--locale /-l<locale>
--parameter/-p <parameterName=parameterValue>
--file/-F <parameter file>
--encoding/-e <target encoding>
\\locale: default is English
\\Parameters in command line will override parameters in parameter file
\\Parameter name can't include characters such as ' ', '=', ':'
\\For RUN mode: we should add it in the end<design file>
--output/-o <target file>
--locale /-l<locale>
--parameter/-p <parameterName=parameterValue>
--file/-F <parameter file>
\\locale: default is English
```

```
\\Parameters in command line will override parameters in parameter file
\\Parameter name can't include characters such as ' ', '=', ':'
\\For RENDER mode: we should add it in the end<design file>
--output/-o <target file>
\t --page/-p <pageNumber>
--locale /-l<locale>
\\locale: default is English
```

For me, this is a major break from the paradigm of "compile and run" software in other languages.

Report Engine API

Embedding the Report Engine API into your application requires a little knowledge of the inner workings of BIRT. The API is outside of the scope of this book, but we will get a brief view of how to do a simple report executor application.

The requirements for this application to work are that you have Java 1.4 or higher set up, and have the BIRT Runtime set up and visible in your Classpath. I am also using Apache Commons CLI to handle the command-line options. The following does not take into account the parameters; it simply demonstrates how to instantiate the Report Engine API.

```java
package com.birt_book;
import java.util.HashMap;
import org.apache.commons.cli.CommandLine;
import org.apache.commons.cli.CommandLineParser;
import org.apache.commons.cli.HelpFormatter;
import org.apache.commons.cli.Options;
import org.apache.commons.cli.PosixParser;
import org.eclipse.birt.core.exception.BirtException;
import org.eclipse.birt.core.framework.Platform;
import org.eclipse.birt.core.framework.PlatformConfig;
import org.eclipse.birt.report.engine.api.EngineConfig;
import org.eclipse.birt.report.engine.api.EngineConstants;
import org.eclipse.birt.report.engine.api.EngineException;
import org.eclipse.birt.report.engine.api.HTMLRenderContext;
import org.eclipse.birt.report.engine.api.HTMLRenderOption;
import org.eclipse.birt.report.engine.api.IReportEngine;
import org.eclipse.birt.report.engine.api.IReportEngineFactory;
import org.eclipse.birt.report.engine.api.IReportRunnable;
```

```
import org.eclipse.birt.report.engine.api.IRunAndRenderTask;
public class ReportExecutor {
private static String BIRT_HOME = "C:/BIRT_RUNTIME_2_2/birt-runtime-
2_2_0/ReportEngine";
private static String IMAGE_PATH = "C:/BIRT_RUNTIME_2_2/images";
private String reportLocation;
private String reportOutputLocation;
/**
* setupCLIParameters
*
* This will setup the arguments
* @return
*/
public Options setupCLIParameters()
{
Options options = new Options();
options.addOption("i", "input", true, "The report file to execute");
options.addOption("o", "output", true, "The name of the output file");
return options;
}
/**
* parseCommandLineOptions
*
* Given the arguments passed into main, this method will use the
* Apache Commons CLI
* to parse those options and return
* a CommandLine object with the options
*
* @param args
* @return CommandLine
*/
public CommandLine parseCommandLineOptions(String []args)
{
//First, parse the command line options using Apache Commons CLI
CommandLineParser parser = new PosixParser();
Options options = setupCLIParameters();
CommandLine line = null;
HelpFormatter formatter = new HelpFormatter();
//Try to parse the command line options, exit the app if there is an
error
try {
//Get the options
line = parser.parse(options, args);
catch (Exception e) {
System.err.println("Parsing failed.  Reason: " + e.getMessage());
```

```
formatter.printHelp("ReportExecutor", options);
System.exit(-1);
}
return line;
}
/**
* startupPlatform
*
* This will startup the Eclipse platform and load any plugins
*/
private void startupPlatform()
{
//Initialize the Eclipse platform, plug-ins, and Report Engine
PlatformConfig platformConfig = new PlatformConfig();
platformConfig.setBIRTHome(BIRT_HOME);
try {
Platform.startup(platformConfig);
catch (BirtException e) {
e.printStackTrace();
//We cannot start the platform, exit
System.exit(-1);
}
}
/**
* createReportEngine
*
* This will create a report engine to use
* @return
*/
private IReportEngine createReportEngine()
{
//Create a new report engine factory
IReportEngineFactory factory = (IReportEngineFactory) Platform.createF
actoryObject(IReportEngineFactory.EXTENSION_REPORT_ENGINE_FACTORY);
//create a new report engine
EngineConfig engineConfig = new EngineConfig();
engineConfig.setBIRTHome("C:/BIRT_RUNTIME_2_2/birt-runtime-2_2_0/
ReportEngine"); //will replace with configuration file
return factory.createReportEngine(engineConfig);
}
/**
* Executes a report with no parameters, only requires report name to
execute
* @param reportName
* @return
```

```
*/
public void executeReportNoParams(String reportName, String
outputFile, IReportEngine engine)
{
try {
//Create the report runnable and runandrender task
IReportRunnable runnable = engine.openReportDesign(reportName);
IRunAndRenderTask task = engine.createRunAndRenderTask(runnable);
//Set Render context to handle url and image locations
HTMLRenderContext renderContext = new HTMLRenderContext();
renderContext.setImageDirectory(IMAGE_PATH);
HashMap contextMap = new HashMap();
contextMap.put( EngineConstants.APPCONTEXT_HTML_RENDER_CONTEXT,
renderContext );
task.setAppContext( contextMap );
//Set rendering options - such as file or stream output,
//Output format, whether it is embeddable, etc
HTMLRenderOption options = new HTMLRenderOption();
options.setOutputFileName(outputFile);
options.setOutputFormat("html");
task.setRenderOption(options);
//Run the report and close
task.run();
task.close();
catch (EngineException e) {
e.printStackTrace();
System.exit(-1);
}
}
/**
 * executeReport
 *
 * This method will execute the report and save the the output file
 * @param reportInput
 * @param reportOutput
 */
public void executeReport(String reportInput, String reportOutput)
{
//Start up the platform
startupPlatform();
//Create a Report Engine
IReportEngine engine = createReportEngine();
//Create a run and render task, and execute report
executeReportNoParams(reportInput, reportOutput, engine);
```

```
//Shutdown platform
Platform.shutdown();
}
/**
* @param args
*/
public static void main(String[] args) {
ReportExecutor re = new ReportExecutor();
//Get command line options
CommandLine cl = re.parseCommandLineOptions(args);
//Get the input file and output file
String reportInputFile = cl.getOptionValue("i");
String reportOutputFile = cl.getOptionValue("o");
//Execute the report
re.executeReport(reportInputFile, reportOutputFile);
}
}
```

Outputting to Different Formats

The BIRT platform supports a plug-in structure based on Eclipse. One of the BIRT Plug-in extension points is the Emitter extension point. Emitters are plug-ins that handle the rendering of reports to different formats.

Out of the box, BIRT comes with several different Emitters. BIRT can output to the following formats with the default Emitters:

- HTML
- PDF
- Microsoft Word
- Microsoft Excel
- RTF
- Microsoft PowerPoint
- Adobe PostScript

In the BIRT Web Designer, the different output formats are available under the **File|View Report** menu.

When using the BIRT Web Viewer, you can specify different report formats by using the __format URL parameter. If you specified __format=pdf it would output in the Adobe PDF format, or for __format=xls, it would output in the Microsoft Excel format.

In addition to the URL parameter, there is also an Export dialog available in the frameset servlet.

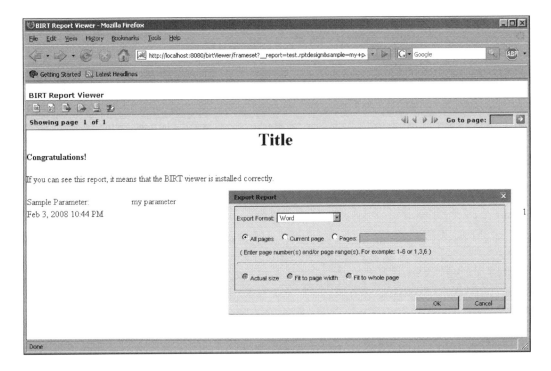

Summary

Although brief, this chapter gave some examples of how to Deploy BIRT reports. The main options are to use the BIRT Example Web Viewer, to use the example command-line tools, or to embed the BIRT Engine API into your own custom web application.

In the next chapter, we will wrap up with a practical series of reports around the Bugzilla platform. We will go over how to create a project and reports from the ground up.

12
Practical Example— Building Reports for Bugzilla

We have seen all the components for building reports with BIRT. By this time, you should be familiar with how to navigate the Eclipse BIRT Report Designer perspective, how to insert components into reports, creating data connections and Data Sets based on queries, Scripting, and various other topics related to BIRT.

As mentioned in the beginning, we are going to look at a practical example for building a reporting site. In this chapter, we are going to look at a scenario where we have a Bugzilla instance set up with a series of bugs related to BIRT. We are going to look at a series of requirements, and build the reports necessary to fulfil those requirements.

The Environment

In this set up, we are utilizing a **Bugzilla 2.22.1** instance set up on **Ubuntu 7.10 (Gutsy Gibbon)**. Bugzilla has been set up to run under Apache, and is connected to a **MySQL 5.0** database.

There is a single product, called **BIRT Book**. Under this product there are several components, as illustrated in the following image:

Requirements

Although we haven't talked about it much, the most important thing to have — prior to building reports — is the requirements. Imagine being a carpenter trying to build a house without any blueprints. We need to have some idea about what we are trying to build before we undertake the task of building reports. Following are the set of requirements that we need for this project. These are actually fairly sparse in terms of requirements. In my experience, requirements range from an extremely detailed set of Use Case documents to mock-ups done in Spreadsheets or some graphic format.

These are the reports that users are looking for:

- Detailed report about a bug. Show who it is assigned to, take in bug ID as a parameter (will be target for all Drill Downs).

- Report to show overall status of issues. Drill-Down to a detailed list of issue.

- Given developer login, show list of bugs assigned to them.

- Performance report for users. Show percentage of issues in finished state versus open state.

Create the Libraries

In the case of these reports, we have a pretty good idea about what kind of things we want to be reusable. First, we know that all of these reports will contain the same Data Source—a MySQL connection to the Bugzilla database. We also want to create a consistent header and layout for the reports. So we will create a Library containing the Data Source and the header, and a Template containing both. We will also create the Style Sheets that we want to use to make things consistent throughout the reports. Let's begin:

1. Create a new Reporting Project called **Bugzilla Reports**.

2. Create a new Library called **bugzillaReportsLibrary.rptlibrary** in the newly created project.

3. Switch to the **Outline** view in **bugzillaReportsLibrary.rptlibrary**. Create a new **JDBC Data Source** called **bugzillaDataSource**.

4. As I am using MySQL, I need to use the **Manage Drivers** Dialog under the Data Source setup to install the MySQL JDBC driver. Following is the Dialog screen where I edited the MySQL Connector-J driver to have a description and Template JDBC URL

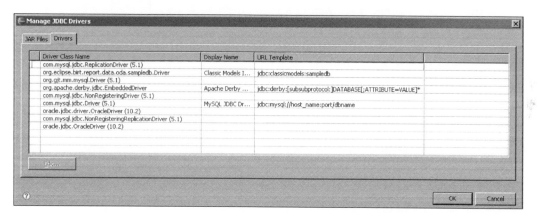

5. Input the correct JDBC URL and Driver for Bugzilla.

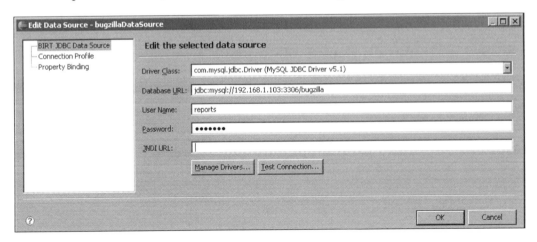

6. Select **Themes** under the **Outline**. Change the name of the Theme to **bugZillaTheme**.

7. Create a new **Custom Style** called **masterPageHeader**.

8. Input the following parameters for the **Style**:

For **Font**:

Color: White

Weight: Bold

Font: Sans-Serif

For **Background**:

Background Color: RGB(64,0,128)

9. Select the **MasterPages** element under the **Outline**. Change the name of the Master Page from **Simple Master Page** to **BugzillaMasterPage**.

10. Select the **Master Page** tab in the Report Designer.

11. Insert a **Grid** into the header with **1** column and **1** row.

12. Insert a **Label** component into the **Grid** cell, and enter the text as **Bugzilla Reports**.

13. In the Report Designer, right-click on the **Grid**, and select **Style | Apply Style | masterPageHeader**.

14. Create a new Data Set called **getAllBugs**. Use the following query:

```
SELECT
bugs.bug_id,
bugs.bug_severity,
bugs.bug_status,
bugs.short_desc,
profiles.userid,
profiles.login_name,
profiles.realname,
components.id,
components.name,
components.description
FROM
bugs,
profiles,
components
WHERE
bugs.component_id   = components.id
AND bugs.assigned_to = profiles.userid
```

15. In the project, create a new **Template** called **BugzillaReportsTemplate.rpttemplate**, and use **Template for Bugzilla Report Project** as the **Display Name**.

16. In the newly created Template, open the **Library Explorer** tab and the Outline (one above the other). "Drag and drop" the **bugzillaDataSource**, **getAllBugs**, and **BugzillaMasterPage** components from the Library to the Template.

First Report—Bug Detail Report

Now that we have the groundwork laid for our project, we can start building the actual reports. In a typical situation, you wouldn't know beforehand every possible element to add to a report Library. So in the next example, we are going to build the report, then go back in after the fact and add some formatting elements—such as Styles—that will be used in the remainder of the reports.

The following report is fairly straightforward. We already have the query to retrieve information about bugs from the Template we will use, so we will need to modify it in two ways. First, we need to parameterize it so that we only return the bug we are looking for. Second, we will also need to store the bug history. These are both very simple modifications; so let's take a look:

1. Open **BugzillaReportsTemplate.rpttemplate**.

2. Save this report as **BugzillaDetailReport.rptdesign**.

3. **Edit** the **getAllBugs** Data Set.

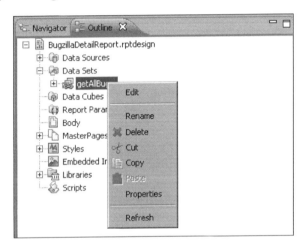

4. Edit the query to read like the following example:

```
SELECT
bugs.bug_id,
bugs.bug_severity,
bugs.bug_status,
bugs.short_desc,
profiles.userid,
profiles.login_name,
profiles.realname,
components.id,
components.name,
components.description
FROM
bugs,
profiles,
components
WHERE
bugs.component_id    = components.id
AND bugs.assigned_to = profiles.userid
and bugs.bug_id = ?
```

5. Create a new Data-Set Parameter, call it **bugID**, and link it to a Report Parameter.

6. Save the changes to the Data Set. From the **Outline**, right-click on it and choose **Rename**. Rename the Data Set as **getBugByID**.

7. Now, we want to create a Table element in the report that displays the Bug information vertically instead of horizontally. To start, drag **getBugsByID** to the Report Designer.

8. Delete the **Header** and **Footer Row**.

9. Insert four rows into the **Detail** section.

10. Move the following fields into the order as illustrated in the following figure. Remove the remaining columns.

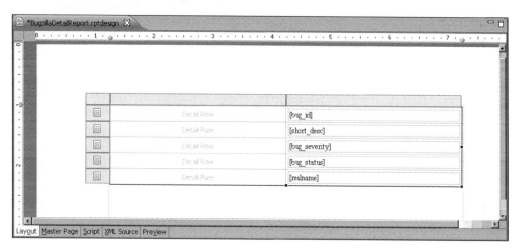

11. Add descriptive Labels to each row as follows:

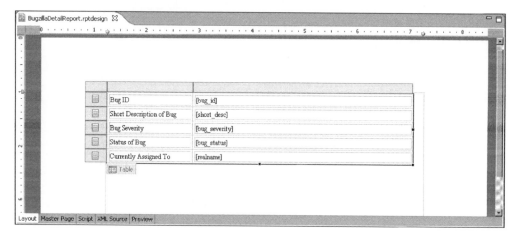

12. Now, we want to create two Styles in our Library, and embed them into the report. This way the Styles will be available in other reports also. Open **BugzillaReportsLibrary.rptlibrary**.

13. Under the **Themes** section, make a new Style called **BugDescriptionHeaderLabel**.

14. Use the following attributes:

    For **Font**:

    Color: White

    Size: Large

    Weight: Bold

    For **Background**:

    Background color: Blue

    For **Border**:

    Top: Solid

    Bottom: Solid

    Left: Solid

    Color (All): **Black**

15. Create a new Style called **BugDescriptionHeaderData** and use the following settings:

    For **Border**:

    Top: Solid

    Bottom: Solid

    Right: Solid

    Color (All): **Black**.

16. Save the Library.

17. I had to close out **BugDetailReport.rptdesign** before the new Styles became visible. Go ahead and do so and reopen **BugDetailReport.rptdesign**.

18. In the **Outline** view, select the Root element. Apply the Theme **bugZillaTheme**.

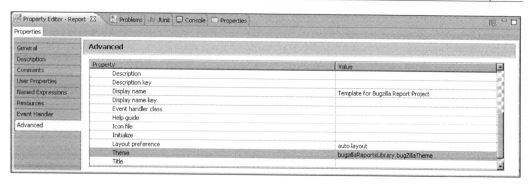

19. In the Report Designer, select the column containing the Labels.

20. In the **Property Editor**, select the **Advanced** tab. Under **Style**, select **BugDescriptionHeaderLabel**.

21. Select the column containing the data, and apply the **BugDescriptionHeaderData** Style.

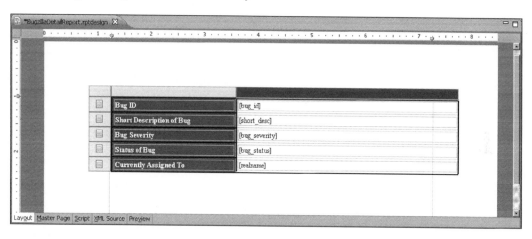

So, we have created the header for the report. Now, we want to see the details of this bug. The details are basically the bug history about who changed the fields, added fields, changed the bug's status, and the resolution.

1. Create a new Data Set called **getBugHistory**.

2. Use the following query:

```
select
bugs_activity.bug_when,
bugs_activity.added,
bugs_activity.removed,
profiles.realname,
fielddefs.name
```

```
from
bugs_activity,
profiles,
fielddefs
where
bugs_activity.who = profiles.useridand bugs_activity.fieldid =
                          fielddefs.fieldid and bug_id = ?
```

3. Add in a new parameter and bind it to the Report Parameter **bugID**.

4. Drag the new Data Set over to the Report Designer.

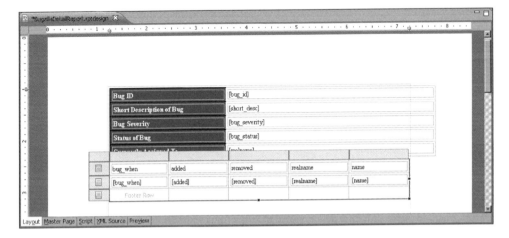

5. Update the header Labels as illustrated in the following figure. In this figure, I also moved the column containing the **Field Updated** field to the second column.

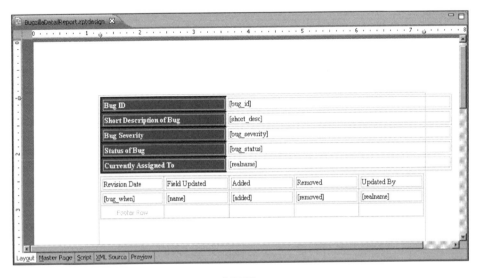

6. Now, we need to create Styles for the Detail Row. We want to create these in the Library also so that they are reusable in our other reports. Open the **BugzillaReportsLibrary.rptlibrary**.

7. Create a new **Custom Style** called **DetailTableHeader**.

8. Use the following settings for the **Style**:

For **Font**:

Weight: Bold

For **Background**:

Background color: RGB(128,128,255)

9. Create a second **Custom Style** called **DetailTableRow**, and use the following settings:

For **Highlights**:

Expression: **row.__rownum % 2**

Operand: **Equal to**

Value: **0**

Background Color: Silver

10. Save the Library. Again, close the **BugzillaDetailReport.rptdesign** and reopen.

11. In the **Header Row** for **getBugHistory** Table, apply the **DetailTableHeader** Style.

12. In the **Detail Row**, apply the **DetailTableRow** Style.

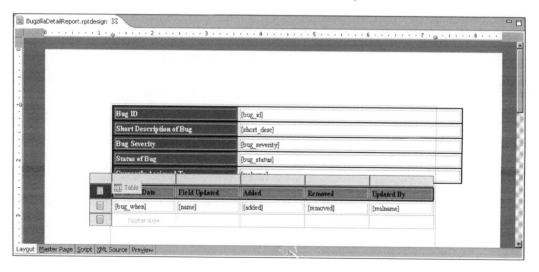

13. **Save** the report, and **Preview**.

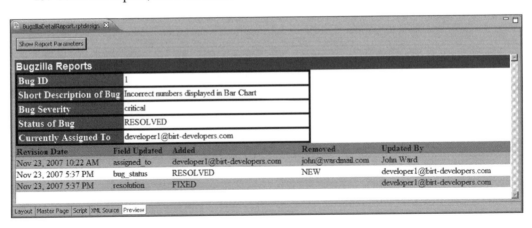

Bug Status

The next report we are going to undertake is the report to show open issues compared to all bugs. What we are trying to build here is a graph that shows — by category — the bugs that are open in relation to the total number of bugs for that category. No other Grouping is required. Under the graph, we also want to show a list of open bugs that we can click on and Drill-Down to the detail for that bug so that we can see the history.

What this means is that we need a bar graph showing all the statuses

1. Open **BugzillaReportsTemplate.rpttemplate** and **Save** as **bugStatusReport. rptdesign**.

2. Drag **getAllBugs** over to the Report Designer.

3. **Delete** all columns except the **bug_status** field and **short_desc** field.

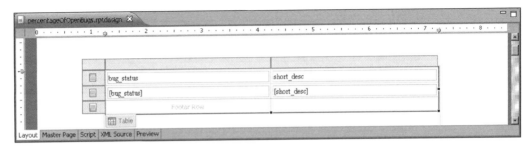

4. In the Table, create a new Group called **groupByCategory**, and group the data by the component's **name**.

5. With the new category created in the Table, insert a new column on the right. Delete the header labels. Move the data fields to look like the following figure:

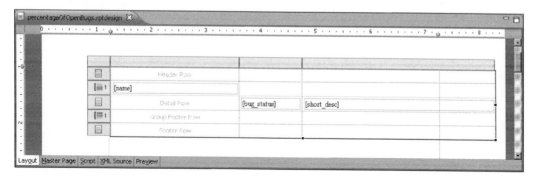

6. In the **Outline**, select the Root element. Apply the **bugZillaTheme**.

7. In the **Group Header Row** with the **[name]** field, apply the **DetailTableHeader** Style.

8. In the **Detail Row**, apply the **DetailTableRow** Style.

9. In the **Header Row**, select all the cells and **Merge**.

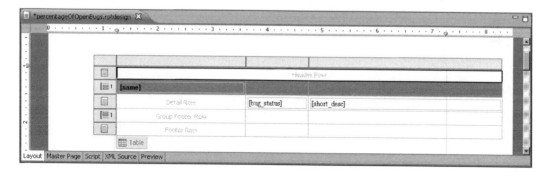

10. In the new merged cell, insert a **Chart**.

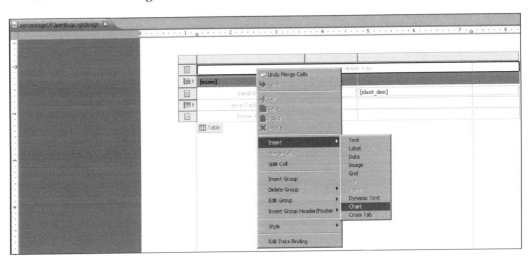

11. Select a **Bar** Chart, and change the **Output Format** to **PNG**.
12. Open the **Select Data** tab.
13. Drag the **bug_status** field to the **Optional Y Series Grouping** slot.
14. Drag the **[name]** field to the **Category (X) Series** slot.

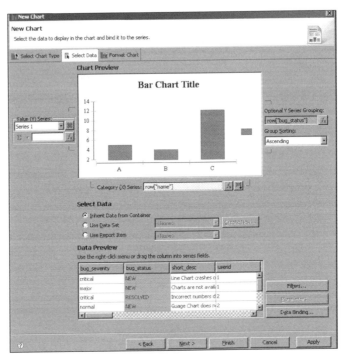

15. Click on the **Edit group and sorting** button.

16. In the **Group and sorting Dialog**, check the **Enabled** check box. Change the **Type** to **Text**, **Interval** to **0**, and **Aggregate Expression** to **Count**.

17. For the **Value (Y) Series**, enter **Series 1**.

18. Under the Aggregate function, select **Count**.

19. Under the **Format Chart** tab, go to **Chart Area | Title** and enter **Bug Status Report** as **Chart Title**.

20. Select **Axis | X-Axis**, and check the **Stagger** check box.

21. Resize the Chart to fit the number of categories.

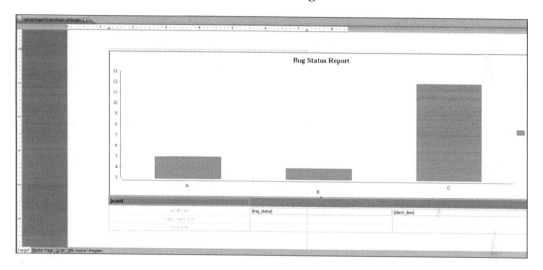

22. The last thing we need is to add the Drill-Through from the descriptions to the bug detail. Select the **short_desc** data item in the Report Designer.

23. Under the **Property Editor**, select the **Hyperlink** tab. Click on the **Link To** button. From the **Hyperlink** Dialog, select the **Drill-through** as type.

24. Select **BugzillaDetailReport.rptdesign** as the **Target** report. Set up the target report parameter **bugID** to be linked to **row["bug_id"]**.

25. Click **OK**, **Save**, and **Preview** the report.

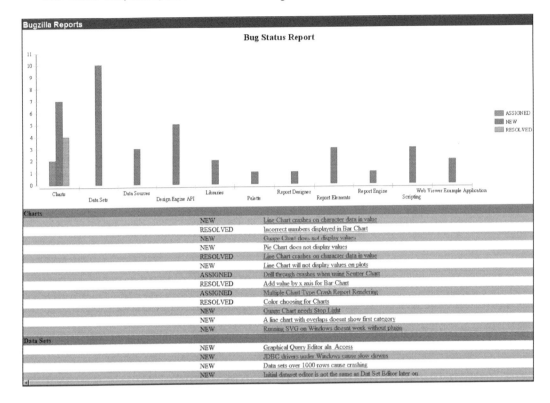

Developer Issues Reports

The next report is a combination of the last two reports in our list. Given a developer ID, this report will accomplish two things: it will show us a Pie Chart of Bugs (fixed versus non-fixed bugs), and give us a list of bugs in an open status assigned to that developer.

1. Open **BugzillaReportsTemplate.rpttemplate** and **Save** as **DeveloperPerformanceReport.rptdesign**.

2. Modify the **getAllBugs** query as:

```
SELECT
bugs.bug_id,
bugs.bug_severity,
bugs.bug_status,
bugs.short_desc,
profiles.userid,
profiles.login_name,
profiles.realname,
```

```
components.id,
components.name,
components.description
FROM
bugs,
profiles,
components
WHERE
bugs.component_id    = components.id
AND bugs.assigned_to = profiles.userid
and profiles.userid = ?
```

3. Bind the Data-Set Parameter to a Report Parameter called **developerID**.

4. We want to use a drop-down list for the **developerID parameter**. Create a new Data Set to display the unique developer IDs using the following query, and call it **developerIDList**.

```
SELECT distinct
profiles.userid,
profiles.realname
FROM
profiles
```

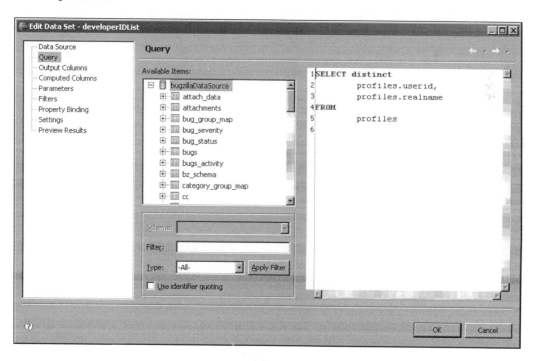

5. Open the **developerID** Report Parameter for editing. The Dialog should look like the following:

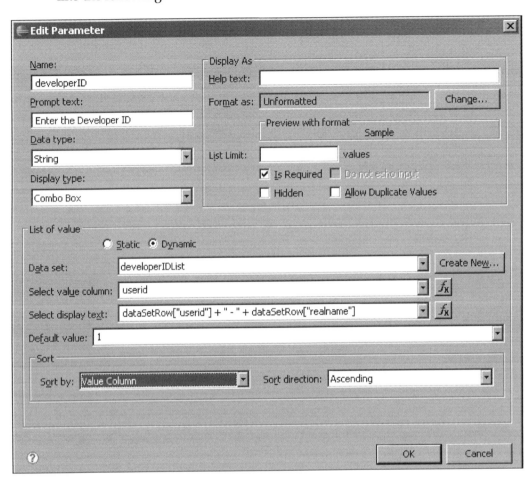

6. Click on **OK** to save the Parameter Edit.
7. Drag **getAllBugs** Data Set over to the Report Designer.
8. **Delete** all columns except **bug_id** and **short_desc**.
9. Insert a new row in the header above the column Labels.
10. **Merge** all the cells in the new row.
11. Insert a **Chart** into the new large cell.
12. Select a **Pie** Chart, and set the **Output Format** to **PNG**.

13. Select the **Select Data** tab. Under the Category Definition, use the following expression:

```
if (row["bug_status"].toUpperCase() == "RESOLVED")
        "Fixed";
else
        "Open";
```

14. Click on the **Edit Group and sorting** button. Check the **Grouping Enabled** check box. Set the **Type** to **Text**, **Interval** to **0**, **Aggregate Expression** to **Count**, and Hit **OK**.

15. Under the **Slice Size Definition**, enter **1** for the value, and change the aggregate function to **Count**.

16. Under the **Format Chart** tab, go to **Title**. and use **Open Issue Chart** as the **Chart Title**.

17. Resize the Chart. Change the Labels for **Bug ID** and **Bug Short Description**.

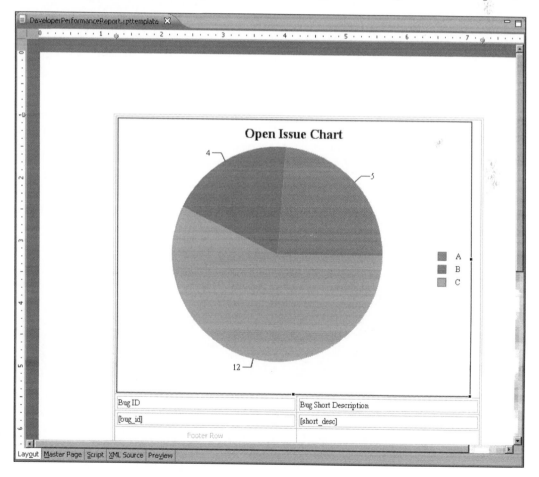

18. Select the **Detail Row** of the Chart.

19. Under the **Property Editor,** select the **Visibility** tab. Check **Hide Element**.

20. Use the **Expression** as illustrated in the following figure:

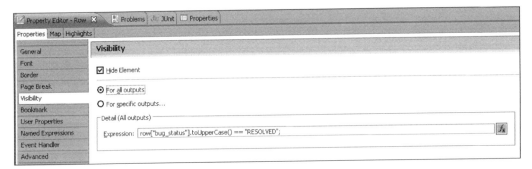

21. Select the **bug_id** data element.

22. Under the **Property Editor,** select the **Hyperlink** tab.

23. Create a **Drill-through** to the **BugzillaDetailreport.rptdesign** using the Table's **bug_id** as the parameter value.

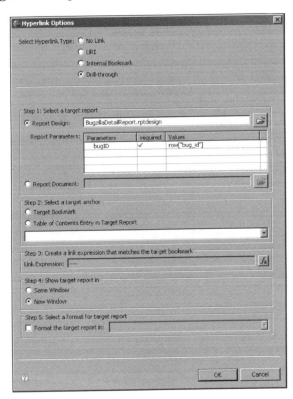

24. Apply the **TableHeader** Style to the report.

25. As we used the Visible Expression to hide rows that are resolved, this will throw the Highlight used in the Detail Row style off. So, we are going to use a little bit of Scripting to apply our Highlight. Open up the **Outline** view.

26. In the Report Designer, open up the **Script** tab.

27. Select the report's Root element, and in the **Script** editor, choose the **initialize** method.

28. Use the following code:

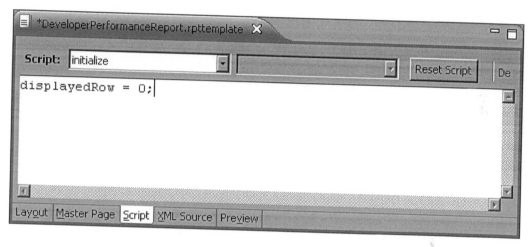

29. Select the **Detail Row** in the **Report Designer**.

30. For the **onRender** method, put in the following code:

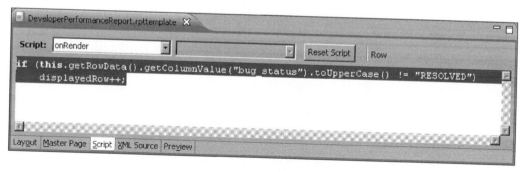

31. In the **Property Editor**, select the **Highlight** tab.

32. Create a **Highlight** using `displayedRow % 2` instead of `row.__rownum`.

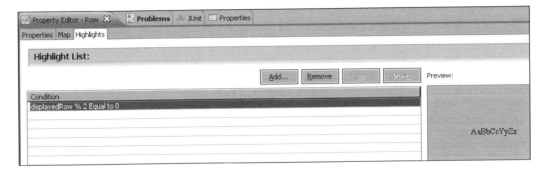

33. **Save** and **Preview** the report.

The reason this worked is because we needed to get the values in the data rows before the visibility rule takes effect. Once we have those components created, we check in the Render phase to see if the value of `bug_status` is the RESOLVED value. If not, then we advance the counter that would normally be advanced by ROWNUM. This keeps it nice and uniform.

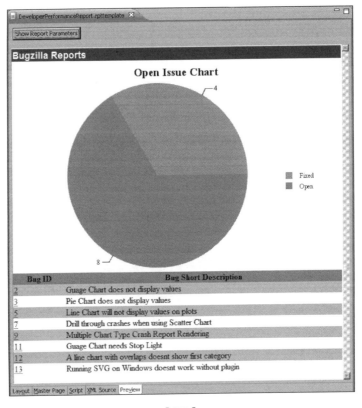

Summary

In this chapter, we looked at a realistic example of a series of reports that could be used in a real-life project. In fact, these requirements were based on some examples of report requirements I have been given in the past.

We illustrated just about every major element of reporting with BIRT—Report Project, Report Components, Charts, Scripting, and Formatting. We even looked at how to look at requirements and find reports with similar specs and data and combine reports. If a single report can take the place of multiple reports, and tell a more complete story, it is always beneficial to do so. In addition, we also introduced the Visibility rule, which is very similar to the Highlight rule. These reports can now be deployed to a report platform and be used for production reports.

Keep in mind that these reports were created in a controlled environment. Many times, data won't be as clean. For example, I based my assumption for the Developer Performance Report on the fact that there would only be two classes of statuses—open and closed. In reality, Bugzilla keeps this open-ended, and there are Open, Resolved, Assigned, and a few others out of the box. This is configurable, and there could be any number of other statuses. While in an ideal world this is the responsibility of the Data Managers to maintain, in the real world report developers' efforts to push back usually result in nothing.

Conclusion

From the beginning: We familiarized ourselves with the Eclipse BIRT Design Perspective. We familiarized ourselves with the various BIRT Report Components. We build some simple reports, and some complex reports. We demonstrated how re-use is possible through Libraries and Templates. We also saw some basic report Scripting.

Hopefully, by reading this book you have gained a good fundamental understanding about how BIRT works, and are now able to build BIRT reports. The BIRT community is a growing one, and there are a number of resources out there for BIRT. There is a growing user community on the Eclipse website. There are a few blogs out there. There are a few developers of extensions for BIRT—such as Tribix, which makes output extensions.

BIRT is a large and difficult "animal" to define and comprehend. While on the surface it seems that it is a report development platform, it is also a set of APIs that can be consumed and extended to meet your needs. If the out-of-the-box output formats aren't enough, then custom Emitters can be built. All sorts of things are possible.

Hopefully, now that you have a good foundation in BIRT, you can begin to extend your knowledge of BIRT depending on your needs.

Index

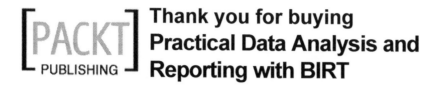

Thank you for buying
Practical Data Analysis and
Reporting with BIRT

Packt Open Source Project Royalties

When we sell a book written on an Open Source project, we pay a royalty directly to that project. Therefore by purchasing Practical Data Analysis and Reporting with BIRT, Packt will have given some of the money received to the BIRT project.

In the long term, we see ourselves and you—customers and readers of our books—as part of the Open Source ecosystem, providing sustainable revenue for the projects we publish on. Our aim at Packt is to establish publishing royalties as an essential part of the service and support a business model that sustains Open Source.

If you're working with an Open Source project that you would like us to publish on, and subsequently pay royalties to, please get in touch with us.

Writing for Packt

We welcome all inquiries from people who are interested in authoring. Book proposals should be sent to authors@packtpub.com. If your book idea is still at an early stage and you would like to discuss it first before writing a formal book proposal, contact us; one of our commissioning editors will get in touch with you.

We're not just looking for published authors; if you have strong technical skills but no writing experience, our experienced editors can help you develop a writing career, or simply get some additional reward for your expertise.

About Packt Publishing

Packt, pronounced 'packed', published its first book "Mastering phpMyAdmin for Effective MySQL Management" in April 2004 and subsequently continued to specialize in publishing highly focused books on specific technologies and solutions.

Our books and publications share the experiences of your fellow IT professionals in adapting and customizing today's systems, applications, and frameworks. Our solution-based books give you the knowledge and power to customize the software and technologies you're using to get the job done. Packt books are more specific and less general than the IT books you have seen in the past. Our unique business model allows us to bring you more focused information, giving you more of what you need to know, and less of what you don't.

Packt is a modern, yet unique publishing company, which focuses on producing quality, cutting-edge books for communities of developers, administrators, and newbies alike. For more information, please visit our website: www.PacktPub.com.

PUBLISHING

Business Process Management with JBoss jBPM

A Practical Guide for Business Analysts

Develop business process models for implementation in a business process management system

Matt Cumberlidge

PACKT

Business Process Management with JBoss jBPM

ISBN: 978-1-847192-36-3   Paperback: 300 pages

Develop business process models for implementation in a business process management system

1. Map your business processes in an efficient, standards-friendly way

2. Use the jBPM toolset to work with business process maps, create a customizable user interface for users to interact with the process, collect process execution data, and integrate with existing systems

3. Use the SeeWhy business intelligence toolset as a Business Activity Monitoring solution, to analyze process execution data, provide real-time alerts regarding the operation of the process, and for ongoing process improvement

JasperReports
for Java Developers

Create, Design, Format, and Export Reports with the World's Most Popular Java Reporting Library

David R. Heffelfinger

PACKT

JasperReports for Java Developers

ISBN: 1-904811-90-6   Paperback: 344 pages

Create, Design, Format and Export Reports with the world's most popular Java reporting library

1. Get started with JasperReports, and develop the skills to get the most from it

2. Create, design, format, and export reports

3. Generate report data from a wide range of datasources

4. Integrate Jasper Reports with Spring, Hibernate, Java Server Faces, or Struts

Please visit **www.PacktPub.com** for information on our titles

Made in the USA
Lexington, KY
17 March 2012